SPORT IN CORK
A HISTORY

SPORT IN CORK
A HISTORY

DONAL O'SULLIVAN

First published 2010

The History Press Ireland
119 Lower Baggot Street
Dublin 2
Ireland

www.thehistorypress.ie

British Library Cataloguing in Publication Data.
A catalogue record for this book is available from the British Library.

ISBN 978 1 84588 970 8

Typesetting and origination by The History Press
Printed in Great Britain

CONTENTS

INTRODUCTION

The history of sport and leisure in Ireland has long been the domain of enthusiasts, many of whom have been industrious in finding sources and have written with considerable style. Recently, this area has begun to attract some academic interest in Ireland, as we can see, for example, in Mike Cronin's *Sport, Nationalism and Ireland: Gaelic Games, Soccer and Irish Identity since 1884* (Dublin, 1999). Of course, there is a considerable body of academic work on sport and leisure in other countries.

This book examines some connections between sport and leisure and social class in Cork in the period 1870-1939. The aim has been to examine thoroughly the primary sources that various organisations and clubs retain (minute books and related material).

The volume of material consulted was quite large, and the common features and differences between the various sporting organisations active in Cork throughout the period under review are discussed in the chapters that follow. An attempt has been made to relate the investigation of sporting bodies and their activities to the wider issues discussed in the academic literature on the social and economic history of nineteenth- and twentieth-century Cork. It is my hope that this book will make a contribution to local studies, as well as to the general history of sport and leisure in Ireland.

I

GAA

THE GROWTH AND EMERGENCE OF THE GAA IN CORK AND SURROUNDING DISTRICTS

When the GAA was established in the 1880s, the founders placed much emphasis on the past, and on the athletic pastimes of those who lived in earlier centuries. Local historians in Cork City and county, when commenting on the early years of clubs following the founding of the GAA, have often made reference to hurling, football and other athletic activities in the earlier nineteenth century and in previous centuries. When Blackrock Hurling Club representing Cork defeated Rapparees from Dublin comprehensively in the 1894 All-Ireland Championship, someone commented, 'How could you beat a team from Blackrock? Sure, they have been playing hurling since the time of Fionn Mac Cuil?'[1]

What needs to be done is to consider the literature on aspects of Cork's sporting history in the earlier nineteenth century, before the founding of the GAA in the city and county. There are of course references to hurling, football and athletic activity in the seventeenth and eighteenth centuries also, and some allusion will be made to these as we ascertain how ripe the situation in Cork was to facilitate the newly organised activity from 1884 onwards.

HURLING, FOOTBALL AND ATHLETICS IN CORK CITY AND COUNTY BEFORE THE GAA

Reference to sports in the early modern period in Cork is found in the action of Sir William St Leger, Lord President of Munster in 1627, sworn as freeman of the city at this time. He proceeded to ban the games of hurling and football, deeming such pastimes 'an uncivil kind of sport'.[2] According to O'Connell, in his history of the Erin's Own club, poets prior to the 1700s referred to the game of 'Goaling', in which 'Caherlag's men ruled supreme'. Caherlag is now the location of the playing fields of Erin's Own. Meanwhile, De Búrca in his history of the GAA, cites the work of local Cork historian Pádraig Ó Maidín, who, writing in the *Cork Examiner*, instances evidence of hurling being played in 1763, 1776 and 1780.

There are numerous references to hurling and football in the first half of the nineteenth century. Ó Maolfabhail, in his history of hurling, cites the Shaw Mason survey of parishes in Ireland from 1813. In the parish of Tracton Union, which is situated between Cork City and Kinsale, the afternoons of the Sabbath and Holy Days witnessed 'goaling parties by the young men in the fields'.[3] He also quotes the following verse from Cork poet J.J. Callanan, who wrote in 1831:

Next Sunday the patron
at home will be keeping
and the young active hurlers
the field will be sweeping.

Sheehan, in his history of Inniscarra, records more definite evidence of hurling in this particular area. He states that the sport was being played in the district fifty years before the founding of the GAA, when there were three teams in the parish. The teams, consisting of twenty-five players each, were Dripsey Goaling Team, Cloghroe, and Inniscarra. Dripsey, with its paper mills, was the most industrially developed of these areas. The manager at the mills was reportedly very enthusiastic about the hurling played by the Dripsey Goaling Team, most of whom worked in the mills. In the 1860s, the paper mills closed and as a consequence the team associated with it disbanded. Sheehan was not able to locate any similarly reliable records for the Cloghroe and Inniscarra teams.

In the middle of the nineteenth century, the *Cork Constitution* carried a number of articles, which, as well as describing hurling matches in and around the city, left no doubt that the paper was opposed to such activity. The edition of 31 March 1831 stated, 'The hurling matches which take place in the vicinity of the South Infirmary on Sundays are most indecent and ought to be prevented. There were several hundred persons collected on the last two Sundays, especially either engaged in that amusement or spectators of it.'[4]

On 11 June 1844, the *Cork Constitution* described a hurling match at Ardarostig, three miles south-west of Cork City. Three teams were involved, Blackrock, St Barrys, and Ballinora, with Ballinora apparently opposing the other two teams. The article depicted a melee in which women participated in the following terms:

> Great numbers were maimed and wounded on both sides and the affair termi-nated after about an hour and half of hostilities, by the retreat of the townsmen. A decent person named O'Brien, from Willow Hill of this City, who was a looker on, had his head laid open by blow of stone and was borne senseless from assailants, and many others received desperate wounds and contusions.

Even the *Cork Examiner*, which was to provide a great deal of coverage on GAA games, did not ignore this rough aspect of pre-GAA activity. Beecher notes that in the *Cork Examiner* of 19 July 1886, when describing a match between St Finbarrs and Aghabullogue, the reporter remarked on the good proportion of old men who 'must have witnessed exciting hurling matches about thirty or forty years ago'.[5] The article also admitted that 'hurling, as played of old was surrounded by many objectionable features – such indeed as were quite suf-ficient to earn for it a reputation that was not commendable'.

Various sources have commented on sporting activity from the Famine up to the 1880s. The foremost authority on pre-GAA activity is Ó Caithnia, and in his book *Scéal na hIomána* he makes reference to hurling in Cork in the decades preceding the founding of the GAA. He cites a reference to a Carrigaline hurler in 1874, and also notes that the term 'hurler' was a deroga-tive term during the tithe wars.[6] He includes the following description of a hurling match between Eaglais and the Barrs from a Canon Duggan, whom he describes as being sympathetic to the game of hurling:

> Sheas na báireoirí i línte mar baghnáth, ach an túisce a thosaigh an cluiche rug an se phéire déag barróg ghrámhar ar a chéile. D'fhan an liathróid gan chorraí ar an talamh, cúpla nóiméad, gach fear acu suite ar a chéile, nó a chéile airsean. Ni ionadh linn, má cheadaití nithe den tsaghas san, gur truaillíodh an cluiche sna seachtóidí ionas gur chuma nó bruíneachas.

It was no coincidence that the aforementioned Canon Duggan was enthusi-astic about hurling, since, according to Ó Caithnia, priests were involved in such games in some parts of Cork right up to the founding of the association.

Ó Caithnia mentions a number of teams that were active in Cork and surrounding districts in the 1860s and 1870s, these being An Eaglais, na Barraigh, Carrig Uí Leighin, Cionn Sáile, Ducharragi, an Seanbhaile, and Carraig Thuathail. From his perusal of the *Cork Examiner* in 1864, it emerges that games were often bitter, with teams reluctant to concede defeat. Ó Caithnia refers to another source, Windele, who in 1864 noted that Kinsale beat fourteen other parishes in hurling. Finally, Ó Caithnia says that there was evidence of hurling in parts of West Cork, such as Enniskeane and Bantry, up to 1880.

THE GAA IN CORK CITY - THE EARLY YEARS

'The Association swept the country like a prairie fire.'[7]

Michael Cusack commenting on the first two years of the GAA

In 1883, against the background of a disagreement at the Cork Amateur Athletic Club's Sports, Michael Cusack came to Cork on what he called 'solely the Gaelic mission'.[8] He had chosen Cork because, as he said himself, 'most of our champion athletes are from Munster', and he proceeded to call the new organisation in Cork the 'Munster Athletic Club'. Cronin, in his centenary history of the Cork GAA, describes Cusack's activities against the background of hurling being played widely in Cork City at this time. He mentions teams such as St Finbarrs (sometimes known as South Parish), Blackrock, Ballygarvan, Ballinhassig, and Cloghroe, who all played regularly in challenge tournaments. He also refers to the playing of an early version of Gaelic football. However, Cusack's actions alone would have been insufficient to establish an organisation in Cork, particularly one which was to grow as strong as it did. One needs to pinpoint, therefore, the key personalities who were instrumental in putting this new organisation on a solid footing in Cork City and county.

Firstly, there was a strong Cork representation at the initial meetings that were held to put the GAA on a nationwide footing. One of the initial group of seven who met at Hayes' Hotel in Thurles in 1884 was a John McKay, a member of staff of the *Cork Examiner*. Only eleven days after this founding meeting, the first athletics meeting under GAA rules was held in Toames, just outside Macroom. The Cork presence at the second meeting of the national association was much stronger. Presiding at this meeting, held in Cork on 27 December 1884, was Alderman Paul Madden, who was the Mayor-elect of Cork City and who was to be a significant personality in the affairs of the GAA in Cork in its early years. Along with Madden and the aforementioned McKay, who was also present at this second meeting, were W.J. Barry, W. Cotter, J.E. Kennedy, J. O'Connor, D. Horgan, A. O'Driscoll and a Dr O'Riordan from Cloyne. Referring to this meeting, De Búrca says that it was attended by a local group of Home Rulers who helped the passing of a resolution that two members of each athletic club in the county should be drafted on to the local GAA executive. De Búrca sees this local support as having been crucial in helping the local Cork organisation get on its feet in 1885 and 1886.

According to Puirséal, John McKay, the reporter with the *Cork Examiner*, became the second secretary of the national association. While there have been few subsequent references to McKay, he was present with Cusack at a meeting of the Munster Football Association when a J.F. Murphy from Cork was removed from his post as vice-president of the GAA. This had occurred at a public protest meeting when McKay and Cusack calmed the furore over Murphy's position. This incident was related to a dispute over the rules of Gaelic football, which we will come to later. However, Puirséal states that the second meeting of the GAA, which was a resumption of the adjourned first meeting of Thurles, took place in Cork's Victoria Hotel, and that Alderman Madden presided over the meeting, which was attended by leading athletes from Dublin and Cork. Mandle sheds a little more light on some of these Cork personalities. According to Mandle, Madden was a member of the Irish Republican Brotherhood, as was John O'Connor, known as 'Long John O'Connor'. Also mentioned is a John King, a nephew of John O'Leary and a Cork grocer.[9]

As regards setting up the local infrastructure for the GAA in Cork, the first meeting to give the association a permanent status in the city and county took place in the premises of Alderman Horgan at 23 Maylor Street. At this meeting, on 23 December 1886, a president, secretary and committee were elected. The County Committee would have the power to decide on questions of affiliation and have the responsibility for arranging ties in football, hurling, handball and athletics. The chairman of the new local association was Alderman D. Horgan in whose premises the meeting was held. The remaining members of the committee were: Sir Edward Fitzgerald from Blackrock; Alderman Phair from St Finbarrs; Mr Scott, NT, from Little Island; Mr Eugene Cotter from Blarney; Mr Dan O'Mahony, NT, from Aghabullogue; Mr T. O'Sullivan, Inniscarra, and John McKay, the first secretary, who was also secretary of the association nationwide. A T. O'Riordan took over from McKay, who resigned from his local post of responsibility, and O'Riordan remained secretary of the Cork county board until 1889. The position of secretary of the board and the identity of the office holder do not seem altogether clear. According to Power, when the 1887 committee was elected, the chairman was Alderman Horgan, the treasurer was a John Slattery and the secretary was a David Walsh, from Riverstown.

Scott, the national teacher on the first committee, represented the area of Little Island, where he was the local headmaster. He was one of a number of personalities mentioned in various club histories who were credited with establishing the local branches of the GAA in their areas. For Blackrock, who were to become one of Cork's foremost clubs, a D.M. Lane was the first secretary in the crucial years from 1883 to 1887, and according to Madden, was also the first secretary of the county board. O'Sullivan, the Inniscarra representative on the county committee, was one of the early secretaries of Inniscarra, though this particular club, like so many others, improvised in its first years with irregular meetings and different secretaries. Jeremiah J. Coffey formally affiliated Midleton Football Club at the third meeting of the national GAA organisation at Thurles on 17 January 1885. Undoubtedly there were other men who were the driving forces in various localities and who were central to the foundation of the GAA in the city and county.

However, in order to understand subsequent happenings within the Cork county board, as well as nationally, there are a number of personalities within the Cork GAA who deserve closer attention. As Puirséal charted the development of the national organisation, he noted that by 1887 the position of two individuals on the executive, Hoctor and Fitzgerald, was coming under increased pressure. Both men were from Cork and had assumed increased power on the national executive, and their strongly republican backgrounds brought them into opposition with the Catholic clergy who then supported Parnell. The clergy also disagreed with the way in which the excecutive had objected to the interference of Dr Croke.

Along with Tim O'Riordan and John Mandeville, the aforementioned Fitzgerald was one of the Cork delegates to the crucial national convention of the GAA in Thurles in 1887, the after-effects of which were to traumatise the association in the years immediately following. While this will be dealt with in more detail later, the GAA came to be split because of a strongly republican element who saw the GAA as being in some way a vehicle for the separatist movement. Opponents to such a move, including the influential clergy, objected to this alignment between republicanism and the association.

Fitzgerald was a member of the IRB and had in fact taken part in the Fenian Rising of 1867. While serving a term in prison, a testimonial had been organised for the benefit of his family in January 1885. The organising committee appointed included the Lord Mayors of Cork and Limerick, six MPs, seven members of the local corporation, and other prominent personages from the worlds of business and commerce, as well as others from the professions. In terms of sporting involvement, Fitzgerald had been closely involved with both his native Midleton and Cork and had served as an umpire with the club.

Another national figure from Cork was Dr Charles Tanner, MP. When Inniscarra, along with over twenty other clubs, entered the 1887 Cork County Championship, they entered as the Inniscarra/Dr Tanner Hurling Club. Dr Tanner was a Cork MP from Inniscarra and was a strong opponent of government policy in the Land War. On 25 April 1887, Dr Tanner arrived in Cork and was greeted by well-wishers and several bands. He condemned the Coercion Act thus, 'You must throw down the gauntlet of defiance at the feet of England – What had the present government done for Ireland? They had disgraced civilization, disgraced England, and forever disgraced themselves and that certainly was as big an accumulation of dirt as could be heaped on any government.'[10]

We can see, therefore, that there were a number of dynamic individuals in Cork who were prepared to give much of their time in setting up the local infrastructure for the playing of the games, as well as those who wanted to make an impact at a national level, not just in the administration of the national organisation, but in seeking to influence how it was to use its power in the larger political milieu.

THE EARLY YEARS

There were a myriad of organisational challenges to be met, both for the national and local units of the GAA, and in the year 1886 the formal structures of the GAA were put in place throughout the country, structures which have remained to this day. It was at the association's national convention on ·15 November 1886, to which eighty-four clubs had sent delegates, that it was decided to set up county boards. Affiliated clubs were to pay annual subscription rates, and the All-Ireland Football and Hurling Championships were also inaugurated. Organising fixtures, enforcing conformity in playing rules and dealing with matters of indiscipline, were the principal challenges to be met. Yet adequate levels of determination and enthusiasm were the basic pre-requisites for the organisation to establish itself. Such qualities were in evidence from earliest stages of the GAA. In Cork City and county, despite difficulties, worthwhile attempts were made to address organisational matters. By August 1886, for example, sufficient progress had been made in organisational terms to host a hurling and football tournament, including ten clubs from Cork and Tipperary.

When the first meeting of the county board (or county committee as it was otherwise known) was held, there were no fewer than twenty-four teams in the draw for the hurling championship. The teams were nearly all from within or just outside the city, with only a number of teams such as Mitchelstown, Aghada, Charleville and Aghabullogue, being from more than ten miles away. There were a number of teams in the draw who had a first and second team entered, such as Aghada and Cork Nationals. This was to be a feature of the GAA for a number of years until competitions were streamlined into senior, junior and intermediate levels. It is also worth noting from this early list of teams, how close geographically some of them were to each other, especially in the city. For example, Tower Street, Evergreen Road, Greenmount, and St Finbarrs were all from the area around the South Parish, while Glasheen was just to the west of the South Parish.

Sheehan, in his history of Inniscarra, says that this club was one of twenty-two teams entered for the 1887 county championship, and notes that the club had paid its affiliation fee. From this, one can see how the county committee was addressing itself financially within the association, and that local clubs would have been making attempts to raise money. The enthusiasm with which local areas in the city formed themselves into clubs continued in to the late 1880s, when the local county board was split into different factions due to internal strife. The main breakaway board, the city board, organised its own championships, such as those played in April 1889. Here, again, two teams from the same club were fielded; the William O'Briens second team played a club called the United Irishmen, while the second team of Nils Desperandum played Davitts from Queenstown. (When referring to Queenstown, as we have done, it is worth keeping the following in mind. Modern-day Cobh was known as Cove up until 1849, after which it was renamed Queenstown after the visit of Queen Victoria, before reverting to Cobh in 1922. Sometimes sports teams from the town continued to be called Cove, possibly anxious to be called by the more nationalist form of the name.) Other teams in action that month were Greenmount and League of the Cross from Charlotte Quay. Just outside the city, and playing in the same championship, were Carrigaline's first team, Shanbally, Ballygarvan and Tracton.

When a football tournament was hosted by the local Ladysbridge and Ballymacoda club in July 1889, a large number of clubs entered. There were also individuals willing to help the association, in terms of providing prizes for tournaments and competitions. Cork Nationals played St Finbarrs Hurling Club on 15 August 1886, for a silver cup worth five guineas, 'given by a gentleman in the city who takes an interest in this old manly game'.[11]

The athletics link with the GAA should not be forgotten. As well as Toames, near Macroom, hosting the first ever athletics meeting nationally under GAA rules, other GAA athletics meetings were held in the early years. On 3 June 1885, a large sports meeting was held in the city, while in October of that year the first national GAA athletics sports meeting was held there also. Cork, was therefore, to the forefront at both a national and local level in terms of a willingness to both embrace the aspirations and undertake enthusiastically the new organisation's playing activities.

Such enthusiasm was also evident in the manner in which organisational matters were addressed. When Inniscarra met Charleville on 12 May 1889 at Mallow, the local Thomas Davis Hurling Club and William O'Brien Football Club undertook the stewarding for the 6,000 attendance, as well as roping off and marking the pitch. Each competing team had one field umpire and two goal umpires. The following July, again at Mallow, Inniscarra played Kenmare in a hurling contest in which the two clubs were representing their respective counties. The pitch earmarked for the game was unplayable, and so another field of twenty acres was offered for the playing of the game, being duly used after the grass had been cut and the field marked.

Some clubs showed admirable organisational skills from early on. The 1887 Minute Book and Statement of Expenses of St Finbarrs is instructive on this account. For example, the club had acquired a clubhouse on the Bandon Road and purchased a new sliotar for 3s 6d. Timber for hurleys had also, in some instances, been purchased and prepared by the club. A field had been rented for £5, while jerseys had been purchased at the Munster Arcade. Two shillings was paid for the washing of the jerseys, and the same sum was paid for an advertisement in the *Cork Examiner*. Finally, in what could be seen as a very progressive initiative so early on in the life of the GAA, the club paid one of their players 15s in sick money for missing work due to injury.

In Inniscarra, the local club organised a clubs competition in 1888, with another competition for juvenile players. The entrance fee for a single team was 7s 6d, and a club would pay 10s if they had two teams participating. The entrance fee for a juvenile team was 2s 6d. The competition was open to every club in the county. Many of the clubs that took part later disbanded or were reformed under another name, such as St Marys Hurling Club, Glanmire Football Club, Queenstown Football Club and a team under the name Charles Underwood O'Connell Club. At the AGM of Inniscarra in 1889 an assistant treasurer and secretary were appointed, specifically for the purpose of running tournaments. A special tournament committee was elected, whereby three members of a committee would form a quorum with full powers to supervise the most important matters relating to the hosting of tournaments. When Inniscarra, representing Cork, played Kenmare in July 1889, the club had unanimously decided that up to twenty-six free travel tickets costing 2s 3d each were to be granted to players and subs travelling to Mallow, and to defray each individual's expenses it was decided that the money be paid out of tournament funds.

Such enthusiasm and organisation did not go unrecognised. A notice from the *Cork Examiner* of Monday, 16 April 1888, announced that, 'Owing to the energetic and efficient management of the County Committee, the contests are now being brought to a close, and Sunday next, or Sunday week at the latest, will see them concluded.'[12]

On Saturday 14 April 1888, Inniscarra played Blarney at Cloghroe. On the previous Sunday, an hour's play between the two teams had produced no score and the county board held the replay on the following Saturday. According to the *Cork Examiner*, the reason for the Saturday game was that the county board did not want to change the date already fixed for the next series of matches where the winners of the game would play Tower Street. In May 1888, at a double fixture, the county board switched the order of the matches involving Blackrock against Doneraile and the Barrs versus Ballyhea. Originally, the Blackrock match was to be the second game but their game went ahead first so that the Rockies team could return to attend the conclusion of a retreat being held in their parish. The tribute from the *Cork Examiner* seems to have been well deserved.

Yet, despite such organisational zeal, there were problems arising for the county committee who were endeavouring to keep matters running smoothly. For example, in 1887, the county board fixed a match for three o'clock on a Friday afternoon between St Finbarrs and Cork Nationals. Not unreasonably, the Barrs captain said the only day his team could play was on a Sunday.

Cronin, referring to the same fixture, explains that the county board's aim was to play the match on a Friday, with the winners playing Passage on the following day and the winners of that encounter to playing Tullaroon on the Sunday.

This was only one instance of organisational difficulties to be addressed in arranging fixtures, especially replays. Often such replays were due to teams not agreeing on playing rules, refereeing decisions or on the authority of the county board. Yet, such obstacles, when looked at in the wider context, were a measure of the development of the GAA in Cork in such a relatively short time.

PLAYING RULES

There were two issues to be addressed as regards implementing playing rules in hurling and football in Cork, and undoubtedly these problems were country wide. The first was that of deciding goals and points and when they were deemed to have been scored. The second obstacle, and one which brought Cork into conflict with the national association, was that of agreeing on the playing rules of Gaelic football and how these should differ from rugby. If the GAA was to establish its own identity the aspect of the playing rules was crucial.

Around the time the GAA was founded in Cork, an early form of Gaelic football was being played in the county. There were various local customs which prevented wrestling, and in both football and hurling there was little positional play. In late 1886, draft rules for the playing of hurling and football in Cork City had been accepted, and on 23 August the first ever game under such rules was played at an open park where the future Páirc Uí Chaoimh was to be built. According to the Rockies historian, Madden, the teams taking part in this football game were Cork Nationals (later known as Blackrock) and Macroom. However, Macroom refused to finish the match, an indication of the early teething difficulties experienced in ensuring conformity to rules and respect for the authorities enforcing them.

The problem with the new codified game of Gaelic football was that it was being played in a manner similar to the game of rugby. In 1886, a rule was adopted under which those playing football under rugby and non-Gaelic codes could not be admitted as members of any GAA branch. Mixing rugby and Gaelic football was a particular problem for Michael Cusack, who was originally at odds with Cork football clubs. They were members of the Munster National Football League whose president had allowed the players to run with the ball. Cusack had described such practices as 'rugby thinly disguised'. As a result, the president of the Munster Football Association had his membership withdrawn as vice-president of the GAA and a public protest meeting dealing with the issue ended in disorder.

Cronin provides more detail on the particular issue of the acceptance of playing rules in Cork. He remarks that the rules for hurling were readily accepted in Cork City, but that Gaelic football rules were not so welcomed. According to Cronin, most players worked in business houses and feared the risk of injury in football, which was considered to be more dangerous than hurling. The football clubs then met to draft a new set of rules at Forester's Hall. The chairman of the meeting, Mr Sutton of the Hibernian Club, said that while the rules of rugby were too scientific, the Gaelic football rules were too loose and dangerous in practice. They decided that rules should be drawn up to make playing in Gaelic football more skilful and well defined.

An open meeting was then held at the Lee Cricket and Football Club at which the proposed new rules were discussed but rejected. Nevertheless, city clubs and adjoining rural clubs played under these rejected rules, which were particular to Cork. However, Cork clubs began to conform to the national rules when a club called the Lees took up Gaelic football in 1886. When the Lees played Emmetts at Cork Park on 6 March 1886, the match ended in a scoreless draw. A reporter at the game compared the game played to rugby and remarked that there was very little scrummaging, and further, that wides did not count.

What exactly counted as a score and who was deemed to be the winner of an encounter in both hurling and football was another matter to be ironed out by the GAA authorities in Cork. On 19 July 1886, at a hurling match between St Finbarrs and Aghabullogue, the ball had to go over the opponents' end line five times before a point was deemed to have been scored. When Cork Nationals played St Finbarrs Hurling Club in August 1886, there was reference to such terms as 'try', 'send-out' and 'overs'.[13] In 1889, when Kenmare played Inniscarra, no number of points could equal a goal. The most common punishable offence at this match was tripping, for which an offender's hurley was taken from him for a minimum of two minutes and a maximum of five. Yet, the game finished controversially because of the disputed winning goal for Kenmare, representing Kerry.

A number of days later, Inniscarra met to discuss the game and condemned, in the 'strongest possible manner', the awarding of the game to Kerry. Inniscarra felt that the referee had not been in a position to judge on the winning goal and the club felt that the central council should have heard the evidence of independent onlookers before making a decision on the awarding of the game. However a speedy reply and explanation from the central council seemed to satisfy Inniscarra. When the club hosted its own tournament, it had to rule at a meeting on 23 July 1889 on an objection by the captain of Kilmurray against Clondrohid, following their tournament encounter. Inniscarra met at their rooms in Cloghroe and unanimously supported the referee's decision. Matters were not always easily resolved as regards the willingness of players and officials to accept either the decisions of a referee, or, failing that, the decisions of the county board or central council when ruling on disputes or replays.

DISCIPLINE, REFEREES AND DISPUTES

The *Cork Examiner* in its report on a match between St Finbarrs and Aghabullogue in July 1886, made the following observation:

> ...under the new rules of the Gaelic Association, and the changed temper of the contestants, which a rigid code of discipline has introduced, trained teams can now meet on the hurling field, play their game vigorously but goodnaturedly and retire at the close without having a man injured in the slightest.[14]

But this match was not without its controversy. There was a dispute over an alleged trip by one of the Aghabullogue players. The outcome of this incident was that the referee awarded his decision to the home team, St Finbarrs. Aghabullogue objected and play ceased while attempts were made to solve the dispute.

Teams did not only object because of foul play by opponents. On 1 May 1887, when Blarney defeated Little Island, the losing team lodged an objection to the outcome of the match because they claimed that the Blarney team contained several players who were not from the parish of the club. In 1887, Midleton played Lisgoold in the senior football championship. Midleton's umpire disagreed with one of the referee's decisions during the match, after which the matter was referred to the county board. There then followed correspondence to the *Cork Examiner* from the secretaries of the two clubs involved and the county board finally decided on a replay.

The problems that objections caused for the administrators of the game could reach almost comical proportions, as in the games involving Cork Nationals from Blackrock and St Finbarrs. Their rivalry was to continue right through the following century, no doubt heightened by events such as the following. According to the *Cork Examiner* of 18 July 1887, Nationals had been fixed to play St Finbarrs to decide who would play the premier hurling team in Kilkenny. But, according to the paper, the match ended in a 'miserable fiasco' after twenty minutes of play.[15] Nationals disputed an equalising point for St Finbarrs and duly left the field. The reporter felt that, 'there ought to be some way out of the deadlock, and those in authority ought to take prompt action'. The replay was fixed for three o'clock on Friday 22 July, the winners to meet Passage in order to select the representative team to play the Kilkenny team.

However, St Finbarrs did not turn up for the game, possibly due to the awkward time, but also possibly due to the county board executive's decision to hold a replay on ruling that a point awarded to St Finbarrs in the first match should have been disallowed. It was then decided that Nationals would play Passage on Saturday, 23 July 1887. But at this point further problems arose, according to the Blackrock historian Madden. Passage could only field fifteen players while teams then comprised twenty-one players a side, and despite Nationals offering to only field fifteen players as well, the championship was not finished. The county board then decided to play the semi-final again between Nationals and St Finbarrs, which actually took place at Tralee and which Nationals won. However, the subsequent final was never played and in 1888 the county board did not present medals either to Nationals or Passage.

It was not just disputed scores that caused the premature ending of games. When Lees from the city met Kilmacabea from West Cork at Bandon, the referee urged the teams at the outset to play an honourable and gentlemanly match. But the omens were not good, if one was to accept the newspaper report that remarked on the 'quarrelsome disposition' of Kilmacabea. As for the Lees, 'a more quietly disposed or amiable team than the Lees it would be hard to find'. When a ball was knocked off a Lee player before going over the end line a 'wrangle' ensued, which was settled by the intervention of a Revd Magner. Kilmacabea then objected to the referee blowing too early for half-time and the match was awarded to Lees, with Kilmacabea lodging an objection with the county board. Nor was the image of the new organisation embellished by events after this match. According to the *Cork Examiner*, players and spectators from Kilmacabea 'swarmed' around the town of Bandon until 7p.m., when presumably their transport was due to arrive. In the meantime, a serious dispute had erupted either among the Kilmacabea followers themselves or involving some of those from Bandon, the reporter not being altogether sure. Several people received wounds from kicks, while a Bandon man had his fingers severely bitten.

On the pitch, some referees were criticised for being too lenient in their application of the rules. In April 1889, at Carrigaline, two matches under the auspices of the city board were staged, one between Carrigaline's first team and Shanbally, and another between Ballygarvan and Tracton. The opposing teams in each match were from neighbouring localities and this was no doubt a factor in what seemed to have been a tempestuous occasion. The reporter present from the *Cork Examiner* was of the opinion that half a dozen men should have been sent off, which would have been the 'proper penalty' for 'flagrant violations of all rules'.[16]

On Sunday, 8 April 1888, Midleton played Emmetts of Bantry in the semi-final of the county championship. The game, described by Corr and O'Donoghue as 'robust', saw a melee developing between the players, who had to be separated by spectators. It was no doubt with such incidents in mind that, when Midleton went on in the same year to play Killorglin from Kerry in the Munster Championship, the president of the Cork county board, Mr Eugene Crean, presented the county medals to Midleton before the game and counselled for a fair and friendly game, stressing the importance of avoiding quarrels.

Events like these were bound to cause concern for administrators at local and national levels, as they strove to promote the image of the association in a positive way. As if such events did not already provide a sufficient challenge for the association, difficulties were further exacerbated by influence of politics within the GAA which split administrators, supporters and players at the end of the 1880s. In this, Cork was to prove no exception.

THE SPLIT IN THE CORK COUNTY BOARD

In trying to understand how different factions emerged in the county board, who then decided to run their own competitions in opposition to each other, one needs to look at events nationally, where the split within the Cork board was mirrored. Within the association in the late 1880s, there were those who saw the promotion of national games as an intrinsic part of a strongly republican separatist movement. Those who took this position were invariably members of the Irish Republican Brotherhood, in some cases former active Fenians. Such a presence in the organisation was anathema to those who were opposed to the GAA's use as a vehicle for militant republicanism. This opposition was found most of all among the clergy. These diverging views were at the heart of the split in various county boards throughout the country, including Cork.

From the beginning of the GAA, parallels were drawn between advancing the cause of Irish nationalism and playing Gaelic games, often symbolised by nationalists carrying a hurley. Mandle, who has studied the links between the IRB and the GAA, instances this link in an article by Michael Cusack entitled 'A Word about Irish Athletics' in the *United Ireland*. In the article, reference was made to Thomas Meagher, who 'darted up from the Missouri on a ray of the morning star and fiercely asked what had become of Irish hurling?'[17] Meagher is supposed to have sworn to Mother Erin, 'I'll take hold of the first camán that comes my way, call the boys together, make a beginning, and ask the avid people to join us.' Also, a James Boland from Blackrock in County Dublin, earlier in 1884, before the meeting in Thurles, had advocated the formation of a nationalistic athletic movement.

However, in more concrete terms, Mandle cites evidence of members of the Irish Republican Brotherhood present at the inaugural meeting at Hayes' Hotel in Thurles in November 1884, concluding that there was a 'suspiciously high proportion of Fenians'. A report from Dublin Castle in the 1880s commenting on the influence of politics on the young association claimed that, 'the question was not whether the association was a political one, but only to what particular section of Irish national politics it could be annexed'.[18]

In early 1887, the new executive began to exert control over the association by appointing members of the executive as ex-officio members of county committees. Maurice Davin met the GAA executive and expressed his opposition to their decisions, saying they had no power to make rules. The executive refused to change the new rules it had introduced and Davin resigned from the executive. The stance of the IRB-influenced executive also alienated the National League, which supported the Home Rule movement, while some IRB men were ambivalent in their attitude to the Home Rule movement. However, it was towards the end of 1887 and the beginning of 1888 that the tensions between militant republicans and their opponents, led by the clergy, first came to the fore. P.N. Fitzgerald and P.T. Hoctor, both IRB men, were now prominent in the GAA and intended to consolidate their position at the 1887 national convention.

Nationally, according to De Búrca, the GAA was now split between pro-Hoctor and anti-Hoctor elements. He states that county conventions leading up to the national convention were packed with IRB supporters. On

9 November 1887, the annual GAA convention was held in Thurles, with two delegates from each of more than 800 branches of the GAA present. The opposing sides first came into confrontation on the question of electing the chairman. Alderman Horgan of Cork and P.T. Hoctor proposed and seconded P.N. Fitzgerald from Midleton and Cork, while Fr Scanlan from Tipperary proposed a Major Kelly of the suspended Moycarkey club. When this nomination was rejected Fr Scanlan and his supporters were ejected; they moved to Hayes' Hotel in the town and held their own meeting. At Hayes' Hotel, Fr Scanlan said that the association was being taken over by a Fenian body also intent on taking over the National League, and he expressed his desire to see Maurice Davin as president.

Back at the convention, the elected chairman P.N. Fitzgerald 'thanked God that there were men in Ireland who would not stand for clerical dictation'. He also expressed the view that, 'Only men ready to die for their country should be at the head of the GAA.' Another IRB candidate, Bennis of Clare, had defeated Maurice Davin on another vote. The convention did however rescind the unpopular rule which gave the executive ex-officio membership of county committees and resolved that the association should be non-political and that no club as a body should take part in any political meeting. Any clubs which at the time were suspended or expelled from the association could be reinstated if there was an apology in writing for breaking the rules.

On the opposite side, Dr Croke wrote to the newspapers disassociating himself 'from the branch of the Gaelic Athletic Association which exercised such a sinister influence on yesterday's proceedings'. Fr Scanlan, who had gathered with his supporters outside the convention, said the GAA was being turned into a Fenian organisation that was attempting to break up the National League, and requested Archbishop Croke to remain as patron of the association. Priests had also signed a letter stating that the convention had been packed. On 16 November, the Blackrock club in Cork condemned those delegates at the convention 'who insulted the priests of Tipperary at the Thurles Convention'.[19] They further added that the club would throw in its lot 'with the Association about to be started with the sanction of Archbishop Croke, the priests and Mr Davin'. A week later the GAA club in Mitchelstown condemned P.N. Fitzgerald for his actions and comments at the convention.

The meetings of such clubs was symptomatic of what was happening nationally, as clubs held their own meetings after the convention, many of these being what De Búrca considered anti-Bennis clubs. There now occurred in fact a swing in support for those who were anti-Bennis and anti-IRB in general, as county conventions met for another convention at the beginning of January 1888. In November 1887, Davin had announced his intention to rejoin the association and the January 1888 convention was fixed. This convention was to have the power to revise the constitution of the GAA and to transact all business connected with the association.

Blackrock referred to the Assocation being formed by Davin and Croke as, not a new association, but an attempt to heal the open split at the 1887 convention. Dr Croke and Maurice Davin had come together and drawn up plans for the reconstruction and organisation of the GAA. A rapprochement had occurred between the executive elected at the 1887 convention and Dr Croke, whereby it was decided that the various county conventions elect delegates for a new general convention in early 1888. An indication of the divisions in the GAA was manifest in that two opposing meetings for delegates were held in some counties, while Ó Riain says that in both Cork and Galway the county committees elected were heavily weighted in favour of the IRB. According to Puirseal, Fitzgerald had approached Davitt and asked for a rapprochement with Dr Croke.[20]

On 4 January 1888, the new convention to reconstruct the GAA and heal the split of the November 1887 convention was held. Maurice Davin was unanimously elected president of the association and Dr Croke praised the rebuilding of the organisation, though he did criticise heavy drinking at matches and the missing of Mass and religious instruction due to attendance at the games. A majority of those elected to the central council were supporters of the National League, while united opposition was expressed towards the RIC. Events also seemed to have taken a turn for the better when the first All-Ireland Final between Galway and Tipperary was held on Sunday 1 April 1888. After what De Búrca refers to as a six-week split, 1888 was a very successful year for the GAA.

And yet, the splits that had occurred hadn't completely healed, nor had the IRB influence lessened in any real way. During 1888, most of the rank and file members who joined the GAA were IRB members, and so at the annual convention of 1889 the IRB were again beginning to dominate. Throughout the country, clubs seceded from the association in opposition to the IRB-led organisation and in support of the clergy and the National League. County boards split, for example, in Limerick and Cork, while in 1889 many county boards seceded from the GAA, either because of the demand of the central council for affiliation fees or because of the political background. Nine counties in Leinster seceded. Priests who had been active in promoting the

GAA in parishes fell away, especially after April 1888, when the Pope condemned the Plan of Campaign.

During 1889, sixty clubs disbanded in Tipperary alone, as the clergy and hierarchy became more forceful in their opposition to the official organisation and towards what they saw as its overt sympathy for militant republicanism. In January 1889, Cardinal Logue criticized the GAA and the 'demoralising effects' it was having on its members. In Meath, Bishop Nulty and the clergy were very hostile to the association, while in Cork a Fr O'Connor took court proceedings against three IRB members of the county board.

When the GAA convention was held in January 1889 the make-up of delegates had changed from the previous convention. Maurice Davin was heckled about the issue of debts of the association and subsequently left the meeting. Ó Riain says that the convention in January 1889 was more in the control of the IRB than ever, though the Cork delegation remained opposed to the new make-up of the central committee. In May 1889, RIC reports stated that in counties Cork, Louth, Clare and Leitrim, far more clubs operated outside the association than were affiliated to it. According to De Búrca, by late 1889 the GAA had declined 'alarmingly', so that at the 1889 national convention only forty-four delegates from nine counties attended.

Through the summer and into the winter of 1890 there was a large drop in the number of clubs nationwide, followed by another steep decline the following year. In 1891, seven counties entered the hurling championship, with only five eventually taking part. At the annual convention of 1892, only eighteen delegates from six counties attended. De Búrca attributes the steep decline in the fortunes of the GAA in 1891 to the Parnellite split, a decline from which, according to De Búrca, the GAA took a decade to recover. The link between the Parnellite split and the previous split was that those who supported Parnell were those who had supported the position of the IRB within the GAA, and these Parnellites only achieved their aim within the GAA in Cork City.

DIVISIONS IN CORK

Figures within the Cork GAA were central to the national split within the organisation. Those prominent figures at the contentious convention in November 1887, Alderman Horgan, P.T. Hoctor and P.N. Fitzgerald, were prominent in GAA in Cork. Also, Maurice Davin, who represented the opposition to the aforementioned delegates, was called a 'renegade' at a meeting in Cork at the height of the controversy. It was obvious, therefore, that the official Cork county board was strongly republican. However, the important question was: did they represent the views of administrators and players throughout Cork City and county?

De Búrca, in his history of the GAA, makes reference to the situation that developed in Cork, recounting how the IRB-dominated Cork county board was in opposition to Fr O'Connor. He also refers to there being twenty-five clubs loyal to the clergy and ninety-seven clubs under the control of the official Cork board. By 1892, there were only fifteen affiliated clubs in Cork following the split between the Fr O'Connor board and the official board, a situation exacerbated by the split over whether or not to support Parnell.

As regards the particular background to the split in the Cork county board, one needs to refer to a statement by Fr O'Connor in which he outlines his reasons for leading a breakaway board. In the following extract, he seems to be suggesting that the members of the Cork county board were informing on others and were in fact in the service of the British government. In the words of Fr O'Connor, there were on the county board:

> ...a few individuals from whom every true Irishman should keep aloof – individuals whose whole efforts were to destroy everything Irish and National, seek their own selfish ends, by the betrayal of a brother and under the pretence of Nationalism and Patriotism, invite with the one hand the list of a few innocent dupes while with the other they are receiving the Secret Service money of Dublin Castle. Those few ruffians who have insinuated themselves into the present county board have also outside it, but unfortunately connected with its operations, about five or six associates – well-known individuals in the city of Cork – who spend the most of the their leisure hours in Captain Plunkett's office, and who supply their regular list of enrolment for the future services of Dublin Castle. Let not the public think that I make assertions of this kind lightly. I solemnly protest as a priest of the city, that I have proof most positive of what I say, and their efforts, happily unsuccessful efforts, even within last month are in the mouths of everyone.[21]

It was following the county convention of October 1888 that the open split occurred within the Cork county board. The president of the official board was a Eugene Crean, J. Russell was the secretary, and David Walsh, the treasurer. The unofficial, or Fr O'Connor Board as it came to be known, had Fr O'Connor as president, a Mr Hickey as secretary, and Sir Edward Fitzgerald from Blackrock as treasurer. To further complicate matters, another board under clerical influence was set up in Mallow for North Cork, with a Revd J. Carver as chairman. This particular board was sometimes referred to the O'Brien Board or North Cork Board. As well as having a clerical chairman, the secretary was also a priest, a Revd C. Buckley, CC, from Buttevant.[22] In 1890, the winners of the championship organised by the North Cork Board, Bartlemy, played the winners of the Fr O'Connor Board, St Finbarrs. It was obvious that both boards were working in tandem, not surprising, considering both supported the position of the hierarchy and clergy on the question of IRB influence within the GAA nationally and in the Cork county board.

Meanwhile, the official Cork county board, sometimes headed by Eugene Crean, ran its own championship, despite the fact that all the city clubs transferred their allegiance to the O'Connor Board. These made up the number of twenty-five clerical clubs, referred to by De Búrca, while the country clubs by and large remained loyal to the Crean board, De Búrca estimating this number at ninety-one. This is directly contradicted by Madden, in his history of the Rockies, who maintains that 90 per cent of the clubs played under the auspices of the O'Connor Board and that Aghabullogue was the only first-class club to stay with the Crean board.

Blackrock, according to this particular club history, remained loyal to the Crean board, as did Inniscarra. On 12 May 1889, Inniscarra played Charleville at Mallow in the official Cork county board championship. In 1889, Inniscarra played Aghada in the Crean Board final, though Aghada never turned up, being of the opinion that the match should have been played in their area. Since Inniscarra were playing under the official Cork county board, they then went on to represent Cork against the Kerry champions, Kenmare, at Mallow on 29 July 1889. Eugene Crean, chairman of the official Cork county board, presented Inniscarra with their county championship medals before the Kenmare match, congratulating them and for the upcoming match 'counselling a fair and friendly game'.[23]

Other national and local historians make reference to the allegations made by Fr O'Connor against the official board. According to Puirséal, Fr O'Connor had alleged that the IRB-controlled county boards were inveigling young men into the IRB, while these members of the board were at the same time paid informants of Dublin Castle. Beecher refers to a letter of Fr O'Connor's on 22 October to the *Cork Examiner*, just after the county convention of 1888. In this letter he claimed that, 'I am influenced by the consideration that in the County Convention held last week a certain self-interested clique had obtained by previous canvass a temporary majority and thereby the election of a committee, the greater part of whom can have no claim to the confidence of the country.'[24] This letter seems to imply that the 1888 county convention was somehow rigged, and anticipates the allegations made at the national convention later on in November in Thurles.

Fr O'Connor, already closely associated with St Finbarrs, received their full support in the form of the following motions adopted at a special meeting of the club:

1. That we are of the opinion that the management of the Cork County Gaelic Sports urgently needs to be reformed.

2. That we decline to comply with the arrangements of the County Board, as at present constituted, knowing that a few of its members are totally unworthy of the confidence of true Gaels.

3. That we call upon all Gaelic Clubs of the County to take immediate steps for the establishment of a truly representative committee capable and willing to direct our sports in the true spirit of the GAA.

Ballygarvan, Ballyhooly and Blackrock all withdrew from the Cork Park tournament in support of the stance taken by St Finbarrs and were thus expelled from the tournament. Little Island, Emmetts, St Peter and Pauls, and Tracton adopted a similar stance. Greenmount, a club that was later to merge with St Finbarrs, adopted the motion indicating that their club would sever its links with the present county board 'until the said Board act in harmony with our clergy and we condemn their action in expelling our city clubs'. The O'Connor Board then went ahead with its own competitions. The *Cork Examiner* of Monday, 1 April 1889, listed the first ties played in the county championship organised by the Fr O'Connor Board (also known as the city board): Ballygarvan, Carrigaline, Shantally, Tracton, William O'Briens, United Irishmen, Nils Desperandum, Davitts from Queenstown, Greenmount, and League of the Cross from Charlotte Quay.

On the following Monday, the *Cork Examiner*, referred to 'The City Board Championships in Park ... in presence of an immense crowd'.[25] In the same competition, Blackrock played Carrigtwohill, while St Finbarrs played Tower Street. The O'Connor Board met in Charlotte Quay from where they organised their own tournaments, and cups and medals were donated. One of the tournaments was for the Fr O'Connor Cup, donated by the priest himself and engraved by William Egan and Sons of Patrick Street for a fee of 4*s*. Of the board itself, Fr O'Connor was president, a Mr Hickey, secretary, and Sir Edward Fitzgerald, treasurer.

Such a split naturally raises the question of which championship was the more representative of the county's GAA activity. There was the anomaly of the situation of Inniscarra, for example, whereby the first team played under the official Crean board, while the club's second team was affiliated with the O'Connor board in 1890 and played in a competition along with thirty other teams.

As to when exactly the split between the O'Connor Board, the North Cork Board and the official Crean board was healed it is difficult to be certain. Puirséal observes that in 1890, county boards estranged from the central council over the IRB versus clergy issue came back under central control. In Cork, Beecher refers to Fr O'Connor coming back from Clontead, near Coachford, approximately fifteen miles to the west of the city, with the words, 'he had been removed from the city, but as long as he had breath in his body he would stand to the Gaels of the country'.[26] This would imply that Fr O'Connor had lost his backing in the city, supported by the fact that in 1891, St Finbarrs, his staunchest supporters, applied to rejoin the official county board. Beecher believes that there were political considerations in such a move, though he found it difficult to uncover hard evidence for this conclusion. Puirséal, referring to the split in Cork, says that in 1893 the City Board and North Cork Board were reunited. However it was unlikely that there was a clear rapprochement, since the split in the county board over IRB control was carried on to the next division in both the local and national association – the Parnellite Split.

THE PARNELLITE SPLIT

In the summer and winter of 1890, there was a large drop in the number of GAA clubs nationwide. In 1891, seven counties entered the hurling championship but only five took part. When the annual convention was held in 1892, only eighteen delegates, representing six counties, attended. De Búrca claims that such a decline was directly attributable to the split within the Home Rule party early in 1891, a split from which he says the GAA took a decade to recover. Puirséal quotes from a P.J. Sutton who, in 1891, commented that, 'The Association would have made wonderful strides this season ... had not the present deplorable crisis arisen and caused our people to devote all their time in the majority of rural districts to politics and fighting one another.'[27]

Puirséal details how the GAA attempted to cope with the fallout from the Parnell situation. Following Parnell settling terms with Captain O'Shea and the release of William O'Brien and John Dillon from prison following the Plan of Campaign, the GAA held a general meeting. A motion was adopted to pursue a policy of independent opposition and to allow freedom of opinion under the leadership of Parnell, the motion being greeted with enthusiastic cheering. According to Puirséal, the majority of national GAA clubs supported Parnell, despite the clergy severing their links with county boards and clubs.

In July 1892, the Parnellite and anti-Parnellite factions came into open confrontation, although according to Puirséal the central council did not intervene. While the majority of the central council were Parnellites, a special meeting of the central council was called on 26 February 1893, when the GAA president asked delegates from the seven counties represented to outlaw political disputes in the association. The president said that emigration and the intrusion of politics into the affairs of the GAA were responsible for the decline in the association's fortunes; it was therefore decided at this special meeting that 'while maintaining a high national standard' the GAA 'must avoid all political confrontations of an internecine standard'.

This was rather different from the proposed stance of a new central council elected in 1891, which declared that the GAA would 'take such action as may be deemed advisable ... in support of the integrity of the national cause'.[28] Whatever about such a strong statement of intent, some of the following statistics only go to show how much the association declined in the following months. The 1892 annual convention was attended by only fifteen delegates, representing Cork, Kerry and Dublin, these same counties being the only ones which had entered the hurling championship. Attendances were low at matches, much of this due to rural emigration. In 1893, Cork had only fifteen affiliated clubs. This was still better than the situation in Monaghan, for example, where there was no county board in operation from 1890 to 1896, a situation which De Búrca said was part of a general nationalist apathy.

In 1893, an attempt was made to reorganise several counties in Munster and Leinster, and in 1894, Cork and Kilkenny increased the number of clubs in their counties, while provisional county committees were set up in Tipperary, Kildare, Louth and Meath. The 1895 hurling championship featured eight counties, three from Leinster and all the counties from Munster except Cork. This was due to Cork's dispute with the central council.

According to Mandle, the division which occurred in County Cork in 1891 over the Parnell issue only exacerbated the previous split involving the rival boards in the county. The November county convention of 1891 was poorly attended; the county board was in financial difficulty, while the GAA structure throughout Munster was collapsing. The number of clerical clubs declined from seventy-two to forty-four while the Fenian clubs declined from sixty-three to fifty. Mandle observes that Parnellites in the Cork GAA were also anxious to keep the Cork GAA under IRB control, but that such a move was only successful in Cork City.

The *Cork Examiner* of Monday 1 June 1891, in its description of the county final between Inniscarra and Blackrock, said that the atmosphere surrounding the match was heightened by rumours of Parnell arriving in the town:

> ...it may be mentioned, some wag hoaxed the police authorities and got them to believe that Mr Parnell would visit the town on Sunday on his way to Kanturk, and address the townspeople, and that it was for the purpose of escorting Mr Parnell and wrecking Mallow – which is thoroughly unParnellite – that the Gaels were assembling! ... for some time on Saturday evening there was great commotion in police circles. It was suggested that information should be sworn as a basis for the prohibition of any assembly of people...[29]

According to the *Cork Examiner*, the excitment 'simmered down' when it emerged that Parnell was not coming. Sheahan also refers to this particular occasion, and its political overtones. He mentions how Mallow was a very anti-Parnellite venue for the holding of the match and how the rumour went out that Parnell was to come to Mallow with thousands of GAA supporters. The majority of members in the Inniscarra club supported Parnell and club patron Dr Charles Tanner. This may explain the previously referred to instance of how Inniscarra's second team affiliated to Fr O'Connor's board.

The effect of the Parnellite split was to be seen at its most pronounced in the case of the St Finbarrs club. Fr O'Connor had been closely associated with the club, and as we have already read, the club threw its full support behind his stance and played under the auspices of his board. However, when the Parnellite issue arose, there were some members of the club who felt so strongly that their loyalty to Parnell superseded their loyalty to the club; therefore they broke away and formed another club: Redmonds.

According to Power, in early 1892, it was twelve members of St Finbarrs first team who left to form Redmonds, a group who came to be known as the Twelve Apostles.[30] Power mentions some of these individuals, including a Mickie Sheahan, whom he described by saying that, 'never a stauncher heart thumped under that grand blue jersey'. He had, states Power, played in all the matches that St Finbarrs had played and 'was one of the twelve men to leave the club they really loved, never to return'. Redmonds were to become one of the strongest clubs in Cork around the turn of the century, but they subsequently declined.

Another club that was to be formed in Cork in the 1900s was William O'Briens, by supporters of William O'Brien, who had been a reporter on the *Cork Daily Herald* and who in 1881 had been appointed by Parnell as editor of the *United Ireland* newspaper. In 1883, he was elected as nationalist MP for Mallow and in 1892 he was elected MP for the city of Cork. After the death of Parnell O'Brien established the 'All for Ireland' League.

At the 1893 national convention, Cork, according to RIC reports, did send delegates, but along with Dublin they seemed to dissent on various policy decisions. Meanwhile, the City Board, otherwise known as the Fr O'Connor Board, and the other clerical board, the North Cork Board, united.

REORGANISATION OF CORK GAA

A new figure in the GAA set about reorganising the organisation nationally. That figure was Dick Blake from Meath. During the Parnellite split, Blake had supported the view that the GAA should take a neutral stance on the issue. In April 1895, there was a major reshuffle within the GAA and Blake became secretary, a role he held until 1898. During this time he visited clubs throughout the country in his attempts at rejuvenation.

However, his relations with the Cork county board were not always friendly. For example, both Cork and Limerick reacted unfavourably to Blake's attempt to lift the ban on the playing of foreign games. Cork became so strict on the foreign games rule that one of the principal figures in the Cork GAA, Thomas Irwin, had been expelled from the Cork county board for playing rugby. He appealed the decision to the Central Council which supported his case. While De Búrca says the 'influential' Cork board had always been anti-Blake, he asserts that the board had always been well organised and that there had always been an even spread of what he describes as constitutional and Parnellite members.

In May 1895, Cork withdrew from the Central Council in a dispute over a match in which the county had been involved. Power, in his brief history of

Nils, which represented the county in this particular match, provides details of the controversy that arose. On 24 March 1895, Nils were to play Young Irelands from Dublin in the All-Ireland Final. Michael Deering, chairman of the Cork board, and other Cork supporters were angry at a Dublin equaliser, since Cork felt that the referee had played forty minutes rather than thirty minutes, and that it was in these extra minutes that Dublin had equalised. The referee then insisted on playing another thirty minutes, which Cork refused to do, and, therefore, Dublin were awarded the match. At the GAA annual convention the following week, it was decided to replay the match at Thurles.

In the replay, Cork were in a dominant position when a spectator struck a Dublin player, which led to crowd trouble. Nils attempted to clear the crowd from the field, since there were only two minutes to go, and they feared not being awarded the match. When the referee attempted to restart the game the Young Irelands team walked off, while the Cork team remained on the field for half an hour hoping that the game would be finished. The Central Council decided to refix the match. This move was a bridge too far for the Cork county board, and on 28 April at a Central Council meeting, Michael Deering withdrew the Cork board from its membership of the Central Council with these words:

> Mr President and Gentlemen, I am authorised by Cork to withdraw from my membership on the Council, and, furthermore, I beg to inform this Council that the Cork people will give to the team that beat Young Irelands, a set of medals as valuable as was ever presented. This is my resignation, as a member of the Council, and the treasurer of the Central Council, Mr David Walsh, will follow in my footsteps. Good evening, Gentlemen.

Cork recognised its representatives, Nils, as All-Ireland Champions, and on Saturday 11 May 1895, the *Cork Weekly Examiner* featured a photo of the Nils team under the heading, 'The Football Champions of All-Ireland for 1894'. At a special meeting of the county board on 16 July 1895, Nils were presented with medals bearing the inscription, 'GAA, All-Ireland Football Championship, won by Nils, 1894'.

The Cork county board then established its own independence by taking affiliation fees from clubs in Waterford and Limerick. Cork delegates disrupted the May national convention of the GAA, but the board subsequently changed its mind and abandoned its independent stance. On 10 May 1896, the Cork county board was invited to join discussions on the rules and regulations for the GAA and its games for that upcoming year. At the end of that same month a special county convention decided that Cork was to return to the national organisation. The county dutifully paid affiliation fees for fifty clubs since county committees had to forward one-third of all their affiliation fees to the central council.

THE COMMITTEE STRUCTURE

At the turn of the century, the administrative structure of the Cork GAA was modernised. It is also significant to note that at this time county committees were being given a certain amount of autonomy as regards implementing policy, particularly in relation to the ban on members playing other sports. At the 1901 national convention a motion was passed giving county committees the power to disqualify from playing those who 'countenanced' sports 'calculated to interfere with the national ones', though at this particular point, Cork did not use this power.[31]

How much power GAA members within Cork were willing to cede to their county committee remained a contentious issue. At the 1906 county convention the motion was discussed that the rule relating to imported games be left optional to the county committee and that the county convention recommend that representatives adopt this position on the issue for a forthcoming national general convention. The motion was narrowly defeated by sixty-five votes to sixty three, with an objection then being raised that some who had voted on the matter had not known what motion was being voted upon. A recount was called for, which the chairman would not allow and 'some disorderly scenes ensued', after which the meeting ended. A group, feeling aggrieved at what had happened, held their own meeting and passed a resolution of protest to be passed on to the Munster Council.

One can see from such events how important the general county committee was. How such a committee could best reflect the county and city was therefore a matter which received great attention at various county conventions. At the convention in April 1901, it was initially suggested that the general committee be made up of six delegates from the city and twelve from the county, but this was amended so that for the following year there were to be eight delegates from the city and ten from the county. The county delegates were to represent East Cork, North-East Cork, North Cork, West Cork and South-East Cork. At the following year's convention it was decided that the county committee would consist of eleven members from the county and nine from the city.

It was also at this time that a number of important decisions were made by the county board to improve the administration in the county, in particular relating to matters of finance. In 1902 the county board decided that:

1. A position of vice-chairman be created.

2. The county board should open a bank account.

3. All bills be submitted to committee meetings.

4. Payment of bills to be made by cheque duly signed by the chairman, treasurer and secretary.

5. Receipts and expenses of all matches be recorded in the minutes of the preceding meeting.

6. Two auditors to be appointed, one for the county and one for the city, each having the authority to examine receipts and expenses of matches at an ordinary weekly meeting.

7. Travelling expenses of teams playing in enclosed grounds for County Championship matches outside their immediate districts be paid as far as possible by the county board.

8. Each club to nominate two members competent to act as referees.[32]

Beecher adds a footnote to these proposals, saying they were 'apparently' proposed by the reform committee of the Eire Óg club, active to the east of the city.

It is clear from these proposed reforms that the finances of the county structure and how best to manage them was of prime importance. To this end, finance committees were established to monitor income and expenditure of the county board. In his address at the annual convention in January 1913, the chairman referred to how three years previously, the board had a balance on hand of £600, but that it now had a balance of treble that amount, a state of affairs for which he thanked the financial committee. At the convention in 1916, the chairman, James N. Down, referred to the previous year as being 'bright and successful', both financially and in the development of hurling and football. Down thanked the finance committee, 'who meet regularly, and who anxiously and jealously scrutinise each and every claim before they claim payment'.[33] Claims for such payment were usually from players claiming for loss of earnings due to injury.

Another example of the work of the finance committee was instanced in 1934 at the annual convention. The report of the treasurer referred to a debt of almost £2,000 owed by the athletics body, the NACAI. The president of the board said he knew nothing of how the debt had occurred, after which there followed a discussion as to whether the debt should be wiped out. It was finally decided that the matter of the debt be referred to the finance committee. In 1924, divisional boards were set up throughout the county, such as a board for East Cork. Within each of these divisional boards a financial committee was established to administer their finances.

The county board's activities began to mushroom, and probably the most important of these was the organisation of competitions, tournaments, championships and leagues in both the city and county. Such organisation was delegated to various boards and committees. As early as 1891, a special board was formed to organise an inter-house competition between the employees of various firms in the city, while in the same year a juvenile board was set up to get younger players involved in the association. In 1901, a special juvenile board was constituted to administer the city section of a hurling championship, and a few years later the Cork Minor Board was charged with catering for players not playing for the first and second teams of their respective clubs. The minor grade had no age limit at this time.

To encourage schoolboys to get involved in Gaelic games, a schools' shield competition was initiated, overseen by a special committee. One meeting of the committee was convened on a Saturday in June 1908, at which a number of issues were discussed. The committee heard from the secretary of a similar committee in Tipperary, who informed them that a representative school team from Tipperary could not possibly play a team from Cork until after the summer vacation, because the boys in Tipperary were then working hard for the intermediate examinations. The committee also expressed regret at the poor response from teachers to the letters that were sent out to enlist their help with school games, and so it was decided to hand the matter over to the county board. The committee also agreed that if a teacher could not form a team, 'any local Gael' could do so, and that boys who were not attending school but were the appropriate age would be allowed to play in the competition.

In 1910, the committee responsible for games in schools and colleges in Cork City and County received a fillip when the Bishop of Cork presented a beautiful cup to the committee and the Bishop of Cloyne made a similar presentation. There were to be senior and junior competitions in both hurling and football, with no age limit for the senior boys and national schools allowed to enter. It was, according to the *Cork Sportsman*'s correspondent, a case of 'the more, the merrier'. There were numerous competitions held to assist charitable causes, such as raising funds for hospitals and churches, and to erect memorials to various deceased national figures. For example, in September 1908, the committee responsible for the running of the Cork Hospitals Cup met and organised a hurling contest between the GPO and Dock Rovers.

Many of these committees had, as one of their functions, the duty of dealing with objections lodged arising from the games played or, as happened in some cases, investigating why games were not played at all. The county board, to expedite matters as quickly as possible in this regard, set up a special appeals and objections committee which ruled on the matters brought to its attention. In his address at the 1913 convention, the chairman referred to how, in April 1912, the Cork delegation made a number of proposals to the national association, one of which being the establishment of an appeals and objections committee. The county board certainly went ahead with setting up its own particular appeals and objection committee. When the board met in January 1920, it heard how the O'Rahilly Football Club had objected to the minor board fixing a match against Brian Dillons during the closed season. The county board decided to refer the matter to its own appeals and objection committee, which was to meet on the following Friday night.

One of the major undertakings of the Cork county board in the new century was a project to open a new playing venue, which came to be known as the Athletic Grounds, down on the Marina, next to the River Lee. It was opened on 11 September 1904, the day it hosted the 1902 All-Ireland Finals which had run behind time.[34] To oversee the project, a private company was established called the Cork Athletic Grounds Committee Ltd, which took charge of the financing of the new venture and appointed a member of the county board as director. The grounds committee still had a debt in the years following the opening of the grounds and the committee held tournaments to reduce the deficit. In the following years, the committee remained responsible for the upkeep and management of the Athletic Grounds. In October 1911, the *Cork Sportsman* advised the committee to repair some corrugated iron to prevent spectators seeking admission without payment as had happened on a previous Sunday.[35]

Among other tasks devolved to committees was the organisation of inter-county matches involving Cork. In February 1909, at a meeting of the county board, a representative of the organising committee for an upcoming match between Cork and Kilkenny, asked that clubs playing league matches have no matches on the day of the inter-county fixture. The representative also asked that those at the meeting advertise the Cork–Kilkenny match in their local districts. Perhaps a more important committee was that which had responsibility for selecting the county team. How the Cork team should be selected was a contentious issue which will be discussed later, but, reporting a meeting of the Cork county board in January 1913, the *Cork Examiner* mentioned how the selection committee gave details of the team they had chosen.

As clubs formed, they appointed their own committees to run club affairs and held both committee and annual general meetings. For example, Nils Football Club held their annual meeting in January 1910, earlier than usual, so that the new officers and committee would have plenty of time to take charge of their respective teams. Committee meetings were to be held every Wednesday evening at 9p.m. at Fr Mathew Hall. Also in January 1910, the Rangers Club wrote to the county board informing the board of the changes that had been made to their executive at their annual general meeting. The work of the club committee of St Finbarrs in the 1930s is worth noting, in that it decided to donate small weekly cash payments to unemployed members of the club at Christmas.

In terms of devolution of power, the most significant development occurred in 1924, when boards with responsibility for various divisions within the county were set up. Previous to this, there had been committees responsible for GAA activity in various parts of the county, but this was not always a satisfactory arrangement, at least for the West Cork area. At a meeting of the county board in January 1910, a letter from the West Cork Committee and a representative of same told the board that it had felt 'keenly' that it had not been treated fairly by the board regarding a guaranteed sum of money, due from the gate of the county final. It had also felt aggrieved that it had not received a fair share of the money generated from the running of special trains for the final.

The chairman of the board, J.J. Walsh, read out the agreement on which the West Cork Committee had based its assertions, and disagreed with their claim, remarking, 'And though we permit your teams to play a single match each for sets of value £30 and pay twice the expenses you are entitled to, you still believe you should get more.' To this, the West Cork representative, Mr O Driscoll, responded 'T'was my Committee that thought so.' Concluding the discussion, a Mr Mackeray said, 'It is a pity that the West Cork Committee should have been led into this trap to be laughed at. The one desire of the Board is to treat honestly and generously with everybody, and develop every department of the county.' This remark was greeted with cries of 'Hear, hear'.

On Sunday, 13 April 1924, the East Cork Board was established with seven clubs represented. The following motions were passed:

1. That officers appointed be 'ex-officio' without the right or power of voting.

2. The officers appointed be independent of clubs.

3. The officers appointed be club representatives, with rights to vote on all matters.

Mr W.H. Murphy, a member of the county board from the Little Island club, was elected an 'ex-officio' member of the divisional committee in East Cork with full powers to act at all meetings during the year.

The position of the aforementioned Mr Murphy remained an issue of contention. He claimed that he was the president of the divisional committee, while remaining vice-chairman of the Cork county board concurrently. The chairman of the committee was of the view that Mr Murphy was a member of the divisional committee. Mirroring the example of the county board, the East Cork Board had its own financial and appeals committees and, by April 1925, it had fifteen junior hurling and four football clubs under its auspices. This devolved form of administration in the county may have encouraged a certain amount of parochialism. At a divisional board meeting in 1933, it was remarked that clubs in the East Cork division had no interest in GAA affairs outside their own division, since at the county convention that year, only two clubs from the division were represented.

The growth of a layered administrative structure from the county board down to the divisional boards and then down to club level was necessary to address various aspects of the running of the GAA in Cork City and county. The most important aspects to be addressed fell into a number of broad categories, namely: finance, the competitive structure, implementation of rules, dealing with objections and appeals, and the improvement of facilities.

FINANCES OF THE CORK COUNTY BOARD AND CLUBS

Prior to the 1900s, there were no more than fleeting references to the GAA's organisation of its finances at club and county board level. At the AGM of the club in Ballincollig in April 1897, the financial report for the year was considered. With regard to the county board, in the 1893-94 period, before it had come back to the national fold, it recorded a balance in its favour of £20.

More detailed information on forms of income and expenditure can be garnered from press reports of county conventions. A selective look at these reports indicates the major sources of income and areas of expenditure. The balance sheet of 1899 showed that the balance on hand from the previous year was £5 12s 5d. The biggest source of income for that year was £147 11s 1d, this being the receipts from the games held at the enclosure at Cork Park. Subscriptions amounted to £16 10s, while gate and train receipts were itemised together and brought in £7 48s 4d. Affiliation fees from twenty-six clubs, at 12s per club, amounted to £15 12s. Fees to enter championships were paid for thirty-eight teams at 2s 6d per team.

While the receipts from games played at the enclosure at Cork Park constituted the biggest source of income, it was also the greatest form of expenditure for that particular year. The cost of erecting the enclosure, plus the cost of labourers' wages, came to £155 12s 11d. Marking the ground cost £3 1s. The board also financed the cost of delegates who attended the congress in Thurles that year and those who attended Munster Council meetings, the cost to the board being just over £10. The board also had to submit some of its affiliation fees to the central council for twenty-five clubs at 4s each. There were other smaller expenses, such as post and stationery, printing and advertising, telegrams and expenses of referees. The balance on hand heading into the New Year was £4 4s 8d.

Generally speaking, these examples of income and expenditure were to remain a constant feature of financial reports to the county board, although the sums involved continued to grow as the board's activities increased. For the year 1899, referees' expenses were 18s, and this sum had increased to £6 3s 1d for the 1901 playing year. Similarly, the cost of printing and expenditure had risen from £3 18s 6d to £7s 11s 7d in these years. Yet, in his address to the 1902 convention, the president of the board reported that the credit balance was the largest the board had had since 1884, despite the giving of grants for the erection of monuments. A grant of £20 had been made to the Michael Deering Fund, he being past chairman of the board, while £10 had been awarded to the National Monument Fund. Another substantial expenditure was that of £9 for the purchase of shields for schools and colleges competitions. But there were now sixty-two clubs affiliated to the board who subscribed to it the sum of £50. The chairman, in justifying the sum on the school shields, said, 'the schoolboys of today would be the Gaelic men of tomorrow'.

The financial report was deemed to be 'audited and found correct' by J. O'Keeffe and W. Curtin (Auditors). However, this did not prevent one delegate from questioning the figures. He was of the opinion that the gate receipts should have been larger, considering the attendances involved. Though the delegate was 'loath to bring charges against any member of the Co. Board', he felt that in future those in charge of tickets should have them properly blocked and arranged so that the county board officers could check them.

Throughout the 1900s, the number of clubs continued to rise, bringing in more revenue in the form of affiliation fees and entrance fees for competitions. The financial report presented to the county convention in January 1906, showed that seventy-seven clubs had paid affiliation fees of 12s each, bringing a total sum of £46 4s, and that ninety-eight teams entered competitions at a cost of 2s 6d each, this amounting to £12 8s. Again, gate receipts were the greatest source of income, amounting to over £300. The increase in playing activity meant a greater need for playing pitches and the board for that year spent £84 6s on renting fields and paid out wages for the care of playing pitches. There were also sums spent on advertising and referees expenses.

This convention of 1906 is particularly interesting for the debate on financial issues that took place. Much of the discussion referred to the best way of checking the receipts of matches. One of the auditors, Patrick O'Sullivan, referred to the checking of gate tickets, saying that the auditors had adopted a different system of checking gate receipts. Vouchers were used, signed by the local committee, which, according to Mr O'Sullivan, would allow a thorough check of the tickets. One delegate, a Mr Kiely of Passage, said the block of tickets should have been presented to the auditors, as without them it would have been impossible to have a proper check on the tickets and receipts. He therefore proposed that the balance sheet be rejected as the block of tickets from matches should have been returned to the auditors in sealed form. There was much agreement with the argument of Mr O'Sullivan but the balance sheet was nevertheless adopted.

There was also discussion on the practice of paying players absent from work, due to injuries incurred playing the games. Up until now, it had been the practice to pay players two weeks of their wages if they had been injured. The auditors now suggested that a fixed sum be paid to injured players regardless of their social position and type of work. It was also suggested that if the sums payable were smaller it would discourage abuse of the system. On the question of the expenditure on playing fields, the auditors were of the opinion that one third of the receipts would be adequate payment to the owners of playing fields. The auditors who had made these suggestions, Messrs O'Sullivan and O'Neill, intimated they would not go forward a second time for the posts of auditors, being of the opinion that different people should fill the post each year. In the circumstances two guineas were moved to cover their expenses.

The question of accounting for the receipts of matches also arose at the county convention of 1908. Total receipts for the preceding year were £383 11s 6d, while expenditure was £360 2s 3d. One of the auditors made the suggestion at the convention that an assistant secretary should be appointed to keep check of the ticket account, and that tickets should be used at the gate of every match. Where there were stands on grounds, the auditors suggested that money taken on those stands be handed over to the county board, rather than being kept by local committees. There then followed a lengthy discussion on the checking of gate receipt money. It was unanimously decided that there be checking on all gates. It was also suggested that the board was being too generous with referees' expenses, but it was pointed out by the board that only necessary and reasonable expenses were allowed.

The income and expenditure figures of the board increased throughout the first decade of the new century. The auditors' report for the 1909 playing year, prepared for the 1910 convention, showed a total income for that year of £727 8s 8d, and a total expenditure of £648 6s 1d. A number of new items of expenditure can be noted in that year's report. As well as sums spent on the rent of fields and on referees' expenses, £84 2s 2d was spent on the travelling expenses for teams (presumably the county teams). A total of £74 was spent on train guarantees, while there was a £5 grant to the unemployed. In terms of income, gate receipts were again the main source, yielding £567 5s 7d. While the board had spent money on train guarantees, this was practically nullified by amounts it received for refunds on trains, a commission on a Bantry train, and a refund on Macroom train expenses. In a circular to be prepared for the upcoming county convention, it was stated that the board had liquidated all of its then current liabilities and had been generous in paying out £33 to injured players, referred to as 'our wounded brethern'.

Perhaps in the light of previous convention discussions on accounting for gate receipts, a detailed report of the ticket situation for matches was to be given to the convention. This outlined the number of tickets printed for admittance to grounds, those sold and those destroyed in error. Also included were the number of passes for admittance printed and those issued. This was presumably to answer any questions regarding the income from matches and how it should tally with the admittance figures. Under the heading 'liabilities', was the sum of £57 11s 6d, due to William Egan and Sons Ltd. Under the heading of 'assets', was £75 11s 2d, which was listed as cash-in-bank, while in the investment account was the sum of £30 in the form of thirty shares in the Cork Athletic Grounds.

The auditors' report made a pointed reference to the 'Secretaryship', saying it was 'out of harmony with an otherwise excellent governing body'. The auditors felt that while the then secretary, Mr Irwin, was receiving £62, a great portion of the work had been performed by others. The report therefore advocated that a Mr O'Leary be appointed as secretary at half the salary of Mr Irwin and that Mr Irwin be appointed assistant secretary on the same salary as Mr O'Leary. This was very much in accordance with a motion on the agenda for the convention that the salary of the secretary of the county board be limited to £30. The motion proposed that two secretaries be appointed on a commission of 5 per cent each on the earned income of the committee.

The cost of renting fields continued to rise during these years. As previously noted, the cost of renting fields for the 1905 playing year was just over £84. In 1911, the rents paid for playing fields was £118, rising to £177 for the following year. Between 1911 and 1912, there had also been a £69 increase in the cost of printing and advertising. The 1913 convention was informed that a profit of £22 12s 7d had been realised from the Bandon Railway Company on trains guaranteed.

It is interesting to note the impact that the outbreak of the First World War had on playing activity and income on receipts for matches. In his address to the county convention in January 1915, James Down, deputising for J.J. Walsh, began with, the 'year just closed has been an ill-starred one, the world over. Nations and individuals have suffered; and our Association has been no exception to the rule.'[36] He referred to how the outbreak of war had affected train arrangements for matches and how the playing grounds near the Renmount depot had been taken over. In addition to bad weather, these circumstances were responsible for a £377 fall in the board's income compared to the previous year. The treasurer added that the final of the Beamish Shield had been played in a continuous downpour and that the receipts had come to £23, when the amount could have been £70.

But the board did spend money on a number of projects in 1914. For example, it erected a pavilion at the marina at a cost of £167, and it secured rooms for meetings on Cook Street and spent £67 furnishing them. There was expenditure on accidents in games and on grants, the deputy chairman noting that most of the money paid for accidents to players were those in the junior grades. One delegate at the convention proposed that the board's account should have been transferred from the Provincial Bank to the Munster and Leinster Bank, which, according to the delegate, 'was controlled by local people'. The treasurer, replying to this, said that the terms were more favourable in the Provincial Bank and that in any event they were working from an overdraft.

Throughout the war years, the board was still in a position to expend money on a number of projects. At the beginning of 1916, the board had a credit revenue of £207 15s 11d. In 1915, £20 had been given to a cross-country committee which sent a running team to Dublin. A sum of £10 was awarded to the senior selection committee (£5 of which was a loan), £5 was spent on training and £8 was given to the Lees Club who were the senior football champions. An additional £5 was given to the O'Leary Memorial Committee. There had been a drop in affiliation and championship fees, especially in North and West Cork, and the chairman recommended that a representative be sent to each of the divisions to inquire into the situation. While accident money was paid out, the chairman stressed that 'every claim into accidents was inquired into carefully'.

The board once again debated the issue of expenditure at the 1917 convention, when the chairman, James N. Down, noted as a 'big question' the number of delegates at that year's convention. He was of the opinion that such expenditure was not justified, as presumably this made a drain on the funds of clubs who paid the expenses of delegates. The treasurer also noted that in the previous year a big game between St Marys and Redmonds had been aborted, which had a 'detrimental' effect on the board's finances. It may be unfair to portray the county board as being always ungenerous, but undoubtedly, there were some who considered it so.

At a meeting of the board in January 1920, a representative of Youghal Football Club told of how, at a match in Kinsale, one of their players had sustained a serious injury. The player had cut his hand on the wire of a goal-post, had kept playing and subsequently had to go to hospital to attend to the injury. At the meeting the club submitted a medical certificate stating that the wound had turned septic. The representative also stressed that this particular player was a poor man with a family and that this had been the first time the club had asked for a grant of money. It was unanimously decided to grant a sum of £8 towards the man's losses. Clubs also took it upon themselves to help their own players when they suffered through injuries. In 1928 Nemo Rangers held a benefit tournament for one of their own players who had lost an eye in a match.

While clubs looked to the board for financial support, the board, in order to improve their major facilities, turned to the Munster Council when large sums of money were needed. At a meeting of the Munster Council in January 1927, Nemo Rangers were granted £50 to enable the club pay off the debt they had accrued in extending their ground. Also present at the meeting was a deputation from the county board, who had a request before the council for a loan to upgrade the Cork Athletic Grounds. A Mr Harrington from the board intimated that they had originally intended to ask for a grant, but would be happy with a loan for which they would give enough security for repayment. He also informed the council that the board would apply to hold inter-county matches at the venue to help pay back the loan. The Cork secretary, in supporting his colleague, said that if the Cork board were to go to the bank for a loan they would have to make repayments at 7 per cent per annum. Another Cork delegate, Mr Buckley, estimated that a sum of £500 was needed to erect a decent stand and to make other improvements. It was decided that Cork's application should be submitted to a forthcoming convention of the Munster Council.

Details of the finances of various clubs in the city are more difficult to ascertain, but there are intermittent details from sources, such as club histories, of expenses and sources of income. One such club in the early decades of this century, was Fr O'Leary Temperance Abstinence Hall, which was attached to a parish centre of the same name. This club was originally set up by a Fr O'Leary in the South Parish, the same area from which St Finbarrs drew their players. The GAA club did not have control of its own finances and on 7 January 1917, a meeting of the committee in charge of the Fr O'Leary Hall received a letter from the secretary of the hurling club asking for a sum of £5 from hall funds. The request was deferred until the next meeting of the hall committee, but the Revd Chairman guaranteed to give the necessary sum needed for the team's affiliation to the county board if such was required. At a meeting of the hall committee on 4 February, it was decided to pay the sum of £5 on the understanding that the sum would be paid back from the funds of a concert in the hall in aid of the hurling club.

Clubs garnered income through fundraising events such these, as well as through membership fees from members. At St Finbarrs, in the 1930s, individual membership cost 2s 6d per annum, while unemployed members were given free membership. The clubs also donated small weekly cash payments to unemployed members of the club at Christmas. In 1933, Nemo Rangers began a fundraising campaign to revive the club after losing some players who had been deemed illegal for playing soccer and who had then transferred to the Evergreen Club. By 1940, the club, through a combination of weekly subscriptions from members and card games, had an income of 60s per week.

One drain on expenses that clubs felt keenly, especially those which were successful, was the cost of training and running teams. A letter-writer to the *Cork Sportsman* in September 1908 complained that playing football was a 'dead loss' from a monetary point of view.[37] According to the writer, players were not getting their fare to the stations nearest the venue of matches, and games were not being properly advertised. The writer further remarked that it was no wonder that players were not ambitious, and instanced the example of the Lees Club, whose activities cost £30 over and above the expenses allowed them by the ruling bodies. A number of years later, St Finbarrs were losing money on training their senior team for the 1926 county hurling final. The club wrote to the county board to clear such expenses, since it had already spent £20 defraying the expenses of training and it felt that to spend any more money was beyond the club's means. In 1928, St Finbarrs complained to the county board that they had to wait to play a match against UCC in the championship because the students had been away on holidays. The club had had its players in training at a cost of £5.

It was no wonder that clubs tried to cover whatever costs they incurred, such as in playing tournament matches. Playing in tournaments demanded travelling expenses and meals for players. But the players could gain some material reward in these tournaments. In the 1930s, St Finbarrs won a Eucharistic Procession tournament where the prize for each player was either £1 or a pair of boots. On 8 March 1931, the club played Blackrock in a tournament in Riverstown for a set of Irish suit lengths.

DEVELOPMENT OF GAA FACILITIES

We have already seen the degree to which expenditure on playing fields accounted for so much of the board's costs as its activities increased. Even before the beginning of the new century the board was very much aware that it was of paramount importance to acquire one central venue for the holding of inter-county games and the more important club matches. They were particularly mindful of how a proper enclosure would be an excellent source of revenue, as the entrance of paying patrons could be properly monitored. However, as we shall see, the transition from allowing free attendance to the advent of imposing admission charges was not a smooth one.

The area earmarked for the erecting of a proper enclosed ground was on the marina, near where the old Cork racecourse was situated. In 1898, the board received permission from the corporation to put up an enclosure in what was then called Cork Park, and on 31 July of that year, the Munster Championship semi-final was held there. Fifteen thousand spectators turned up; the four turnstiles were totally unable to cope. Patrons climbed the wire fencing and a gate was also knocked down, allowing many free admission. On the following Monday, the *Cork Examiner* described the scenes at the enclosure. The paper blamed the board rather than the spectators, saying they had been waiting since 1.30p.m. to gain admission to the ground due to a delay in the starting time. This hold-up had been caused by the breakdown of a train carrying supporters from Tipperary. Stating the attendance figure to be 15,000, the paper said that less than half that number paid the admission price. It described the event as a 'serious loss' to the county board and the result of 'faulty arrangements'.[38]

The following year the board decided to erect a second enclosure at the same location, but the problem of admitting crowds remained and the board incurred further losses. At this juncture the board decided to take out a lease for that year and the following years. The problems with spectators at Cork Park was raised at the county convention in March 1900. Tom Dooley, a member of the county committee, addressing the delegates, told how the board had gone to 'considerable expense' to erect an enclosure at Cork Park but that their efforts to ensure that spectators paid their entrance admission had been frustrated by what he referred to as a 'contemptible section'.[39] He said that such people would pay train fares to matches, but would not pay the 'small tariff' charged to gain entrance to the venue. He also remarked on how the matter was not helping businesses in the city which could gain from inter-county matches, since various county committees would willingly send teams to play friendlies against Cork Park, which would thereby bringing spectators into the city.

The treasurer of the board, Mr Wren, also raised the matter at that convention and expressed similar views to Mr Dooley. For example, the Limerick county team had come to play Cork to help finance the enclosure, but this gesture had only resulted in a loss to the board. At the match, the enclosure had been torn down and, according to Mr Wren, a 'considerable' number did not pay admission.

However, the board remained determined to have a major GAA venue in the city. To raise funds for the erection of a proper stadium a limited company was formed called Cork Athletic Grounds Committee Limited. The county board invested in the venture and a county board member became a member of the company's board. After subscriptions for share capital had been raised, a lease for six acres was drawn up between the Cork Agricultural Society, Cork Corporation and the county board treasurer, John Fitzgerald. At this time the grounds were intended to cater for all sports, and it was envisaged that a rugby international between Wales and Ireland would be played there.

The result of the board's redoubled efforts to secure a major venue came to fruition in 1904, when the delayed 1902 All-Ireland Finals were played at what was now called the Cork Athletic Grounds. The Lord Mayor of Cork, Augustine Roche, formally opened the grounds while the Barrack Street, Butter Exchange and Midleton Bands provided musical entertainment. Yet, the inability of the venue to cope with crowds manifested itself once again. A crowd of 20,000 was present, but again there were not enough turnstiles to cope with the numbers. Some of the spectators climbed on to the corrugated iron surroundings which resulted in one of the refreshment rooms collapsing from the weight of people standing on it. In its account of the event, the *Cork Examiner* noted how the congestion in front of the entrances was 'extreme' and estimated that 1,000 people had climbed over the enclosure.[40] Commenting on the field itself, it noted that it was a 'fine surface', after the grass seeds had been sown the previous spring.

At this time, the Athletic Grounds were run by a private company who leased the grounds for sporting occasions, the rent being one third of the net receipts. For example, the grounds were let out for the playing of hockey and association football. A number of initiatives were undertaken to promote use of the grounds. The company in charge installed a weighing machine and shooting gallery and wanted to arrange tramway access to the venue. Some time after the opening, ladies were admitted free of charge, and advertising was being placed at the ground by 1906. However, by this time, it was decided by the county board secretary that the grounds were to be used exclusively for hurling and football. The grounds remained the principal venue in Cork City and county throughout the following decades, setting the scene for some major spectacles, as will be seen later.

The board did not concentrate its efforts exclusively on the Athletic Grounds, however, and when the venue had been properly established, it continued to use other pitches in the city for inter-county and club games. At the turn of the century, the county board had been looking at a number of sites, in particular following the loss it incurred at the Cork–Limerick game of 1899. At the county convention in March 1900, the president, replying to a delegate, said that the board had tried to secure a number of sites during the year, not just at the Cork Agricultural Grounds, but also at a site at Blackrock, though the owner of one of these sites had objected to the county board's plans. Mr Wren, the president, stated that the site they had in mind in Blackrock, in the Ballintemple area, was especially attractive because it was particularly suited to the electric tramway system. However, a gentleman living nearby claimed that the games would be a nuisance to both his family and himself.

Another major venue in Cork was the grounds at Turner's Cross, used up until 1912 as a pitch for Gaelic games, after which date it came to be used as a soccer grounds. In the period from 1922 to 1925, the Nemo Rangers club gained control of the grounds and intended lengthening the pitch, for which it needed financial assistance. The club asked for a grant of £35 to develop the grounds, which was approved by the finance committee but subsequently reduced to £20 as the board was financially insolvent at the time. The club also asked for financial assistance from the Munster Council, based on the fact that the council had taken almost £5,000 in receipts from a Cork–Tipperary game held at the grounds, but this request was refused. The county senior football final was also held at Turner's Cross in the 1920s, though other clubs continued to have reservations about the size of the ground. Nemo Rangers had held discussions with the city commissioner about lengthening the pitch. In May 1929, the county board used the venue for a national hurling league game against Galway, but this only increased the frustration of Nemo Rangers, who had lost more than £41 over the previous twelve months and eventually the club felt that it had no option but to close the grounds. A week after the aforementioned national league game, the club committee refused to allow a senior hurling championship game at the grounds and Turner's Cross was no longer used for Gaelic games.

With regard to acquiring venues for meetings and conventions, various locations throughout the city were used. For example, a meeting of the Cork county board was held at the Municipal Buildings in September 1896. In 1898, it used a new venue for meetings – the courthouse at Anglesea Street. Committees in charge of various leagues used other venues. In December 1897, the Cork City League Committee met at the Catholic Young Men's Society Hall. It was in 1915, however, that the county board acquired permanent premises for its meetings when it acquired new rooms at Cook Street, in the centre of the city. These rooms were to be used by the board until the opening of Páirc Uí Chaíomh in 1976 and were known as the 'Parliament of Cook Street'.[41] For county conventions, the board chose a number of different venues across the city. For the 1900 convention, the premises of the Nils Football Club were used. In subsequent years, larger public venues were availed of. In January 1913, the board's annual convention was held in the Fr Mathew Hall. The city hall came to be used in the following years. The 1915 convention was held there, using the council chamber. In 1934, the GAA celebrated its jubilee year, and under the headline 'Jubliee Year of a Great Movement', the *Cork Evening Echo*, described how the annual convention of the county board was held at the Cork County Council chambers in Washington Street and was attended by 300, including former officials and officers.[42]

CLUB PITCHES AND FACILITIES

Clubs could avail of venues overseen by the county board for championship or league matches, but finding pitches on which to practice was altogether more haphazard, especially in the case of clubs from within the city. At a meeting of the committee of the Fr O'Leary Temperance Abstinence Hall, in the south inner city, one of the members mentioned the necessity of procuring a field for the hurling team affiliated to the centre. The committee unanimously agreed to give further assistance in meeting the requirements of the team. However, this seemed to be easier said than done, because the following May the same Mr O'Donovan was still reminding the committee of the necessity of procuring a field for the hurling club.

In the early days of Glen Rovers every alleyway was used, in particular a piece of ground known as 'The Gardens', just off Spring Lane, where the club was founded. In 1926, the club procured a playing field in Kilbarry, which it rented for a sum of £10 a year from a Mr Tim Twomey. In its early years, Nemo Rangers, situated in the south of the city, practised at a quarry on Windmill Road. As Blackrock prepared for a particular championship, two trial teams played each other in what was known as the Hockey Field, which was almost certainly more suitable than the patches of ground being used by other clubs in the city. Brian Dillons, who began playing activity at the beginning of the century, were in a somewhat more fortunate position, in that, although a city team, they were near the countryside to the north of the city. There were a number of grounds around this area in which Brian Dillons played, such as Bell's Field, near an area known as Madden's Buildings, and one known as Kelleher's Field. As can be seen from the names of these grounds, they either belonged to individuals and families at the time or had so belonged previously and were now being used communally.

In terms of acquiring playing equipment, clubs more often than not improvised in whatever way they could, though items such as Gaelic footballs were being sold in the city from a relatively early stage in the life of the association. In the *Cork Examiner* of 23 June 1894, Murray & Co. of Patrick Street advertised Gaelic footballs for sale. They were described as 'Murray's GAA Registered' and were either 'Endless or with End Pieces' and came in various sizes. Those interested in purchasing were invited to write to the shop for a price list. There is little information in club histories on whether or how clubs purchased or improvised in the making of footballs, though, as will be seen later, if a ball burst, as sometimes happened, matches had to be abandoned. It was in the purchase and making of hurleys that the improvisation of clubs can best be seen.

When the Grenagh Club, some miles to the north of Cork City, began GAA activity in the early 1900s, sticks were used instead of camáns and were made ready for use by being pared into a suitable shape. When the club re-emerged in the 1920s, after lying dormant, hurleys were purchased for a number of years at Eustace's of Leitrim Street. Money was raised by holding dances and through player subscriptions, but when initial fundraising ideas ran out, hurleys came to be made locally. Nemo Rangers improvised in a similar way, in that in the early years of the club, members cut saplings from trees known as 'brooks' and used them for hurleys. When Glen Rovers began their activities they had their jerseys knitted at the convent of St Maries of the Isle and purchased their hurleys from Collins' Shop in Leitrim Street and from a Myles Glen, who had a hardware store on North Main Street.

Clubs came to various arrangements as to where to host meetings and social events. The first club room of Glen Rovers was over a pub in Bird's Quay owned by a Dan Dorgan and his wife, and this was to remain a social meeting place for club members until 1969. Brian Dillons and nearby club Riverstown decided to pool resources in the 1920s to make the most of each other's facilities and they went under the club name of Sarsfields. The new club used the pitch at Riverstown and the clubhouse at Dillon's Cross. As a Brian Dillons' member recalls, 'The idea was that, with the pitch at Riverstown and the clubhouse at Dillon's Cross, Sars had an anchor at both ends of the district, although Mayfield remained independent in between.'[43]

However, the effort to reap the best of each facility did not prove a long-term success. Club members from Sarsfields became disenchanted with having to attend meetings up at the Brian Dillons Club, while those from Brian Dillons were not keen on travelling to Riverstown for training as they had to hire sidecars to do so. The final break came when the Brian Dillons players felt they were not getting their fair chance to play. Brian Dillons, after the split, acquired the premises of the Dillon's Cross Pigeon Club and knocked a partition where hitherto a pony had been kept. The clubhouse on Stream Hill then acted as a community centre, holding regular céilís, as well as modern dancing and what the club historian calls 'fireside banter'.

St Finbarrs were able to use the facilities of the Fr O'Leary Temperance Abstinence Hall for meetings, though this caused some annoyance to the committee in charge of the running of the hall. This facility had been officially opened in the South Parish in 1906 after a decade of fundraising. St Finbarrs was a separate hurling team to the team associated with the temperance hall, which went under the same name as the hall. In the late 1930s, the matter of the St Finbarrs club using the rooms of Fr O'Leary Hall was given quite a bit of discussion among the committee in charge of the affairs of the hall. The minutes of the hall from 4 April 1938, show the secretary pointing out to the committee that, as a body, St Finbarrs Hurling Club were not members of the hall, but the meeting decided that the privilege of holding their weekly committee meetings should be extended, though a member of the committee dissented on the matter. The secretary was then directed to remind St Finbarrs that this was confined to simply meeting, and he was directed to ask the club for the names of committee members who were allowed to make use of the meeting-room concession. It seems that other members were gaining access to the Fr O'Leary Hall's facilities; at the same meeting the hall committee reaffirmed that only members of the hall should be admitted and a determined stand be taken to expel intruders.

From April to September 1938 the committee of Fr O'Leary Temperance Abstinence Hall discussed the use of its rooms by the St Finbarrs Club. They had agreed to give use of the rooms to St Finbarrs GAA club on condition that the club submitted the names of its committee to the Fr O'Leary Hall committee. St Finbarrs had not replied to these demands and, following further communication by the Hall's committee, when they finally did, they refused to comply with their wishes.

The fact that the hall had its own separate hurling team since the early part of the century may have meant that there was a keen sense of rivalry between the two teams, since they were both based in the South Parish. This rivalry may have manifested itself in the way St Finbarrs were less than cooperative with the committee of Fr O'Leary Temperance Hall on the issue of the meeting room.

PLAYING STRUCTURE: COMPETITIONS, TOURNAMENTS, CHAMPIONSHIPS AND LEAGUES

While the latter-day structure of the GAA, which revolves around the playing of championships and leagues, began in the last decade of the nineteenth century in Cork, tournament games held for a variety of causes were just as popular, if not more so, in terms of getting teams involved in organised games. Tournaments were organised by clubs to raise funds and to generate money for the erection of monuments, churches and for charitable causes.

Tournaments held by neighbouring clubs were particularly popular as they allowed the opportunity to play local rivals without having to travel too far from home. For example, in 1896, the Ballincollig club played in a number of tournaments hosted by clubs in Bride Valley, Cloughduv, and Coachford, as well as one hosted by the Gaelic League. All these clubs were from the same area to the west of Cork City. In the Cloughduv tournament, held on the 9 February 1896, it was the junior teams from Ballincollig and the host club Clougduv who met in one semi-final. In 1902, Ballincollig entered the Cork City Harriers Tournament, the National Monument Tournament and the William Ahearne Memorial Tournament.

Another significant tournament at the turn of the century was held in conjunction with the Cork National Exhibition in 1902. Inniscarra was one of the clubs that entered, enticed no doubt, by what the club historian calls a 'massive cup', plus medals for the winners.[44] On 10 September 1904, the *Cork Examiner* referred to an upcoming special tournament called the Cork Hospital Gaelic Football Championship. The rules for this competition were adopted from those of the Dublin Saturday League, and the chairman of the organising committee, in looking forward to the competition, spoke of the 'sportsmanlike spirit which is likely to prevail'.[45]

The importance of tournaments around this time can be gauged from the fact that a special meeting of the Geraldine Rovers GAA club was held in September 1904 to elect officers who would be in charge of the hurling and football teams for forthcoming tournaments.

Hosting and entering tournaments was one matter, but it seems that they were not always finished in good time. For example, in a circular issued by the county board before the county convention of 1910, reference was made to various changes in the organisational structure in the county, and it was mentioned that the board had cleared up outstanding tournaments.[46]

In the years following the 1916 Rising, a number of local competitions were held throughout the county to raise money for the Prisoners' Development Fund. In Cork, in July 1920, a Cork Selection defeated St Finbarrs in a tournament held to help the Cobh Republican Prisoners' Development Funds. In 1927, Nemo Rangers played in a competition for the Morsecock Cup, which had been run to raise funds for the dependants of those who had drowned when the SS *Morsecock* had sunk. In 1932, the emerging Sarsfields Club, to the east of Cork City, played St Finbarrs four times to decide the winner of the Fever Hospital Cup.

Although, as will be seen later, league and championship formats were long established throughout the city and county, right into the 1930s many tournament games were being played. Erin's Own, to the east of the city, were one of the clubs who took advantage of these playing opportunities, and at the AGM of Glen Rovers in January 1934, the secretary, reviewing the previous year's activity, noted than when the senior team had been knocked out of the championship, it had instead concentrated on the Beamish Shield and tournament matches.

LEAGUES

More so than championships, leagues, especially in the city, seem to have been the main form of organised competition, particularly in the early days of the association in Cork. The popularity of the league structure was espoused by the *Cork Sportsman*, in a piece written on 11 July 1897. The writer, calling himself 'Sport', had asked the people in West Cork what benefit a league structure would be to them, the reply to which the writer reported as, 'We want something more attractive than a mere County Championship chance – something making for prolonged interest. Nothing else will ever succeed in moulding and developing our material.'[47] The same paper made reference to an East Cork Hurling League in August of the same year.

This theme of the league structure being the best way of encouraging and facilitating teams was taken up by the *Cork Sportsman* in 1908. In September of that year, the writer of the paper's GAA notes said, 'Everybody seems to think that if Gaelic football is to assert itself locally more senior teams are necessary. Indeed, there are dozens of fine young fellows only bursting for an opening, as last year's league proved, and it is simply criminal not to get them going.'[48]

This is not to say that leagues were not already being run that year. In June 1908, a writer for the same paper, under the section entitled 'Leagues', said that the 'Cork Suburbs are waking up and the Leagues are bringing out great teams'. The following August he stated that, 'There is no end to the number of football leagues we are going to have before we're done.'

Evidence of the number of leagues being run can be found in an excerpt from the *Cork Sportsman* of Saturday, 1 January 1910, which proposed that the

Preparing for the throw: a Gaelic football match in the early twentieth century. (Image courtesy of *Irish Examiner*)

secretaries of the various league committees meet around the table, the leagues mentioned being the Saturday Hurling and Sunday Hurling Leagues. A most upbeat summary of league activity was given by the chairman of the county board at the annual county convention on 27 January 1913. He remarked that, 'No efforts have been spared for the infusion of vigour' and that 'Half-holiday, Saturday and Sunday Leagues are everywhere and assistance is always forthcoming from central funds when the occasion demands.'[49] Yet it seems it was important that the leagues did not detract from county championship matches. A meeting of the organising committee for an upcoming match between Cork and Kilkenny in February 1909 asked that clubs should have no league matches on 21 February, when the inter-county match was due to take place, and that board delegates publicise this inter-county match in their own districts.

At the same 1913 convention, the chairman also spoke admiringly of the new speed with which the championships had been completed during the preceding year. This was not the first time that the board showed a determination to finish their championships in good time. At the county convention in March 1900, the board secretary referred to how the county championships in hurling and football in Cork were being adversely affected by having to wait for championships in other counties to be completed. A circular distributed before the county convention of 1910 noted the 'drastic change' in the administration of the board's affairs, which ensured that all championships had been completed in seven months.[50]

The board considered various ways of running championships, taking into consideration the city and the size of the county. At the convention in February 1908, the decision was taken unanimously to have an open draw in the championship as opposed to a divisional one. The county board also experimented with running the championship on a league basis, but this necessitated too much travelling, and in 1911 the format reverted to that of a knockout competition. In the aftermath of the War of Independence and the Civil War, the original divisions within the county were reorganised and in the 1924/25 season, divisional boards were formed which ran their own championships.

An important aspect of the competitive structure was the evolution of various grades to cater for different ages and abilities. The growth of such a structure is indicated by the fact that in the years from 1912 to 1914, the county board was administering five grades of competition, namely senior, intermediate, middle grade, junior and minor. Junior and senior grades had existed at least as far back as 1895 and in that year a number of bye-laws were passed stating that players who took part in senior tournaments would not

then be allowed to play in minor tournaments. The first junior championship was run by the Cork board in 1890. In 1905, a minor championship was
introduced specifically for players who had not played with either the first or
second teams of their clubs.

What was known as the middle grade was also introduced both in
league and championship formats. In January 1910, the *Cork Sportsman* gave
notice that Cobh were to play St Finbarrs in middle-grade competition
at the Athletic Grounds in the Cork City Football League. For a county
championship semi-final in the middle grade in October 1911, a 'lack of
suitable railway arrangements' meant Youghal were deprived of 'many of
their men'.[51] It was finally decided at the 1914 county convention to abolish this middle-grade competition. This was possibly due to the fact that at
a previous convention in 1910, the board had introduced the intermediate
grade to accommodate teams between the senior and junior grades. There
continued to be changes to the competitive structure, such as in the 1930s,
when the county board gave the opportunity to junior players to play at a
senior standard by allowing junior clubs to come together and form a senior
team in their division.

Competitive activity for juvenile players was not ignored, either outside
or within the school system. As early as 1890, a meeting of the county board
resolved to hold juvenile championships; participating players were not to be
more than sixteen years of age and teams had to pay an affiliation fee of 2s 6d.
A juvenile board was formed in 1891 and another was formed in 1901 which
ran a special city section hurling championship. The secretary of the county
board, Mr Tom Irwin, speaking at the February 1908 convention, expressed
pleasure at the continued progress of youth shields, which, he said 'form a
practical way of educating the useful aspirants to the ranks of the GAA'.[52]

The *Cork Sportsman* reported a meeting of the schools shield committee in
June 1908. Members of the schools shield committee expressed their regret at
the poor response the committee had received from teachers to letters they
had sent out, and said that if a better response was not forthcoming they would
hand over the matter of schools activity to the county board. They decided
to send a deputation to the county board to discuss the poor response from
schools. To compensate for the poor response from teachers the committee put
forward the proposal that if a teacher could not form a team then 'any local
Gael' could do so, and furthermore, that boys who were not going to school
but were of the proper age could also play in the schools competitions.

The county board also liaised in other ways with schools, with long-term success. In the early 1900s, the North Monastery School, run by the Christian Brothers, had banned the game of hurling in the school, rugby being the main game played there. However, two Christian Brothers and a lay teacher formed a hurling team. The Brothers were then approached by the county board, who asked if the students could compete under the name of the school in the future. The board also liaised with clubs such as Nemo Rangers, whom they asked in the club's early years (around 1910) to organise juvenile leagues in their local area in the south of the city. Individuals in clubs also encouraged juvenile activity; much of the credit for this work in the early years of Glen Rovers goes to a Paddy O'Connell, who organised street leagues and who helped that club's profitable links with the North Monastery School. He also attempted to establish similar links with Farrnaferris and Presentation schools.

Another opportunity to promote playing activity was through the organisation of competitions between the various business houses in the city. It is significant that when a juvenile board was formed in 1891, an inter-house board was formed in the same year. Since many businesses took a half day on a Wednesday, a league called the Wednesday Half-Day Gold Medal Hurling and Football League was begun. In 1899, Tom Dooley, one of the prominent members of the Cork county board, founded the inter-firm board to organise matches between business institutions, as well as government institutions, such as the GPO.

RULES, ENFORCING DISCIPLINE, APPEALS AND OBJECTIONS

When the county board was brought back into the fold of the national association in the 1890s, after the various splits, it was bound to implement national policy on a number of issues, most notably in relation to rules on foreign games, which will be discussed later. From its earliest years the GAA had enforced rules relating, for instance, to how football should differ from rugby or to who was entitled to participate in athletic events run by the GAA. For example, the rule on athletics participation read, 'That after 17 March 1885, any athlete competing at meetings held under other laws than those of the Gaelic Athletic Association shall be ineligible to compete at meetings held under the GAA.'[53]

Another rule that the GAA attempted to enforce nationally related to how Gaelic football should be played, with this directive being issued:

We have to remind those who played football that the ball is not to be passed or carried in any way. It may be caught but it must be kicked or put on the ground at once. It may also be hit with the hand. The passing and carrying is entirely foreign, having been imported from rugby…

Aside from these national directives, the Cork county board also introduced its own bye-laws in the mid-1890s, which were as follows:

1. Teams more than fifteen minutes late to forfeit games.

2. Players who take part in senior tournaments cannot revert to the junior grade.

3. Parish Rule: A player working in one parish but living in another could play with either one parish or the other.

4. The board's permission needed before player transfers, after which he cannot play or another three weeks.

5. All members of the same team to wear the one colour.[54]

The parish rule was one which occupied the minds of the county board right up to modern times, as it was constantly adjusted to ensure fairness and prevent poaching of players. In 1911, GAA in West Cork was practically non-existent and players without clubs were being recruited by teams in the city, such as Nils and Lees. In order to stop this practice the board modified the parish rule.

Some years later another directive from the county board was issued on the question of wearing sports clothes of Irish manufacture. This occurred at the county convention in 1901, when a Mr Curtin remarked on a how a particular team of Gaelic footballers had not worn jerseys of Irish manufacture. He proposed a resolution that it be incumbent on teams to do so. It was decided that it be communicated to clubs that the wish of the county board was that, wherever possible, a club should wear jerseys of Irish manufacture.

The aforementioned rule on punctuality, with its intention to begin matches at the appointed time, did not seem to have had any long-term impact. The lack of punctuality was a constant criticism of the board that continued into the new century, and one which the board itself acknowledged. At the 1908 county convention, the county secretary, Tom Irwin remarked, 'we admit that want of punctuality is one of the greatest drawbacks to our Gaelic pastimes'. At the county convention in January 1910 two motions were submitted to deal with the issue. One proposed that any team who failed to line out to the minute of the appointed hour would lose any claim to consideration in the case of accidents during the game. A slightly more flexible motion proposed a similar penalty, except it would allow fifteen minutes grace after the original fixed time of the match.

Such measures were no doubt proposed in response to the criticism the county board was receiving on the late starting times of matches. In a piece in the *Cork Sportsman* in January 1910, entitled 'Carelessness and Lack of System', the writer made this caustic remark, 'Reference is not made here to punctuality which seems hopeless of attainment.' A week previously, in the same paper's GAA notes, the correspondent, while praising the way the county board had finished the championships, criticised the board for the lateness of matches, saying, 'That eternal Gaelic half-hour is as much in evidence as ever'. He also noted that the board had never taken 'the stringent measures they promised'.

Another important matter which had to be addressed by the board was that of rough and dangerous play and how it should be disciplined. Tom Irwin referred to it in his address to the county convention in 1908, when, in dealing with a number of matters, he said, 'We also refer to the tendency of rough play practised on our Gaelic field and so often referred to by our referees.'[55] There were already procedures laid down by the national association for dealing with errant players. For example, at the annual national convention on 24 February 1907, a motion was adopted whereby players who were ordered off the field of play should remain suspended until reinstated by the committee in charge of the match at which the player or players were ordered off.

But it was not always easy to define whose authority was final. For example, at a match between St Finbarrs and Midleton on August 1913, encroachment from spectators on to the pitch led to the match being abandoned. At a meeting on the following Tuesday night to discuss the match, the chairman of the county board, J.J. Walsh, laid the blame on the St Finbarrs club and labelled the troublemakers a 'bunch of savages'.[56] The match was awarded to Midleton, but St Finbarrs appealed the decision to the Munster Council, which ordered a rematch. J.J. Walsh responded that this decision was a licence for vandals.

Such incidents bring up the whole issue of the use of appeals by clubs and counties against what were perceived to be unjust decisions by either the central council or by the county board. One way in which clubs sought redress if a match was lost, was to question whether the team lists of the opposition were accurate and tallied with the team actually playing. At the county annual convention in 1906, a motion was passed that in county championship matches, a list of players taking part should be signed by the referee in charge of the game and that it should be compared to the register. The use of lists would help in the implementation of another motion passed at the same convention – that any club playing a man on the second team who had already played for the first team should be suspended for six months.

The accuracy of these lists was questioned at a meeting of the committee of the Saturday Hurling League, which was convened to discuss how, in a match between Nils and Rangers, one or both lists did not correspond with those actually playing. The chairman of the committee agreed with a Mr Mullins, who raised the matter, that there were inaccuracies, but nevertheless he said he could not deprive Nils of the points. It was, however, decided that in future the referee was to be empowered to give a copy of the list supplied to him on the field to the captain of the opposing side if requested to do so.

At a meeting of the county board in January 1913, a motion was passed that players be registered in Irish as a measure to encourage the Irish language. At the same meeting, there arose an argument over whether the motion on registering players in Irish was actually written on Irish paper. A number of years later, in November 1924, Nemo Rangers had a grievance over a match they were to play against St Finbarrs at Turner's Cross. The club appealed to both the Cork county board and the Munster Council but the appeal was not dealt with on the grounds it was not written in Irish.

The Nemo Rangers club history refers to how there were constant objections being lodged in the 1920s. For example, a championship in which Nemo Rangers was involved was held up for five months when the club lodged an objection that was rejected on the grounds that the envelope used was not an Irish one, though Nemo Rangers claimed that the rules did not necessitate this. But, it would appear that the rules did so state, if one refers back to the meeting of 1913 cited above.

There were, throughout the overall period of 1880 to 1939, various examples of objections lodged by clubs on a range of issues, and the following examples give some indication of what these were, as well as the rules being enforcing by the board at any particular time. One matter was that of what venues should be used in championships and how neutral they should be. For example, at the county convention in 1916, the Fermoy club had proposed a motion that a bye-law relating to semi-finals and finals be deleted, and that in future fixtures should be fixed for neutral venues by the governing body. The motion was defeated, however, and the treasurer moved a direct negative to it, saying that the proposal would not help the receipts of the association and the proper carrying out of matches. It would seem that the board was intent on hosting matches (particularly in the latter stages of championship) at central venues, most probably in or near the city, where they hoped the biggest crowds would attend and where the facilities were best in terms of turnstiles, hoardings, etc.

This issue had been put into sharp relief a few years earlier, in August 1913. St Finbarrs were due to play Midleton near Cobh, a game which did actually go ahead, attended by 6,000 spectators who came in three special trains. However, the Barrs had earlier objected to playing the match, claiming that by hosting the match in Cobh the board was not complying with its own bye-law that championship semi-finals should be played in the city. However, any doubts over whether the match would take place were assuaged when the captain of the Barrs team wrote to the *Cork Examiner* assuring the public that his team would travel to Cobh for the match.

As previously mentioned in the section on committees, there was in existence a special appeals and objections committee to deal with such matters as they arose. For example, in January 1920, at a county board meeting, the O'Rahilly Football Club objected to the fixing of a match between themselves and Brian Dillons, the O'Rahilly club claiming that this was in contravention of the rule relating to the closed season, when matches were not to be played. The matter was referred to a meeting of the appeals and objections committee the following Friday night. The Brian Dillons club history also refers to the game, which Brian Dillons won to secure the O'Rahilly Cup. While the outcomes of various appeals lodged are not always detailed in club histories, some appeals do seem to have been successful for clubs. In October 1911, the *Cork Sportsman* referred to a replayed match between St Patrick's and Little Island, noting that three weeks previously, the St Patrick's team had been disqualified, the match being part of a tournament inaugurated by the Mayfield club.[57]

Numerous appeals were lodged on the outcome of matches. For example, at the Carrigtwohill tournament, Little Island lodged an objection against Bartlemy after the game and it was subsequently refixed. But on this occasion Bartlemy did not turn up, after which Little Island claimed the game. The winners of the Bartlemy versus Little Island match were due to play Carrigtwohill, but although Little Island had claimed the match, it was Bartlemy who finally played Carrigtwohill.

Another example of appeals disrupting and causing confusion in the games fixtures occurred in July 1887. St Finbarrs, taking part in the semi-final of the county championship, were ordered to replay their match when a point they had scored was deemed to have been disallowed by the county executive. The replay was scheduled for the unusual time of three o'clock on a Friday, the winners to play Passage in the final the next day. Either because of feelings of injustice or the inappropriate timing of the match, St Finbarrs never turned up.

Another indication of the types of appeals and recourse to redress undertaken by clubs can be found at a meeting of the county board which took place in September 1896. At the meeting, the secretary of the board read an objection from a club called Ballindangan to what they saw as the illegal constitution of the Fermoy team that they had played. The Ballindangan club also felt aggrieved that whenever a dispute on the field occurred, a Fermoy man named O'Leary entered the playing area and struck the Ballindangan goalkeeper. When they had listened to the objection, the board postponed dealing with the issue until the next meeting of the board, when the match referee would be present.

At the same board meeting, a letter was read from the Doneraile Hurling Club on behalf of one of its members named O'Regan, denying that this O'Regan had held any hostile feelings towards the Kanturk Club. The letter from Doneraile further stated that O'Regan had been expelled from their club and that such a move should now satisfy Kanturk. O'Regan's expulsion was then ratified by the board. One interesting question arises in such matters, namely the issue of who had the final jurisdiction on matters of discipline – the club, divisional board or county board. In the early 1930s, Aghada played Leeside, these being two clubs from East Cork. Leeside had a player sent off during the game; the club objected to the East Cork Board but lost. The club then appealed this decision to the county board and had the decision of the East Cork board reversed.

The county board also had to deal with objections on more bureaucratic matters of procedure. At a meeting of the board in February 1909 some delegates raised the issue of the legality of delegates representing a number of clubs, and whether these delegates should be admitted to meetings. The clubs objected to were St Finbarrs West Intermediate Club, the Catholic Young Men's Society Club, the Munster Arcade and GPO clubs. The chairman acknowledged that some of the named clubs were illegally constituted, since members were also playing with other clubs, yet the chairman said he would allow these clubs to be represented at the meeting and this was agreed to.

Clubs offered a variety of explanations for failing to fulfil fixtures. At a weekly meeting of the Cork county board in January 1910, the Dungourney Club from East Cork informed the board that they could not play in the Accident Cup unless a special train was provided. Accordingly, the South-East Selection whom Dungourney were to play were given a walkover. In November 1914, Blackrock were due to play Midleton at Mallow. At Glanmire Station, the Blackrock players turned back because they were under the impression that the match would not be played, and supporters who had paid for train tickets were given a refund. At a subsequent county-board meeting the Blackrock delegate did not blame the county board in any way but he insisted that Blackrock had done no wrong in their actions.[58]

However, when looking at the whole issue of how the board enforced rules and dealt with objections to same, the most outstanding issue that arises is that of the question of foreign games, the degree to which they were banned and how such a ban was received by players and clubs in the city and county.

THE BAN ON FOREIGN GAMES

As we have noted, Michael Cusack had particular difficulty enforcing conformity to the new rules of Gaelic football, as distinct from the type of game being played in Cork, which was a mixture of rugby and football. However, the 1890s saw the county board being particularly fastidious in enforcing the ban on foreign games. Tom Irwin, one of the foremost personalities in the Cork county board, was suspended in 1896 by the board for playing rugby, though this ban was rescinded by the Central Council. At the county convention in the same year, it was decided by a vote of seventy-nine to three to ban rugby players from the association. The pro-ban rule of the Cork county board could also be seen in the unfriendly reaction they made to the circular which had removed the foreign games ban in the 1890s.

The overall policy of the GAA changed at the beginning of the new century, and hardened. In 1901, at a national annual convention, a motion was passed which gave county committees the power to disqualify those who 'countenanced' sports 'calculated to interfere with the national ones', though, according to Mandle, Cork did not make use of this power at the time.[59] Another convention in 1902 heard the following proposal, 'Any member of the Association who plays or encourages in any way Rugby or Association Football, hockey or any imported game which is calculated to injuriously affect our National pastimes, be suspended from the Association; and that this resolution apply to all counties in Ireland and England.'

This particular convention was reconvened in 1903, where a further resolution was adopted, though Tom Dooley of the Cork board objected to it, saying that it violated the GAA's non-political rule. The resolution that passed at the reconvened convention of 1902 read that, 'police, soldiers and sailors on active service be prevented from playing hurling or football under GAA laws'.

At the 1903 convention proper, the ban on police, soldiers and sailors in the navy playing GAA games or attending athletics meetings under GAA control was extended to militia men and naval pensioners, but, the option of enforcing such a ban was left with individual county boards. However, at the annual convention for 1904, held in 1905, a general ban was sanctioned to be enforced countrywide, and penalties were outlined for those who infringed it, both from then on and in the past. At the national convention of 1906, the Cork board expressed its wish that the optional power of enforcing the ban be restored to the county boards and also asked that an amnesty be given to those who had previously infringed the ban on foreign games.

In 1909, a delegate from the Cork county board to the national convention asked that the various bans imposed either on who should play the games, or on what games could not be played by GAA members, should all be lifted. However, this independent and lenient stance of the Cork county board changed with the 1910 election of the strongly republican J.J. Walsh as chairman of the board. He quashed any opposition to the ban and actually extended it to cover jail warders. In Mandle's words, Walsh wanted to ensure that 'there was not so much as a soccer ball, outside the British garrison in Cork County'. An indication of how much Walsh wanted to enforce these rules can be gauged from the mention of a county-board meeting in the *Cork Examiner* in January 1913. Mr Walsh could not be present at this particular meeting, but wrote asking that any changes to the foreign games rule be postponed until he was present.[60]

The ban came up for discussion again at the 1919 annual congress, when counties Dublin, Cork, Kerry and Limerick took a neutral position on the issue. At the Cork county convention for that same year, a vote of sixty-eight for to eleven against was taken in favour of abolishing the ban. Tom Dooley, who previously had been an advocate of the ban, was now one of those who voted to abolish it. De Búrca notes that some years later, in 1927, there was a strong preference in Cork for abolishing the ban, despite popular feeling being anti-Treaty after the Civil War. Again, this was contrary to national GAA policy; at the previous year's congress the association had voted to retain the ban by a majority of eighty to twenty-three, and also decided to only vote on the ban every three years.

Perhaps the best indication of how the ban caused division and friction within Cork is to be found in the exchanges that took place at the Cork county convention in 1926. The discussion arose out of a proposal from St Finbarrs, St Annes and Redmonds that the ban on playing foreign games, and those that already played them, should be lifted. A Mr T. Ryan of the Redmonds club attacked the level of hypocrisy within the association, citing how he had been attacked for his opposition to the ban, yet his critics supported foreign games themselves. The representatives from St Finbarrs and St Annes, in supporting the motion, pointed out that against the background of the ban, all teams in the city were illegal.

These delegates, who opposed the ban, elaborated on their reasons for wanting its removal. Mr Ryan of Redmonds said that if the ban was not in the rule book there would be less trouble, remarking that, 'They were all born with the sin of disobedience and like the apple in the garden they were all making for it.' Mr J. Lynch of St Finbarrs told the convention that he did not believe there was a single legal team in the city and attacked those at conventions who opposed the ban yet fielded teams with illegal players. Mr J. O'Brien of the St Annes club said every team his club fielded was illegal and the chairman, in responding to these remarks, said, 'You are speaking for the city clubs of course. If not, I won't contradict you', to which Mr O'Brien replied, 'I include some of the country clubs as well'.

Those who supported the ban then spoke. A Mr Beckett of the Lee's club opposed the removal of the ban, saying that, 'efforts were being made to keep English dances out of the county and if dances were to be kept out, English games should kept out' – words which drew applause. A Mr Barry, also opposing the motion, said:

Why did the British send their armoured cars to Croke Park on Bloody Sunday? Why were they not sent to Dalymount or Ringsend? [hear, hear] As regards the argument that the ban rule was being broken too often, if that was a reason for abolition, why should they not abolish one of the Ten Commandments that was being broken too often?[applause]

The county board chairman also spoke against removing the ban, outlining his reasons thus:

In the past the arguments in favour of the abolition were nothing more or less than a request to the Gaels of the county to break the rule because it was being broken … when Englishmen came to Ireland they became more Irish … the reverse was now taking place and the Irish were becoming more English than the English.

After these various arguments had been, made the motion to remove the ban was defeated by eighty votes to forty-seven.

Yet the ban continued to cause problems for clubs in the later years. When Brian Dillons played St Anne's in the city junior final, St Anne's objected to one of the Dillons players, a Mossie Keenan, because they alleged he had played soccer. Brian Dillons could offer no defence, and the club historian quotes from a Dillons club man who said about Keenan, the player in question, 'In fairness to him, he told the club when he was joining that he had played soccer but it had been a while back so they took a chance and played him anyway.'[61]

Nemo Rangers were put in a very difficult situation over the ban in October 1932. On 17 October 1932, the Nemo Rangers senior hurling team were to play Ahane from Limerick in the semi-final of a tournament in Charleville. The Cork team had many prominent hurlers who had already been suspended for playing soccer. Before the match in Charleville, the team did not pose for a team photograph, no doubt for fear of identification. For the legal players this was the last straw, according to the club historian, and these legal players left the club and simply played challenge games. The Nemo Rangers players who had been illegal went to play with Evergreen instead, possibly to escape detection for their previous activities.

SELECTION OF THE COUNTY TEAM

Another issue, which may not have caused quite as much friction as the ban, but was nevertheless a divisive one, was the question of who should take responsibility for the selection of the county teams. Clubs such as Inniscarra and Nils had represented Cork in hurling and football in the 1890s, but it seems that in the new century this practice caused division in the county. The county champions, when representing the county, could also select players from other clubs to play on their team, and this undoubtedly caused friction among other clubs who may have felt that their own players were being unjustly ignored.

One instance of how the county board attempted to select a county team that was not taking part in the All-Ireland series, occurred in September 1896, when a special meeting decided to send two teams to Tralee to play in a benefit match for the O'Connell memorial church. There was a long discussion as to whether an individual club should represent the county, or whether players should be selected from various clubs. It was eventually decided to draw from various clubs, and so the make-up for the hurling team was as follows: Redmonds (five); Blackrock (three); United Nationals (four); St Finbarrs (three), plus a substitute. For the football team, six players from each of two city clubs were selected, plus five from another club and the substitute from a third. Evidence of the friction can be gauged by the following proposal from the county board chairman at the county convention in 1910:

> Whereas the present system of selecting inter-county teams has frequently resulted in dissension, and consistent demoralisation, it is thought that the interest of the game would be enhanced by the introduction of an alternative whereby the County Committee may have the option of placing the responsibility in the hands of a Selection Committee.[62]

However, this proposal did not seem to solve the friction to which the chairman referred. At a board meeting in October 1911 the Mitchelstown club objected to the selection of the Cork team being left to the Lees club. Nevertheless, it seems that at this time, the power of selection that the county champions had hitherto enjoyed was now in the hands of the county board. For a team such as Blackrock, which had been particularly successful, this seems to have caused division. One of the club's great players particularly opposed it and, in the words of the club historian, the issue created a 'Cloud over the Mahon Penninsula'.[63] There followed several meetings at the club and it was decided that anyone from Blackrock who had been selected for Cork and wanted to play could do so.

It was only in 1919, when Cork contested the All-Ireland Final in September of that year, that the responsibility for picking the county team was given to nominated selectors rather than the club champions. This was also the first time that Cork wore red and white colours, which were the club jerseys of the Fr O'Leary Hall team. At a board meeting held five days before the All-Ireland Final, a representative of St Finbarrs raised the question of whether his club was entitled to captaincy of the team. The reply as was as follows:

> ...it was pointed out that the Barrs would have that recognition, but that in

the interests of what was at stake next Sunday, as well as the interest of the prominent Barrs player who would himself be playing on Sunday, it would not be advisable to change horses crossing the stream. The jerseys worn on Sunday would remain unchanged, but they had come from the Barrs parish and the Barrs would be the All-Ireland Champions should Cork win on Sunday. The Barrs representative accepted this assurance, stating that they had no desire to cause friction.

GEOGRAPHICAL SPREAD OF CLUBS

The Cork county convention of January 1934 was an auspicious occasion, as it was the silver jubilee of the founding of the association. The convention was to be held in the council chamber of the courthouse and a solemn Mass was to precede it at 11.15a.m. According to the *Cork Evening Echo*, every one of the 173 clubs in the county were to send delegates to the convention.[64] This represented a major increase, if one looks at the county convention in 1900. Here, the clubs listed at the convention were: Blarney, Kilshannig, Nils, St Finbarrs, Blackrock, Skibbereen, William O'Brien FC, Redmonds Hurling Club, Cork Young Ireland, Castlemartyr FBC, Passage West, Carrigtwohill, and Lisgoold. These clubs encompassed all parts of the city and county and the president of the board expressed his pleasure at the large attendance of delegates, despite the long distances they had to travel.

At the following year's convention in April 1901, the clubs represented were: Macroom, Lees, Crosse and Blackwells, Cobh, Ladysbridge, Skibbereen, William O'Brien Football Club, St Finbarrs Hurling Club, Aghinagh, Dungourney, Doneraile, Lisgoold, Nils, Redmonds, Fermoy, and Cork Young Ireland Society Football Club. The pesident expressed his pleasure at the 'large and respectable gathering'.[65] The chairman outlined various reasons at the convention why more clubs were not affiliating, instancing the break-up of clubs, emigration and clubs amalgamating.

Despite the chairman's remarks, there was a larger representation of clubs at the following year's convention. Clubs represented in 1902 were: William O'Brien FC, Blackrock, Sarsfield Hurling Club, Young Ireland Society Football Club, Lisgoold, Fermoy, Lees, Inniscarra, Kanturk, Banteer, Dromtariffe, United Nationals FC, St Finbarrs HC, Ballincollig HC, Nils, Gurtroe FC, Queenstown FC, Evergreen National FC, Redmonds HC, Passage FC, Sibbereen FC, Crosse and Blackwell, Newmarket FC, Killeagh

FC, Macroom, Blarney, and Carrigtwohill. Clubs from almost every part of the county were represented in this list, though significantly, no clubs from West Cork were represented. It is now worth studying in greater detail how these clubs were spread geographically and the cluster of clubs that there was, particularly in the city and to the west and east within a radius of approximately twenty miles.

To the immediate west of the city, a cluster of clubs formed, directly related to centres of employment in the area, such as the Ballincollig Gunpowder Mills and the Dripsey Woollen Mills. The clubs directly related to these centres were Carrigrohane, a forerunner of the Ballincollig Club, and Inniscarra, which, even before the founding of the GAA, had its forerunner based on teams representing the Dripsey Mills. For example, these two clubs met in the county championship in March 1888 with twenty-one-man teams.[66] In 1890, Ballincollig Gladstonians entered the inaugural county juvenile hurling and football championship along with another team from the area, Bride Valley. Ballincollig then played in tournaments hosted by Cloughduv, Coachford and Bride Valley, all of whom were based within a twenty-mile radius, west of the city.

Within a similar radius to the east of the city, clubs sprang up in the late 1880s. At a meeting in July 1889 to organise a football tournament hosted by Ladysbridge and Ballymacoda clubs, a large number of clubs sent representatives, including two teams from around Cloyne called Churchtown South and a team from Youghal. The opening of the tournament was postponed so that Midleton could play as well. The following September, Carrigtwohill, approximately ten miles to the east of the city, held a tournament in which the neighbouring Little Island Club took part, as well as Bartlemy from North Cork.

New clubs or old revitalised clubs were formed in the new century in the East Cork area. In January 1910, the *Cork Sportsman* noted some new clubs in East Cork. These included the Midleton Young Men's Society Football Club, who were to enter that year's forthcoming intermediate championship. The paper also noted that Carrigtwohill were to form a new team, and that there were new clubs a little further east in Ballymacoda and Shanagarry.[67] By the 1920s, there were sufficient clubs in East Cork to warrant setting up the East Cork board, which took place on Sunday, 13 April 1924, and at which seven clubs were represented. On 6 June 1924, a team representing the East Cork division played Blackrock.

However, it is with the city and its geographical distribution of clubs that we are most concerned, and the best method of studying this distribution is by examining the north and south sides of the city. On the south side of the city, some of the most important clubs to emerge were Nemo Rangers, Redmonds and St Finbarrs. St Finbarrs were based in the area of the city known as the South Parish and gradually came to be the dominant club there. However, there were a number of clubs which were formed in this area from the earliest years of the GAA in Cork, the majority of which were later subsumed by St Finbarrs.

This trend was noticeable from as far back as the 1880s and 1890s, when both Greenmount and Bishopstown joined St Finbarrs. From 1906 to 1918, there were two senior hurling clubs in the South Parish – St Finbarrs and Fr O'Leary Total Abstinence Hall. But at the end of this period there was a consensus that the area could not support two senior hurling clubs, and on 19 March 1919, the Fr O'Leary Hall club played its last game (though the club colours of red and white were adopted by Cork at the time the club was folding). However, this did not mean the end of the foundation of smaller teams in and around the south inner city. In the late 1920s a team called St Anthonys were active around Wycherley Terrace and Bandon Road. This was also the traditional catchment area for St Finbarrs.

Numerous references have been made to the Redmonds club that broke from St Finbarrs during the Parnellite crisis in the early 1890s, and which became one of the most prominent teams in the county in the following decades. The club, which declined as the new century progressed, was also based in the south inner city and moved its premises frequently, being sited at various times in Princes Street in the city centre as well as the south-side locations of Sullivan's Quay and Barrack Street. In between the countryside and the south inner city, the club known as Pouladuff was formed and it was in existence in the late 1920s.

From the 1900s, the area at the eastern side of the South Parish also saw the formation of a number of smaller clubs, most of these in time being subsumed into the Nemo Rangers club. In the 1900s, the Rangers team – forerunner of Nemo Rangers – played matches against teams from around the same area, such as Dunbar Street and Reads Square. When Rangers did not field a team in the 1903/04 season, some of its members played for another team in the area called Evergreen. In the period around 1915, the Rangers team were drawing players from Hibernian Buildings, Douglas Street, Anglesea Street and Dunbar Street, and it held its meetings in White Street. Evergreen eventually faded in the 1930s and some of the members of the old club formed the Turner's Cross club in 1934. By the early 1940s, clubs in the South Parish such as Redmonds, Evergreen, Turner's Cross, Hillside and Inisfail had all faded away.

Further east of the South Parish catchment area, heading towards Blackrock, a team from Albert Road called the Geraldines was in existence until 1928. At the south-eastern tip of the city was one of the foremost Cork sides, Blackrock. As it grew in strength in the 1900s, the club picked its best team from the various parts of the parish, such as Ballintemple, Ballinure, Ballinsheen, Boreenmanna, Skehard, Ballinlough and Brick Yard.

To the north of the River Lee, the dominant team to emerge in the new century was Glen Rovers. In the late 1880s, over two decades before Glen Rovers was founded, William O'Brien's from the north inner city and Sarsfields from Glanmire to the immediate east of the city, intended to join, but this proved impractical. The original William O'Brien's teams did, however, have a contingent of Glanmire players. The eventual companion football team to Glen Rovers hurling team was St Nick's, which was founded in 1902 and had a room in York Row. The club split in 1910 due to political upheavals between the O'Brienites and Redmondites that surfaced at the 1910 general election, though the split was healed in 1917. In 1912, the original St Nick's club had moved to premises in Wherlands Lane, remaining in the Blackpool area, but in the 1930s they left this site and had their premises with Glen Rovers in Bird's Quay.

Along with St Nick's, there were various other teams located in the north side of the city at the turn of the century, such as Maddens Buildings, Lansdowne Road and Commons Road, though it is that unlikely such teams were affiliated to the GAA. There was at least one team from the area where Brian Dillons was to emerge, to the north-east of the city, which was active in the early 1900s, and played matches against Maddens Buildings. There were a number of other north-side teams mentioned in the 1915 minor championship, including the Thomas Davis club, later to merge with Glen Rovers, as well as Fair Hill and Mayfield, the latter being situated in the north-east of the city, sandwiched between Sarsfields and Brian Dillons.

THE GAA AND THE TROUBLES

The political upheavals that affected the GAA in Cork from 1914 to 1923 can be grouped into two time periods, 1914 to 1918 and 1918 to 1923. The period from 1914 to 1918 saw the concurrent events of the First World War and the 1916 Troubles affecting GAA activities, though these were not as traumatic as the events surrounding the War of Independence and the Civil War.

The first issue to affect the running of the county board's activities concerned the position of the chairman, J.J. Walsh, who was an ardent republican and, as seen earlier, a fervent supporter of the ban. In 1914, Walsh had objected to the conferring of the freedom of Cork City on the British Viceroy to Ireland. Mr Walsh, who worked in the post office, was given the option of a job transfer to Bradford or deportation. Instead, he moved to Dublin. The county board in Cork never accepted his resignation and he became the honorary president of the board, but after the 1916 congress, on his way back to Cork City, he was arrested and brought to prison under heavy guard.

Thus, when the county convention was held in January 1915, James N. Down presided, 'in the unavoidable absence of our chairman J.J. Walsh'.[68] The presiding chairman also referred to how outside events had affected the board's work, saying, 'the year just closed has been an ill-starred one, the world over. Nations and individuals have suffered; and our Association has been no exception to the rule.' He also referred to how, in the preceding year, the championships had been disrupted because the war had upset train arrangements. Furthermore, the grounds near the Renmount depot had also been taken over by the army.

The issues of train disruption and the use of grounds continued to be vexing. In 1918, at the annual congress, the GAA discussed an attempt to get train services back to normal for matches, which had been carried out through the lobbying of Irish MPs who had met with the Chief Secretary, H.E. Dunlea. As regards the issue of grounds being occupied, Mandle specifically refers to the situation in Cork. During the War of Independence, the football grounds were occupied in Cork and, in one instance, spectators were refused admission to a widows' and orphans' benefit match at the Cork Athletic Grounds. To counteract this measure the players played in an open park, where a collection was taken up for the fund. Mandle also cites incidents from 1920; an unauthorised GAA meeting which was to have taken place at the Mardyke had to be abandoned when police and soldiers intervened, while the Munster hurling semi-final for that year was switched from the Cork Athletic Grounds to Riverstown.

These events were played out against a national background whereby special permits had to be obtained before games were allowed to proceed. In Cork, in 1918, a J.J. Buckley, manager of the Cork Athletic Grounds, had enquired if a permit was necessary to allow a junior hurling championship match between Glen Rovers and Nemo Rangers to go ahead. The GAA nationally addressed the issue, when, at a meeting of the Central Council in July 1920, it was decided that permits should not be requested and that anyone who did so would be indefinitely suspended from the association. On 4 August 1918, games were held simultaneously right throughout the country, all beginning at the same time which was meant to show the authorities that games would go ahead without permits.

O'Toole refers to other activites in Cork, such as the aforementioned Munster hurling championship match on 29 July 1920 between Limerick and Tipperary, which was to be played in the Cork Athletic Grounds but was instead moved to Riverstown to the east of the city. This was the last major game to be held in Munster that year. In July 1920, all public assemblies and gatherings had been banned in Cork. In the preceding months of May and June 1920, matches had been regularly held in Cork. Mandle has also noted from a *Cork Examiner* of May 1919, that the police had become more oppressive in trying to prevent the playing of hurling in the streets and open places in the city and county.[69]

Apart from the issues of permits and the takeover of major grounds, there was also the major issue of players and officials being in jail or on the run from the authorities. For example, in September 1922, two principal officers of the county board, the chairman Sean McCarthy and secretary Pádraig Ó Caoimh were both in jail. This, along with the other problems associated with the Troubles, led to the county championships being abandoned and leagues for senior and intermediate teams in or near the city being held instead. The Nemo Rangers historian refers to instances in 1923 when players sought by the authorities would turn up at venues for games and disappear immediately afterwards. Players in prison actually brought about the formation of the modern Nemo Rangers club, when on 15 March 1919, the Rangers and Nemo clubs amalgamated. Membership of both clubs had fallen, partly due to the number of players that were in prison, but the catalyst for the merging of the clubs was a friendship forged in prison by Denny Hegarty of Rangers and Paddy O'Keeffe of Nemo.

The hunger strike and death of prisoner Terence McSwiney had a major effect on GAA activities in the city. The county board adjourned its games shortly after McSwiney went on hunger strike and there was no further activity from August 1920 to January 1922. When McSwiney died, Sunday 31 October 1920 was designated as a closed date for the games as a gesture of sympathy. O'Toole says that this Sunday was considered to be a day of mourning for McSwiney, but that it was only in County Cork that all GAA fixtures were called off.[70] The death of Tomás Mac Curtain in 1920 caused further tension and precipitated the British army's takeover the Cork Athletic Grounds, thereby preventing a Munster hurling championship match between Cork and Tipperary. Also at this time, the prominent secretary of the county board and well-known referee, Tom Irwin, had his life threatened and consequently he left for South Africa. It was then that Pádraig Ó Caoimh took up the vacant position of secretary.

In July 1921, with the declaration of a truce, GAA activity was resumed throughout most parts of the country, but the Cork county board did not want to resume games in the county because it feared that the truce would not last. According to county-board historian Cronin, the other counties came round to the Cork board's view and the playing of Gaelic games was put in abeyance until 1922, when matches resumed. When activity recommenced, the number of junior clubs in Cork city had doubled.

However, the Civil War was set to cause further disruption. In December 1922, the Cork county board passed a resolution asking the central council of the GAA to convene a special congress and form a subcommittee to mediate between the Civil War sides. The central council held a special meeting in January 1923 to try and bring about a rapprochement between the two sides. However, there was still the question of republican prisoners in jail, and both Sean McCarthy of the Cork board and Austin Stack of the Kerry board would not allow their respective counties to resume playing until all republican prisoners were released, and as a result these counties were suspended from the association.

August 1924 saw the release of these republican prisoners and the suspended counties were readmitted to the association. According to Ó Murchú and Brosnan, Cork, along with Kerry and Limerick, did not take part in the 1923 All-Ireland series held in 1924 due to the internment of prisoners.[71] De Búrca, in commenting on these events, says that in July 1923 the Cork board had refused to send a junior team to play Offaly in the junior hurling final until such time as the county board chairman, Sean McCarthy, was released from jail.[72] Mandle, remarking on the same issue, notes that due to Cork's refusal the central council promptly awarded the title to Offaly.

SPECTATORS

While it is vital to study the growth and evolution of the administrative structure of the GAA as well as the political background against which its activities took place, it is when one looks at the games themselves that one sees the most immediate impact of the GAA on the lives of the citizens of the city and the surrounding country districts. This impact can be studied by looking at the behaviour and appearance of both players and spectators, particularly in the context of local rivalries. An important source of study in this respect is the coverage of games in the local press and how the newspapers allowed both journalists and those with an interest in the games to express their views.

Let us begin by looking at the quality of facilities for the playing of the games. We have already noted the attempts by the county board and clubs to acquire playing fields and the rents expended on same. The quality of playing fields, particularly in the early decades of the GAA, was variable. In April 1888, a hurling and football double bill was held at Shortcastle, Mallow, involving country teams from Buttevant, Bartlemy, Fermoy and Dromtariffe. All the teams met some way from the actual field and marched to it, accompanied by the brass band. The *Cork Examiner* described the field as a meadow given by a Mr Richard Lombard, TC, and went on to add that 'A better field for any sports could not be found in the country.'[73] A little later that month, when Bandon hosted a match between Lees and Kilmacabea, the ground, along with the weather, was described as 'of the most favourable character'.

On the other hand, some fields were unsuitable, either because of their location or their degree of access. Grass not being cut was one particular problem. When Cork played Kerry in hurling and football at Mallow in 1889, the match reporter said the ground itself was well laid out, but that the long grass told against the players. At a hurling championship match in Mallow in July 1890, the field was uneven and the grass very high. This would certainly have militated against the quality of a hurling match. Bad weather created difficulties for spectators as well. In April 1895, when Nils from Cork played Young Irelands from Dublin in Tipperary, the approach to the field was very muddy and, if a car passed, mud covered everybody.

Grounds were beginning to be laid out with flags to mark the pitches, as well as ropes to keep spectators on the proper side of the field. Mallow, as instanced above, was a particularly popular venue in the first decades of the GAA in Cork, used on a number of occasions for matches involving the Cork and Kerry champions. In 1889, when Inniscarra met Kenmare, the Mallow club was in charge of stewarding, which involved marking and roping off the pitch. Mallow was also the location for the county final in 1895 between Blackrock and Ballyhea, and Madden cites the *Cork Examiner's* description of the field, 'which is of very large dimensions, was marked with flags and well kept, and a charge of 3*d* was made for admission by the county board'.[74] In Mallow, a new field was procured for matches in 1908 and when Waterford played Cork there, in the semi-final of the Munster football championship, the match correspondent reported that the field looked in 'splendid order'.[75]

It is interesting to note how the major new venue in Cork approaching the end of the nineteenth century, the Cork Athletic Grounds, coped with crowds. At the Munster championship between Cork and Tipperary in 1898, there were only four turnstiles to cope with a crowd of 15,000 spectators, when with hindsight it was suggested that twenty were needed. A crush resulted when the turnstiles could not cope, so patrons climbed over the barbed wire, but this was insufficient to allow access to those seeking entry, and eventually a door was broken down, through which spectators entered. By 1911, people were accessing the same venue without paying, as the *Cork Sportman's* correspondent reminded the county board. He also advised that they repair the corrugated iron which had been damaged in the process of the patrons gaining free admission.[76]

PLAYERS

References to players, which appeared both in club histories and newspapers, could include their physical fitness and appearance, as well as to humorous incidents in which they were involved. When Nils from Cork played Young Irelands from Dublin in the All-Ireland Final in 1895, the match correspondent was impressed at how well-built and athletic the players were.[77] When Cork played Dublin in 1914, the *Cork Examiner* again commented on the physical prowess of the Dublin team in particular, noting their 'well-adjusted balance of weight', as well as their smart appearance.[78] In earlier years, teams came in for praise when they were togged out in distinctive jerseys, emphasising the fact that much of the time the appearance of teams left something to be desired. When Collegians played Cloughduv it was noted how effective the distinctive colours of the players' jerseys were.[79] Again in 1906, the writer of a piece on a match between Macroom and Fermoy was fulsome in his praise of the teams in this regard, 'First of all it must be mentioned that the thirty-four players were neatly attired in complete football outfits that reflected very great credit on their clubs.'[80]

RIVALRIES AND CONTESTS

It did not take long for a sense of rivalry to build up within the GAA in the city and neighbouring country districts, this rivalry nearly always being due to contesting teams being from neighbouring areas. Rivalries were also formed from the practice of issuing challenges and counter-challenges, and when teams came to oppose each other frequently.

In April 1889, the Cork City board hosted a double bill of matches in Carrigaline between neighbouring teams to the south of the city. Carrigaline's first team played Shanbally and Ballgarvan played Tracton. It was to the latter game that the correspondent of the *Cork Examiner* directed his comments, thereby indicating that the rivalry contributed to incidents during the game. 'The spirit displayed on both sides was not at all commendable', read to the match report, which opined that the referee should have put half a dozen players off, which would have helped the cause of hurling.[81] The blame was largely laid on the Tracton team, which was described as 'undoubtedly a slashing team, if they would only play with better temper'.

Proximity of opposing teams, leading to over-exuberant play on the field, was again seen at a match in 1889 involving a double fixture, this time Blackrock versus Carrigtwohill and St Finbarrs versus Tower Street, the latter pair being from the south side of the city. It was almost certainly with reference to the latter match, with its neighbouring opponents, that the match correspondent addressed his comments. The behaviour of the spectators suggests that feelings ran high between the two south-side neighbours, as there was 'an immense crowd, [a] portion of which was not as orderly as it should be, but of course allowance must be made for partisanship among the spectators when local teams have the field'.[82] When Tower Street scored, their supporters engaged, not surprisingly, 'in wild cheering'. As regards the field of play, the reporter referred to 'collisions' but these did not seem to be accidental, as referees were urged to ensure that such incidences should not take place during games.

Another 'robust rivalry' emerged in 1889 between two teams to the west of the city, namely, Aghabullogue and Blarney. One of their matches was held in Blarney, the village being thronged with people and the match watched

by the supporters with 'great anxiety'. While there was alot of 'hard puck-
ing', it was reported that 'not a single incident occurred during the game'.
Aghabullogue, which was a major hurling force in the late nineteenth century, had also developed a keen rivalry with Blackrock. There was great
interest in their match in November 1897, because some months previously
Aghabullogue had defeated the city team, although Blackrock claimed that
on that occasion they had only a scratch team. Special trains were laid on for
supporters from the city and there was a very large crowd in attendance, but
the *Cork Examiner* reported that very good order was kept by the spectators,
also noting the very good feeling between the players.[83]

On 12 August 1895, the *Cork Examiner*, in its report of a match between
the Lees and Nils Football Clubs, detailed the background to the rivalry that
had developed between the two teams, not to mentioned the large numbers
of spectators who came to the game. The report began with the observation,
'Naturally, the more often that two teams meet, the rivalry becomes intensi-
fied after each occasion, and judging yesterday by the competitors and the
followers of the teams, we should say that it had reached its zenith.'[84]

It was, therefore, no surprise that each of the teams had a very large following at the match. The considerable crowd and the tension of the rivalry
led to encroaching on to the field at one of the end lines. There was further
interference on the goal line, as the paper described, 'What also added to
the blocking of the goal line was a plethora of men, who were in on the
field under the false pretence of clearing the goal, whilst others suffered from
occasional fits of over-officiousness.'

A rivalry which developed between Blackrock and Redmonds caused
particularly eventful incidents in 1896, leading to a public order ban on their
match and the intervention of police to uphold the ban. These events had
their roots in a rivalry that had begun in 1893, when the two clubs had met
and the *Cork Examiner*, cited by Hassett in his Blackrock history, reported
that there had been a lot of money staked on the match.[85] The impact of the
events surrounding the 1896 meeting of these teams can be gauged by the
fact that it was covered in a report in the *Cork Constitution*, which normally
devoted little coverage to Gaelic games. The match itself was the semi-final
of the city division of the county hurling championship. Stakes to the value
of £40 were competed for, according to the *Constitution*.[86] Against this background of betting, the authorities feared public disorder, and a court order
was obtained ordering that all public houses in and around Passage be closed
from 10a.m. to 10p.m. on the day of the match. Twenty-nine public houses

and hotels were affected by the ban and to ensure compliance four police-men were stationed at each public house. To follow this course of action, 160 policemen were drafted into the district. The paper concluded its piece by saying that, 'persons who came from long distances to witness what they believed would be a most exciting match were more or less disappointed'.

In its report on the match, the *Cork Examiner* said that the crowd was prob-ably the largest ever assembled at a hurling contest and while the spectators were mostly from Cork City, there were 'immense' numbers from other areas as well.[87] Both teams had won the All-Ireland championship in previous years and they had originally been drawn to play in Cork Park in the city. Blackrock, for some reason, were not happy to play there and had waived their claim to the match but would still play Redmonds, with the losing team to forfeit £20. Many people came to the match who had never been previously interested in hurling and it was inevitable that the whole background to the game would express itself on the field. The *Cork Examiner*'s report said the 'first minute's play was distinctly lively and a petty skirmish took place in midfield'.

According to Cork sports historian Power, the chief of police had acquired a judicial order, not alone banning the opening of public houses, but banning the game itself, a course of action which caused tempers to rise, as people had come from every part of Cork to watch the game.[88] According to Power, Michael Deering, chairman of the county board, took responsibility for the crowd and any disorder that might ensue, which satisfied the police. As Deering 'slipped away quietly to bring on the teams, "shillelaghs" were taken from their hiding places, down the legs of trousers and thrown away'. Of the game itself, it was said that it was 'rough at times' but was 'nevertheless a good, clean exhibition of ball-playing'.

Mention has already been made of the rivalries in the south of the city, such as that between St Finbarrs and Tower Street, but rivalries also devel-oped in the north of the city. For example, in the area from where Glen Rovers drew its players, there was a small club which rarely met with suc-cess, called The Commons (which was also a specific area). However, on one occasion, they scored a shock win over Glen Rovers and duly celebrated by travelling through the heartland of Glen Rovers, into Thomas Street and Spring Lane, on a side car with a banner which read, 'The World Beat the Commons, But the Commons Beat the Glen.'[89] Another rivalry developed to the north-east of the city between Brian Dillons and Mayfield. When they met in the semi-final of the city championship in 1936 the *Cork Examiner* observed, as cited by Horgan:

…both teams came from the same parish and naturally there was a double dose of the club spirit thrown into it. It was evident that both sides had trained hard for the engagement … hard knocks were given and taken … there was not an unsporting or unclean bit of play in the whole hour…[90]

More rivalries formed between clubs on opposite side of the River Lee, the major one being that between Glen Rovers and St Finbarrs. This rivalry began in earnest in 1934, when Glen Rovers beat St Finbarrs in the senior hurling championship final and, when the cup was brought to the north side of the city in that year, thousands danced at the crossroads and the local sergeant granted an exemption to the public houses.

Another strong rivalry developed between two teams in the Inniscarra region to the west of the city – Inniscarra and Shournagh Valley. At one stage, the teams had joined together but this did not last, and when they met in a replay of their match in September 1934, Sheehan describes the tension before the game, exacerbated by the fact that players from both teams worked in the woollen mills in Blarney.[91]

ATTENDANCES AND BEHAVIOUR

We have already noted the influence of rivalries that developed based on geography, betting, and repeated meetings of the same clubs. Further study of spectator behaviour will follow here, but let us look first at other factors which may have influenced spectator attendance.

Fine weather did seem to be associated with larger attendances, though not invariably. For a Saturday hurling league match in October 1911, between Douglas Hurling Club and St Mary's Hurling Club, fine weather prevailed, and the *Cork Sportsman* described the attendance as a 'fairly large body of spectators'.[92] However, the same edition reported on a match the previous Sunday, between Sunday's Well and Geraldines, when there was 'delightfully fine weather' but the crowd was of 'meagre dimensions'.

Conversely, when Inniscarra played Donoughmore in September 1935, there was torrential rain up to the beginning of the match but there was nevertheless a large attendance. It should be borne in mind, however, that the game was played on a Sunday and was the Mid-Cork junior semi-final. The day of the week on which the game was played and what was being played for were therefore two obvious factors affecting attendance, in addition to the weather. For example, in October 1911, there was a small number of spectators at the Athletic Grounds for a match in the Saturday Hurling League. Numbers who turned up to watch tournament matches could also be disappointingly small. For a match between neighbouring teams of St Finbarrs and Redmonds in October 1911, in the St Anthony's Hall tournament, the *Cork Sportsman* correspondent commented on the small attendance, complaining that more should have come to the match and urging bigger attendances for the rest of the tournament. (The writer did also highlight the fact that rain threatened in the morning.[93]) This tournament match was followed by another between the Douglas and Emmetts second teams and the crowd for this was 'exceedingly sparse'.

A few years previously, St Finbarrs had met Redmonds to play for a special cup presented by William Phair, a notable personality from the area from where the two clubs also came. While there were a lot of spectators, it was thought that the crowd could have been larger, 'considering the high status of the teams engaged'.[94] Again, it is possible that the crowd was smaller because this was not a championship match.

Spectators contributed a great deal to the atmosphere of games; they both influenced, and were influenced by, events on the field of play. For example, when Young Irelands from Dublin played Nils from Cork in the All-Ireland Final in 1895, Cork scored a goal and this is how the reaction of the Cork followers was described, 'There followed a scene which baffles description. Hats were flung up in the air, danced on; waived sticks were flung up, and men who never saw one another before danced with one another.'[95]

All eyes on the ball: a junior hurling match from the 1930s. (Image courtesy of *Irish Examiner*)

We have already discussed the attempts by the county board to fence in the major venues so as to ensure payment and to keep supporters from encroaching on to the fields of play. For the majority of games in this period of study, there was at most a rope to separate players from spectators during a game. The following piece from the *Cork Sportsman,* reporting on a match between Juverna and Cobh, exemplifies how near spectators were to the field of play, 'Still pressing, Kilkeary added another. "Evens All" was shouted and the followers of both teams rushed up and down the sideline urging on their respective sides.'[96]

With regard to spectators, reports of matches mainly noted whether or not they encroached on the field of play, and this was the case from the very early years of the GAA. In August 1886, at a match between Cork Nationals and St Finbarrs, the crowd was described as most orderly, despite the fact that it had been the largest crowd seen on any occasion for many years, and also despite the fact that the match had lasted for two hours (including stoppages) and that there had been a delay of an hour and a half before the game began at all.[97] When Buttevant played Bartlemy in a hurling match, a Fr Barry was in charge of Bartlemy, while a Fr Buckley was with the Buttevant team. Fr Barry claimed the match since Buttevant was not at the ground at the appointed hour, but the match did go ahead, Buttevant's excuse being that there were at twelve o'clock Mass and could not have been there any earlier. Despite this dispute, and the large crowd present, the *Cork Examiner* writer remarked that 'a more orderly and well-conducted crowd … it would be hard indeed to find'.[98]

However, the important presence of the clergy contributed in no small way to such good behaviour. When Cork and Kerry clubs met in the Munster finals in Mallow in July 1889, the crowds were as much as five or six spectators deep, yet there was not a single instance of the line being broken and even when excitement rose to a high level the crowd remained most orderly.

The fact that reporters commented on the absence of encroachment suggests that it happened frequently. We have read of the encroaching at the match between Nils and Lees in the county championship of 1895, which was set against the rivalry between the teams. When spectators did encroach it greatly annoyed sports writers, such as occurred in April 1888, when an estimated crowd of 10,000 people gathered to watch a double bill of fixtures involving Aghada, Ballygarvan, Tower Street, and Inniscarra. The matches took place at the Cork Athletic Grounds near the River Lee and the section of the crowd on the river side of the ground was particularly guilty of encroaching. This prompted the *Cork Examiner* to comment, 'surely when such persons come to see a hurling match they ought not themselves be the cause of stopping the game'.[99]

If events became particularly tempestuous on the pitch, spectators could find it difficult not to become involved. When St Anne's played Nemo Rangers for a cup presented by the Cork Branch of the National Athletic and Cycling Association, fights broke out between opposing players and accidents were frequent, the *Cork Examiner* attributing much of the trouble on the field to the behaviour of the spectators. When, in the closing stages of the match, a St Anne's player was ordered off and two other players began fighting, spectators encroached from inside the paling but the referee succeeded in clearing the field, an action for which he received praise from the newspaper. In 1915, when Brian Dillons played Queenstown in Cobh it was alleged that followers from the visiting team, Brian Dillons, struck a Queenstown player at the end of the match.[100]

Spectators could also engage in disputes and fights without events on the field precipitating such actions. Nils played Kilworth in a hurling match in Mallow in July 1890, and, while overall events had been very successful, the *Cork Examiner* remarked that the only regrettable thing about the day had been the number of squabbles and disputes that had cropped up, which it stressed did not occur among the players, but among the spectators, whom, it said, 'very frequently showed a most turbulent disposition'.[101]

It was the conclusion of a match that spectators most commonly attacked players or spectators from the opposing team. In April 1888, the city team Lees played a team from West Cork, Kilmacabea, in Bandon. The match itself had been a tempestuous affair and the referee found it impossible to control the game. Both sets of teams and supporters had travelled by train to Bandon and the Cork team left for home on the 4.30p.m. train. The Kilmacabea train was not departing until 7p.m. and while waiting, trouble began. It was unclear whether the trouble began among the Kilmacabea contingent or whether it involved a dispute with a Bandon man regarding a previous match. In addition, the window of the carriage of the Kilmacabea train was broken. The *Cork Examiner* summed up the events, saying that, 'altogether it was a most disgraceful piece of rowdyism'.[102]

Again, in 1906, in giving a full description of an incident after a match between Fermoy and Macroom, the newspaper reporter summed up by saying that, as far as could be judged, the trouble had been caused by spectators and not players. There were probably signs of trouble to come during this particular match, since one match reporter noted how 'the spectators displayed very keen interest in it as it progressed, and now and then party spirit ran high in certain knots of rival enthusiasts'.[103] There then followed a description of what happened:

The teams were then retiring to their respective pavilions when a very lamentable incident took place. It may be difficult to point to the guilty parties, but a couple of facts cannot be questioned. Some parties broke in from the offside of the field and threateningly pursued the Fermoy men, the majority of whom ran for the pavilion. A crowd followed, and several encounters took place outside and inside the pavilion, the glass was smashed and one individual was seen to throw a piece of board he carried in his hand, in among the crowd. Most commendable efforts were made by a few prominent gentlemen present, who, too, were representative of the clubs, to bring about a cessation of such disgraceful conduct, and with the assistance of a few police, happily succeeded.

In the same day's edition, the *Cork Examiner* remarked on the language being used by both players and spectators at a match between Inniscarra and Shanballymore:

A few players and over-excited spectators were heard to indulge in blasphemous and abominable expressions that were extremely hurtful to all others who went for enjoyment. It is to be hoped sincerely that the Gaelic authorities will take cognisance of such disedifying behaviour, and use measures, best known to themselves, to cope with players who seem to take pleasure in giving utterance to such filthy expressions, as were heard yesterday.

Taking to the field: note the number of players on each team. (Image courtesy of *Irish Examiner*)

INCIDENTS OF INDISCIPLINE

Instances of indiscipline occurred on the part of a whole team not co-operating with a referee or lodging an objection, or on the part of individual players who stepped outside the boundaries of what was acceptable. If a team was not satisfied, the match often had to be abandoned, either because it would not play on in protest, or because the referee could not control matters.

An example of the latter occurred at the game between Kilmacabea and city team Lees, at Bandon in April 1888. The *Cork Examiner* remarked on the 'combative disposition' of the Kilmacabea team and noted how this was not the first time that Kilmacabea had played with such an attitude. Trouble began when Kilmacabea claimed what was described as a 'free knock', since the ball had gone over the end line off what they believed was a member of the opposing team. However, the referee awarded a kick out. A Fr Magner, who was present, intervened to allow the game to continue. This only settled matters until half-time; the reporter described how the Kilmacabea team got 'very excited' when the referee blew for half-time, presumably because they did not feel that the correct amount of time had been allotted for the half. By this stage, Fr Magner was no longer able to impose his will on matters and the Lees team was awarded the match.

There are examples from the earliest years of Cork GAA of matches having to be abandoned because teams disagreed with the decisions and judgements of the referee. In July 1886, St Finbarrs played Aghabullogue at St Finbarrs pitch. A tripping offence was allegedly committed by an Aghabullogue player. The referee concurred and gave the decision to St Finbarrs, which prompted Aghabullogue to object and play was then terminated. St Finbarrs were involved in another controversial match the following year, when they played Cork Nationals. The match ended in what was described as a 'miserable farce' after twenty minutes. Cork Nationals had objected to an equalising score awarded to St Finbarrs, the dispute centring on whether the ball had gone over the goal line, and the incident led the referee to leave the field. The winning team had been due to play a team from Kilkenny and, after the match had been abandoned, the *Cork Examiner* felt that, 'There ought to be some way out of the deadlock, and those in authority ought to take prompt action.'

In a match between Evergreen and Blackrock in August 1895, there had been a number of disputes, and in one instance play was held up for a quarter of an hour. The match report was critical of such long delays, saying, 'it would be well that the referee's decision, on matters in dispute, should be accepted without the interference of outside parties'. Referring to a match played the previous Sunday in Bandon, twenty miles to the west of the city, while acknowledging that generally in Gaelic games 'anything untoward is rare', the reporter found it 'sad to say there was more than good hurling played within the hour, and men lost their tempers'.[104]

There are also specific references to individual players fighting in games. On Sunday 21 November 1909, two matches were played at the Cork Athletic Grounds, but due to the first match being delayed by the late arrival of Blackrock players, the second match between Barrs and Redmonds took place in semi-darkness. A row developed between two players, one from each side. Another two players, one from each team, then joined in and these four players were sent off. It was noted that several other players helped the referee to end the row.

When Inniscarra played Cloughduv in the deciding game of the 1911 Mid-Cork League, where the winners were to receive a set of medals, two opposing players began fighting, sparking a melee in which the supporters joined, though a Fr White helped to restore order. The referee sent off two players and received an undertaking that there would be no more trouble. Similarly, the prompt action of the referee prevented an escalation of trouble when, in a match between the city teams of Geraldines and Rangers in 1914, two players 'had once assumed a fighting attitude'.[105] At a match in 1928, between Leeside and Sarsfields, two players dropped hurleys and engaged in fisticuffs, according to the Erin's Own historian, but were ordered off the field of play and order was promptly restored.[106]

Perhaps because of a bias towards the Cork teams, the Cork press, on a number of occasions, criticised what was perceived as a lack of discipline on the part of teams from other counties. For example, Midleton played Kinsalebeg from Waterford in the Munster Hurling Championship in 1890. Corr and Donoughue, the Midleton club historians, quote from a newspaper report which said that the referee had been too lenient with the Waterford team and that Kinsalebeg had given the 'kind of display which cannot be condoned'.[107] In 1895, in the All-Ireland Final between Nils from Cork and Young Irelands from Dublin, the *Cork Examiner* noted how, on a number of occasions, Young Ireland players picked up the ball and ran with it as in rugby. It also instanced an occasion in the same match when a Young Ireland player caught a Cork player by the neck and slung him to the ground, as well as an incident when a Dublin player had struck a member of the Cork team, and when a Cork supporter had shouted 'foul' and was charged by the Dublin player.[108]

As well as being ordered off, players and their clubs could incur suspensions for a number of months if it was felt that indiscretions merited such a measure. Following an intermediate championship match between Little Island and Ballinhassig in which a player was sent off, a county board investigation took place into the use of bad language during the game. The Little Island club was originally expelled after the investigation into the match, but this was amended to a six-month suspension for the club. After a match involving two north-side teams, Brian Dillons and Fair Hill, played around 1917, the county board imposed suspensions on several players.

The St Nick's Club was expelled from the GAA altogether in 1918, after an investigation into their game with Fermoy in the senior county football championship. The *Cork Examiner* blamed St Nick's for the foul play and attributed the behaviour to bets made on the outcome. According to the paper, 'Fermoy were tripped, beaten and kicked without the slightest provocation having been given and no doubt very serious results would have followed only for the prompt action taken by the referee.'[109] Some time later, a general amnesty was granted to clubs that had been expelled from the GAA in Cork and St Nick's were allowed back into the association.

GAMES AS EVENTS

While we will study press coverage of the games in more depth later, it is worth noting here the sense of spectacle that was conveyed at some of the matches. A sense of excitement and anticipation was conveyed, as crowds gathered at venues to watch and this was often heightened by accompanying musical entertainment. At the 'enormous gathering' at Mallow for the hurling championship match between Nils Desperandum and Kilworth, held under the auspices of the O'Connor and O'Brien boards, the match report noted that, 'A very entertaining feature of the day's programme was the playing of the Barrack Street Band on the field.'[110] When the two East Cork teams of Knockraha and Lisgoold played in 1902, the Lisgoold team travelled with a band from their own area, and according to one press report, 'Seldom if ever was there witnessed at the place such an enormous gathering of people, contingents arriving from all the adjoining parishes to witness the contest.'[111] Another scene of keen anticipation in the lead-up to a match was to be found before the county final in Mallow in 1895. Hassett quotes the following piece from the *Cork Examiner*, which describes the arrival of crowds for the match between Ballyhea and Blackrock:

The gathering was one of the largest seen since the inception of the Association. Two special trains were run by Cook's Agency from Cork, which brought a very large contingent, including a big following of the Blackrock team … people poured into Mallow by train and car from all surrounding districts.[112]

One particular event which generated great excitement and comment was the opening of the new Cork Athletic Grounds in 1904, headlined in the *Cork Examiner* with the words, 'International Matches in Cork, New Athletic Grounds Opened'. Under the headline were the words 'Immense Attendance'.[113] The article went on to describe the period before the match, 'Long before the hour fixed for the opening, large numbers could be seen wending their way in the direction of the grounds, while the trams plying to Ballintemple on the one side, and the Lower Road on the other side, were packed to an uncomfortable degree.'

A band from Midleton, as well as the Barrack Street and Butter Exchange Band from the city, played at the game, while there were spectators who watched from on top of the corrugated roof of the refreshment rooms, which collapsed, though without serious injury to anyone. At two o'clock, the Lord Mayor of Cork officially opened the grounds, at which time the attendance was estimated to be 20,000. In the hurling game, Dungourney from East Cork played London Irish, while the football game featured Bray Emmetts and London Irish. A special train from Dublin brought 1,000 people, and, as for the games themselves, there was 'not a single untoward incident'. That evening the Lord Mayor hosted a dinner in the vestibule of the municipal buildings for ninety guests, including representatives of the Irish teams which had played earlier in the day and guests from Munster, Leinster and Connacht. There was no representation from the London Irish team, although they had been invited. During the course of the evening, the guests gave what was described as a time-honoured toast to 'Our Native Land'.

The build-up to a match added to the idea of the games as public events, the scenes afterwards were no less important. No doubt, all teams and their supporters celebrated after major victories in championships or wins over rivals, but the celebrations in the north side of the city when their teams were victorious were particularly noteworthy. This is how a Teddy O'Donovan, in the Glen Rovers Club history, described the after-match scenes in the Blackpool area of the city in the 1930s:

As the leading side-car bearing the proud captain with, of course, the cup, reached Blackpool Bridge, shouts of 'Here They Come!!' brought hordes of women-folk spilling from the cavern-like mouths of Slatterys' and Fosters' Lanes to overfill an already packed Thomas Street. The Dalys and the Deanes, the Lynches and the Leahys were proud to come forward to pay homage to their victorious sons, waving black shawls and tricolours, even pillow slips and papal flags to add their own particular touch to a very colourful scene.[114]

When the sister football club to Glen Rovers, St Nick's, won a county final in 1938, the St Nick's historian said the 'celebrations were mighty' and that absence from work for a week or two by the players was ignored by understanding bosses.[115]

TRAVEL AND TRANSPORT

From the earliest years of the GAA in Cork, the train was the most important mode of transport for players and supporters who wanted to get to matches that were not within walking distance. Special trains were laid on for the more important matches. For the hurling and football matches involving clubs from Cork and Kerry at Mallow in July 1889, patrons came on the normal trains as well as four other special trains laid on for the day. When Kilworth from North Cork played Nils Desperandum from the city in a hurling championship match in Mallow in July 1890, approximately 2,500 tickets were purchased at Glanmire Station, the main city terminus. An ordinary train and two special trains carried supporters to Mallow, though that was considered to be hardly sufficient to accommodate everyone. A special train also came from Fermoy for the Kilworth supporters. As for the arrangements from Cork, the *Cork Examiner* had this to say, 'the arrangements made for the lease of tickets at the Cork terminus were admirable and there was in consequence comparatively little overcrowding or confusion'.[116]

In the new century, trains were similarly important. Often, special trains were also requested by clubs. For the All-Ireland final in November 1912, which involved Blackrock representing Cork against Kilkenny, there was anger at the Great Southern and Western Railway that the company would not grant a special train for the Saturday night for those who were going to support Blackrock. On the Sunday of the game, Sunday morning specials were laid on for the estimated 1,000 to 1,500 patrons who went to support Blackrock. When trains were not available, attendances suffered. For a final in Ballinhassig to the west of the city, between Ballymartle and St Finbarrs, the attendance was 'fairly large', however, 'not quite as large as the importance of such a match demanded but this was to a large extent, due to the want of train facilities'.[117]

The following piece from the *Cork Sportsman* shows how a train was used by the Juverna team from the city which travelled to play Cobh:

> Notwithstanding the unpleasant atmospheric conditions prevailing on Sunday last ... Juverna men travelled to Cobh. Their Selection Committee installed themselves in a special compartment, and after a short glance over the Dublin Evening Papers, and a brief chat over the Elections, the work of overhauling the team began. It was found that thirteen of the original team were on board and the difficulty of filling four places from sixteen eligible was a formidable one. The selectors found this so but as Rushbrook docks appeared, they had given the finishing touches to their side. On arrival at the field, heavy cold rain fell in abundance, and some time elapsed before it was possible to start the match.[118]

However, trains were not the sole means of transport. For those who played with or supported the Grenagh club, some miles to the north of Cork City, those who had bicycles were considered to be in the upper-class bracket, but everyone who wished to get to matches always seemed to manage it, whether it was by bicycle, lorry, or horse and trap.[119]

NEWSPAPER COVERAGE

> The whole secret of the success of the *Cork Sportsman* lies in the fact that its contributors are all practical sportsmen who know their subject inside out. Fine, honest, clean-living men who physically and mentally are always in training, men whose enthusiasm for their subject is only equalled by their capacity for putting their views and feelings into words for the benefit of other followers of sport.[120]

This was how the *Cork Sportsman* described its contribution to the coverage of sport in general in Cork, and Gaelic games received plenty of such coverage. From the earliest years of the GAA in Cork, the local press, in particular the *Cork Examiner*, covered the games and meetings of the association. In the late 1890s, this coverage was extended by the founding of the *Cork Sportsman*. Press coverage did not just consist of simply describing how the game was played, detailing the scores, etc. and leaving it thus. Indeed, much of the coverage was in the form of correspondents admonishing what they felt to be behaviour that was detrimental to the GAA. Coverage also consisted of praising the Gaelic games and attributes which they developed.

A lack of punctuality and poor organisation were particular sources of annoyance to those who covered the games. Commenting on a championship match in 1890, the Erin's Own historian quotes from a *Cork Examiner* report which showed annoyance at the late starting of the game, 'A good deal of gambling would have been avoided if there had been more regard for punctuality ... proceedings were to commence at 1p.m. but it was twenty minutes past five before the two events on the cards finished.'[121]

The *Cork Sportsman* was very strident on this particular point. Discussing the board's attitude to punctuality in its edition in January 1910, this is what the paper had to say, 'I shall give them a hot "rubbing up" before the Championships start. Yet the Board never took the stringent measures they promised the sluggards – here they were weak and weakness meant failure. Otherwise we have done well.'[122]

Newspapers were also quite unforgiving if the organisation of fixtures was not what it might have been. At a double bill in 1906, St Finbarrs were to play the Inniscarra second team in the first match and the Inniscarra first team were to play Shanballymore's first team in the second match. For the first match the Inniscarra team did not turn up and St Finbarrs were awarded the victory. The Shanballymore team arrived late for the following game because of the timing of the train, but Inniscarra waited and the match was played. Commenting on the day's events, the *Cork Examiner* concluded its piece with the comment, 'So much for the hurling fixtures.'[123] In 1909, a similar situation arose in which Little Island were to play Aghada in a league match which never took place. Commenting on the incident, the *Cork Sportsman* remarked, 'Aghada thought it better to wait 'till the "ball was over" and not write 'till Monday morning. The excuse was that the weather was too bad. I'll say no more, but I hope the league will take a tip, and not allow teams to be codding them.'[124]

The *Cork Sportsman*, in particular, adopted a paternalistic attitude towards the players, especially in hurling, constantly encouraging them to practise and not ignore their skills. In the course of reporting a match, one columnist, writing under the name 'Carbery', gave this piece of advice, 'Get your hurleys out lads; get into the open fields and play the game of your fathers and you will be the better men everyway for it.'[125] Again, in the GAA notes of the *Cork Sportsman* of January 1910, the writer noted that it was a very quiet time for hurlers, but he hoped that the players were not neglecting their practices.

In the *Cork Sportsman* later that month, the writer calling himself 'Clan Desmond', began his column on hurling by talking of how the 'reeking political atmosphere has thrown into miserable insignificance every other pleasure in the life of the "man on the street"'.[126] It was noted that even the hurlers 'have caught the fever', but the columnist continues:

> But now that much of the excitement is over, it behoves our hurlers to return to their old love. The days are lengthening already. The muddy weather appears to be over for a time at least, and dusty hurleys should be introduced to their old friend the springy leather to rudely kiss it with rupture once more. I hear of a good few general meetings coming on in the course of the next week or two, and once these are over, practice should start at once.

While, as we have seen, newspapers were not slow in condemning foul play or indiscipline, there were also occasions when a degree of sympathy was shown for the teams which had transgressed. In March 1936, Mayfield, from the city, and Castlemartyr, from East Cork, played in the county junior hurling final. Incidents during the game were looked into by an investigating committee and recommendations from the committee led to the clubs being suspended as from the date of their match. The correspondent on the *Cork Evening Echo*, commenting on this judgement, said, 'I rather feel for the clubs in the position in which they now find themselves but incidents of the nature brought under notice cannot be treated with leniency.'[127]

In the same day's edition of the paper there was also sympathy expressed towards Redmonds, who were knocked out of the championship, 'My own sympathy goes out to the Redmonds whom I had expected to see stay some distance in the county Championship … There must be something wrong somewhere … It seems inconceivable but it is true.'

There was also praise for the qualities that Gaelic games fostered in those who played them. In the 22 January edition of the *Cork Sportsman* of 1910, the following paragraphs praised hurling, 'As to the practical, muscle-building lung-strengthening and limb-supplying of the game, practical experience is the proof … hurling is the only game of such an apparently strenuous character which never kills through sheer vigour.'[128] Elsewhere the paper said:

> From the view point of physical culture it is seen that hurling complies with three essentials for a beneficial outdoor sport – played under healthy conditions, calls into play almost every faculty of muscular activity and demands to a larger

degree the intelligent and simultaneous co-operation of the higher faculties of sight and skill. Its pursuit is attended with health-giving conditions – a fact that is self-evident. A better knowledge of the country and fraternal feelings have been created to a large extent by inter-club and inter-county contests.

In January 1934, in previewing an upcoming football match in the Railway Cup between Leinster and Munster, the writer going by the pen name 'Iomanuidhe' recalled the previous match between the two provinces, 'Everything that is best in Gaelic Football was fully exemplified, and the struggle illustrated beyond question that no game requires greater physical traits, combined with quick decision and elusive movements than Gaelic Football.'[129]

When describing the action on the field, press reports tended to focus on the style of play of the various teams. Here is how the *Cork Examiner* described the Mayfield and Brian Dillon teams, who would also have been close rivals, 'the Mayfield Boys are smart and scientific hurlers but lack dash. Brian Dillons play with great courage and verve. Such are the chief traits of both teams.'[130]

Summarising a match between Cobh and Juverna, the correspondent in the *Cork Sportsman* concluded that 'the match, considering the sodden condition of the pitch, was a good one. Cove were nicer footballers and physically stronger, but in bustling and vigour, Juverna triumphed.'[131]

Early reports on matches show there was no great scientific method in the styles of play. Describing a match between Cork Nationals and St Finbarrs, the *Cork Examiner* noted that 'there was a great deal of rushing for the next 10 minutes'.[132] The early reports tended to describe the play in general, rather than singling out what individual players did. Here is a description of the controversial meeting of Blackrock and Redmonds which had been over-shadowed by a court order to prevent the game from going ahead because of the fear of trouble:

> From here it was then transferred to the eastern line, where some close play took place. Again, the ball touched the Redmond ground, and as quickly was it sent spinning into neutral territory. The puck out sent the ball to the eastern side line, from which the Redmond wing men brought the leather opposite the Blackrock posts and a very stiff tussle here resulted in the Redmonds scoring.[133]

A very interesting aspect of the newspaper coverage was the opportunities it provided for followers and players of the games to write in to the local press, either praising the coverage of Gaelic games, or, as happened on other occasions, to take issue with match reports. The following are excerpts from a number of letters written to the *Cork Sportsman* for its issue of 8 January 1910. The first mentioned here relates to a report of a Cork versus Tipperary match:

> Dear Sir,
> I read 'Carbery's' description of the hurling final, and on the whole considered it to be a fair and impartial account. There were a few points on which we would differ, but everyone is entitled to his opinion. I also read the article, by 'Old Sportsman', in which he (the first so far as I know) accused the Tipps of showing the white feather. It would hardly be wise to make such a charge over one's name. There was no justification for such an assertion. Prejudice may lead one to extremes, but should not go so far as slander...[134]

There was another letter on behalf of the St Finbarrs club, regarding the coverage which their game against St Colmans had received:

> Dealing with the report, which was impartiality in the extreme (I don't think!), it states that 'O'Connor, the Colmanites' speedy right winger, got a bad blow on the instep, and had to retire'. Now I wonder, did this very impartial reporter see what Mr O'Connor did just previous to his retirement from play? Would it surprise him to know that the speedy right winger rushed at one of our players and hit him a most ferocious blow on the knee with his hurley ... Further down we read – 'The Barrs now scored a point, but the pace was evidently telling on them, while the college lads were keen and speedy as ever'. Well, now, if our team were so fatigued, how does the writer account for the fact that our team outclassed St Colman's in the last five minutes, jumped the paling and ran to the station to catch the train for home?

This letter then prompted a reply from a representative of St Colmans. The reply was written a few weeks after the letter from St Finbarrs appeared, but the letter writer at the outset said he had not seen the paper for a few weeks as he had been on holidays. This letter took issue with various points in the earlier letter, such as the following, 'Regarding Mr O'Connor's instep: he spent four days in bed after the match. I believed the Finbarr player finished it and possibly even "leaped the paling", whatever that may be, in spite of the "most ferocious blow on the skull".' The writer concluded his letter saying he did not want to arouse bad feelings between the clubs, but did stress 'that never was a more gross injustice committed, whether intentionally or otherwise, than that against St Colmans at Mallow'.

One of the most significant letters to appear in the local press was that written by James Kelleher from the Dungourney Club, relating to four players who were due to represent Cork and who were suspended for not turning up for the match. 'Carbery', writing in the *Cork Sportsman*, said he had received 'several communications' on the issue, but would not discuss it in greater detail because he said the newspaper for which he wrote 'has for its sole object the encouragement and development of healthy sport in Munster, and all other interests are subservient to this great mission'.[135]

Yet, a central figure, who was one of those suspended, a James Kelleher from Dungourney, used the medium of the *Cork Sportsman* to write a lengthy letter defending himself and those other players who had not travelled for the match. It is significant in the way it highlights differences between players and the county board and the sense of injustice the players felt at how they were being treated:

> I have been asked by your correspondent in the last issue of the *Cork Sportsman* to give my reasons for four picked men not travelling to do battle for Cork against Limerick on Sunday week last.
>
> The principal objection in the way is the distance to Ennis. Imagine a man travelling 120 mile by rail, to play a match which should be played thirty miles from the City of Cork. Starting from Dungrouney at six o'clock in the morning, walking six miles to the railway station, going on to Cork, Mallow, Limerick, then into county Clare and playing a hard hour's game, starting from the latter place at half-past-six in the evening, and arriving home at two, or perhaps three, o'clock next morning. We have done it before and will be prepared to do it again if we are required by any of the hurling teams in Cork. Give me the name of the County Board, Munster or Central Council man who will do it? Would they walk half-a-mile from the station to the playing ground without a car while the players have to rely on shanks mare? I have seen, to my disgust, the players draw the crowds, make the money, lose their sweat at many a hard hour's game, while those gentlemen, at the head of affairs, take charge of the bag and jump on their cars again before the match is over – off to count the coin made by the rank and file.[136]

The letter then went on to complain about inadequate compensation to players for injuries during games, and it finished with these rousing sentences:

It is time for the Gaels of Ireland to wake up, take the bags from these gentle-men, show them the outside of the gates, and have men of the type of Austin Stack, Maurice McCarthy, Dick Fitzgerald, and Dan Fraher at the head of the association in Munster. The governing body has been captured by non-players, and the players themselves – the men who pay the freight – seem to have no direct representation on it. As Dungourney were champions for 1907, and this year is yet unfinished, I think they were entitled to as many representatives as any club in Cork.

There are a number of final points worth remarking on, with regard to newspaper coverage of Gaelic games. From the point of view of the press, a significant development took place for the opening of the Cork Athletic Grounds in 1904. For the occasion, a special telegraphic service was pro-vided at the new grounds to facilitate journalists, having been put in place with help from the acting postmaster in Cork and the Superintendent of Telegraphs.

Following the great spectacle of this particular match, the *Cork Examiner* had an editorial devoted to the success of the day. The editorial referred to how heretofore there had been inadequate provision for outdoor sports and that major facilities had long been required. It also referred to the crowd of 20,000 present and continued with reference to an upcoming international to take place in the Mardyke grounds, involving England and Ireland, saying that 'Sport, like music may be said to be cosmopolitan, so all who admire sport for sport's sake will be pleased to learn that great progress has been make with the Mardyke Field'.[137] The editorial then went on to praise sport, its associated qualities and Gaelic games and rugby facilities:

> It will thus be seen that practical steps are being taken to provide whole-some amusement for all admirers for various kinds of sport, and the taunt that emigration was to some extent caused by the dullness existing is now, to a con-siderable degree, being removed. Physical culture and outdoor games are now recognised as being necessary for the well-being of the rising generation…

As one reviews Cork's GAA story from the latter half of the nineteenth century to the 1930s, a number of salient issues emerge. During the period, rivalries reached such intensity on numerous occasions that the very core function of the association was put at risk and in exceptional circumstances put into abeyance. Yet the remarkable fact was that the attraction of the games and dedication of successive cadres of leaders among administration, referees and players, not to mention the sheer popularity of sports among citizens, were sufficiently strong to withstand even the most seismic of political splits.

By the 1930s, while residual elements of older political rivalries were still present, it was within and between parishes, clubs and counties that rivalry was now principally located. By this time, issues which had been there from the beginning relating to rules, discipline, finance and facilities constituted the agenda of the organisation and field of commentary of its enthusiasts and its detractors. Its nationalist origins were unambiguously clear, but party -political loyalties no longer featured as a key determinant of its rivalries.

The development of facilities and the increasing professionalism of its financial management and its arrangements are clearly reflected in the sources that have formed the basis of this chapter, though there continued to be a challenge in enforcing uniform, acceptable standards in all of these areas. Old habits die hard.

With regard to spectators, the lack of references to the attendance of women suggests virtually all-male attendances. Whether the silence of the reporter on gender deserves comment is something one cannot say.

There a number of other issues which deserve comment. It is noteworthy that the GAA, from an early stage and right throughout the period of this study, showed a concern on behalf of the clubs and the county board to recompense those who lost out financially through injury caused by their participation in the games. There was also an element of social concern in the way donations were made to unemployed members, both by individual clubs and the county board. The same concern extended to the payment of travelling and training expenses.

As one scans the development of the GAA across this timescale, there is evidence of a greater degree of discipline exhibited by both players and spectators. Instances of spectators encroaching on pitches and breaking down barriers were more common in the earlier years, and the graphic descriptions of injuries to players and spectators in the earliest years of the games were not repeated in the press as the time progressed.

II

ASSOCIATION FOOTBALL AND RUGBY

GROWTH OF SOCCER IN CORK

On 24 August 1901, the association football clubs in Munster met at premises called the Referees Room, in Marlboro Street, Cork City, and formed the Munster Football Association. Clubs were to pay an annual subscription of 10s towards membership and the first match to begin the official season in 1901 was one between the Kings Royal Rifles and a selection from the affiliated clubs in Munster. With regard to Cork's representation in the new association, there was a major contingent of army and navy teams based in Cork. These were the Royal Engineers, 6th Provisional Battalion from Fermoy, HMS *Black Prince*, RE Camden, and the Army Service Corps.

The civilian teams from Cork in the new MFA were Cork City, Cork Celtic, Aubeg, Passage, Haulbowline, and Millfield. Even the civilian teams showed the influence of the British navy presence, since the Passage and Haulbowline teams were from Cork Harbour, where the influence of the navy was strongest; in all likelihood these civilian teams had already been playing navy teams before officially affiliating with the Munster Football Association.

Various cups and leagues were initiated to facilitate competitive activity. The *Cork Sportsman* of 19 October 1908, under the heading 'Association Football', listed a match between Cork Celtic and the Royal Engineers to be played at Turner's Cross, while Cork City were to play Church of Ireland at Blackrock in the second division of the Munster League. The same day's edition listed matches taking place in competitions in Leinster, such as the Leinster senior and junior leagues, as well as the County Dublin leagues, and it also gave the results from the English League, Division 1.[1] The *Cork Examiner* of Monday 22 November 1909, mentioned that in the third round of the Irish Junior Cup,

HLI Reserves were to play Church of Ireland, while in the second round of the Berkeley Challenge Cup, the 10th Company RGA defeated the 30th Company Royal Engineers. In yet another fixture, the 49th Company RGA defeated the 43rd Company RGA. Munster Leagues had been initiated with three divisions, with Cork teams in each, and by 1914 there were four divisions of the Munster League – senior, intermediate, junior and minor – while there had been two separate divisions for military teams.

In the first decade of the century, the army and navy teams were dominant in the league tables, such as outlined by the *Cork Sportsman* on Saturday 12 December 1908, where the following teams played in the first division of the Munster League: RW Fusiliers, Sherwood Foresters, Haulbowline; 2nd S/L Regiment, 31st Brigade RFA, and Cork Celtic. Army and navy teams dominated in the second division also, where the only two civilian teams were Cork City and Church of Ireland. For example, in 1911, the East Surrey Regiment alone were able to field four teams.

COMPETITIVE STRUCTURE IN THE 1920S AND 1930S

In March 1922, the Munster Football Association was reorganised. Teams from Cork, which affiliated, were Fordsons from the Henry Ford Factory, Barrackton and Clifton, and they were accompanied by other Munster teams such as Limerick, Clonmel, Cahir Park, Tipperary Town and Tipperary Wanderers. For the 1922/23 season, a South Munster League was begun consisting of ten teams, all of which came from either Cork City or Cobh. The strength of soccer in Cobh showed the influence of the British navy still stationed there, and in the 1920s, soccer was strong enough in the district to hold a league of its own.

In the 1920s and 1930s, teams continued to play in various leagues and cups. Cork teams such as Barrackton, Cork Utd, and Freebooters were junior soccer teams, which entered the Munster Senior Cup of 1926. The *Cork Evening Echo* of Friday 9 March 1934, listed the various leagues and cups that were to be competed in on the following Sunday. These were the Munster senior league, Munster junior league, minor league and minor cup. There were also Munster junior league fixtures on the Saturday of this particular weekend and, significantly, an inter-house league. It is interesting, as Carter notes, that in the 1935/36 season, junior and minor competition soccer matches were attracting bigger crowds than League of Ireland matches.[2]

GEOGRAPHICAL SPREAD OF SOCCER CLUBS
IN CORK CITY

A sense of the geographical distribution of teams in Cork City can be gauged by noting the teams listed as taking part in various leagues and competitions from the early decades of the twentieth century. Reflecting the military origins of the game around Cork, the second division of the Munster league was arranged in three sections, these being 1. Cork and Ballincollig, 2. Queenstown and Haulbowline, and 3. North Munster. The greater participation of civilian teams is reflected in the number of teams who played in the South Munster League of the 1922/23 season. These were: Barrackton, Shandon, Bohemians, Fordsons, YMCA, Tramways, Clifton, Cork City, Parnell Rovers, and Blackrock Rovers. The local background to teams such as Barrackton, Shandon and Blackrock Rovers can be readily seen, while Fordsons and Tramways were work-based teams.

Many of these teams are also to be found in Carter's list of teams active in the mid-1920s, and playing in and around Cork City. These were: Bohemians, Fordsons, Bridewell, Barrackton, Cork City, Cork Celtic, Grattan, Great Southern Railway, Fermoy, Mallow, Cobh Ramblers, Southern Rovers, Rangers, Springfield, Burtonville, Tramways, Dwyers, Belville, Ardfallen, Central Utd, Glenview, Rockmount, and Victoria Celtic. Dwyers and Great Southern Railway were new work teams to enter the competitive fray.

Some of the foregoing teams were among those listed by Carter as taking part in the Munster Junior League of 1930, these being: Gas Company, Southern Rovers, St Marys, Crosshaven, Barrackton B, Bridewell, Cork Bohemians B, Cork Celtic B, Burtonville, Glenview, Grattan Utd, Rockmount, Bellville, Springfield, Cork City B, Suttons Utd, Dwyers, and Blackrock. Apart from the work teams of Gas Company, Suttons Utd, and Dwyers, it is difficult to associate the other teams with a definite geographical location, with the exception of Crosshaven and Blackrock. However, Carter does throw light on the origins of the some of the teams. For example, Rockmount were founded in the Blackpool area in the 1920s and a team called Southview, formed in 1936, originated in Reid Square.

According to Carter, in 1933, a team called North End were the 'pride of Quarry Lane', Quarry Lane being situated in the Blackpool area. By the mid-1930s there was a team active from the Bandon Road area in the south of the city called Rockwell. This particular side had split from Greenmount, also from the South Parish in Cork City.

GROUNDS AND PITCHES

While a number of recognised soccer grounds were established in Cork City, in the period from 1900 to 1939, in a trend similar to that of the GAA, various open spaces and grounds were used if more formal venues could not be found. In some cases, these facilities were lent by owners, as in the case of a game played between Cork Celtic and the Black Prince Ship at a venue called Lansdowne Park, in April 1901, which had been lent for play by a Mr Meehan. When a second-round tie of the Irish Army Cup was played in Kinsale in December 1901, between the East Surrey Regiment, which was stationed in the town, and the King's Own Light Infantry, stationed in Cork Barracks, the ground used was described as 'very spacious'.[3] This facility quite possibly belonged to the army, who were probably at an advantage in having their own patches of ground on which to play their games. For example, in January 1910, the Cork team HLI Reserves played a team from Belfast called Celtic Strollers in what was known as the Camp Field, situated on the north side of Cork City. Civilian teams, even when taking part in official competitions, had to use whatever patches of ground were available. In October 1911, Freebooters played Rockwell in the 3rd Division of the Munster League. Up to then, Freebooters had not been able to procure their own ground and, according to the *Cork Sportsman's* report for this game, 'retreated to the open Park to fulfil their engagements'.[4]

One of the main central venues used for the playing of soccer in Cork City was Turner's Cross, which, as we have seen, was also used as a G.A.A. venue. On 28 September 1901, when the first official soccer season began, an exhibition game between the King's Royal Rifles and a team comprised of affiliated clubs from throughout Munster played at Butler's Field, Turner's Cross, which up until then had been used for GAA matches. As noted already, the Nemo Rangers club used the venue for Gaelic games in the 1920s, as did the Cork county board, though it was lost to Gaelic games for good at the end of the 1920s. Changes were made to the facilities, though these were not without some problems. Commenting on a match held the previous Sunday, the soccer correspondent for the *Cork Evening Echo* noted some of the difficulties encountered by spectators:

> Many people were badly disappointed with Turner's Cross, last Sunday. The arrangements were very imperfect, but that could not be helped in the circumstances, as the changeover was rather hurried. On the next occasion, however, many improvements will be seen. For one thing it will be easier to obtain admission.[5]

Improved fencing was to be erected at the ground and 'last Sunday's scenes of crowded touch-lines will not be seen again'. The report predicted that the projected improvements 'should make it one of the finest in the south'.

Another central venue in Cork for soccer matches was Victoria Cross, in the west of the city. In January 1910, Cork City were to play Cork Celtic there, though just before the game was to take place, the match ball burst and could not be replaced because there was no time to find a new one. The same ground was used in 1926 for the Free State Cup semi-final between the Cork team Fordsons and Bray Unknowns. This match was originally to be played at the University Grounds, in the Mardyke, but the terms for which the university granted the grounds were not acceptable to the Free State Football Association. According to the *Cork Examiner*, there was 'some disappointment' at the change of venue, since crowd accommodation was more limited at Victoria Cross, and yet 10,000 people attended 'and the stewarding arrangements were so perfect that there was no undue overcrowding at any part'.[6]

Fordsons, the Cork team who entered the Free State League in the early 1920s, had procured their own ground for matches on the Ballinlough Road. The venue was surrounded by high walls and sheets of corrugated iron, while the pitch itself was separated from the rest of the enclosure by five-foot-high stakes. It was conveniently situated only a few minutes' walk from the Douglas tram terminus.

However, when Fordsons were due to play St James Gate in the semi-final of the Free State Cup, the rugby pitch of the University Grounds in the Mardyke was used. When Fordsons were drawn to play Shelbourne in 1926, the Mardyke venue was used again, though rain which fell before the match made the pitch a 'veritable quagmire'.[7] This pitch at the Mardyke was to become the venue for all the major soccer matches played in Cork in the late 1920s and right throughout the 1930s. Crowds at the venue, especially for Free State Cup matches, were so large that instructions were issued in the local press some days before, advising patrons on the procedures for entrance to the venue.

The *Cork Evening Echo* of Friday 20 January 1933, commented on the large crowd that had attended the previous Sunday's match at the Mardyke, between Cork FC and Shamrock Rovers, noting that it was 'one of the record crowds of the season', and estimating the attendance at 12,000 spectators.[8] The same teams were to meet again at the Mardyke the following weekend and it was predicted that a large contingent of Dublin supporters would attend. Arrangements for entrance to the ground for the forthcoming cup tie were to be altered and these were the instructions given to patrons:

> Entrance to the stand will be at Wellington Bridge stile, but only ticket hold-
> ers will be admitted there. Gates will be opened at 1.45p.m. and patrons are
> requested to have the exact amount of admission ready, to facilitate the stile-
> men, whose instructions are not to hold the crowd up seeking change, so that
> no change will be given.

Similar advice was given to intending spectators for the local derby match
between Cork FC and Cork Bohemians, which was also to take place at the
Mardyke, 'There is certain to be a huge crowd and accommodation in some
parts of the ground is certain to be much overtaxed. First come, first served,
from your own point of view, and of great convenience to the much worried
men at the turnstiles.'[9]

In March 1936, Cork were to play Drumcondra in the Free State Cup, and
this was again preceded by a piece in the *Cork Evening Echo* telling patrons of
the admission arrangements at the Mardyke. There were to be twelve turnstiles in operation and stand ticket holders were to be admitted by a members'
gate, with another special turnstile being set aside for the 2s entrance fee. Five
turnstiles would be in operation at what was called the Mardyke end and
another five turnstiles for what was called the 'popular' 1s enclosure. As was
the case for previous matches, patrons were asked to have the correct change
ready for admission, so as to prevent unnecessary delay.

However, there were problems with the Mardyke venue, due to the fact
that spectators had found ways of watching matches without paying the
admission charge. As a result, Dublin teams being unwilling to play there,
since they noted that their share of the gates was not as large as it should be.
Spectators were able to watch for free by standing on railings around the
grounds, standing on grass slopes at one end of the ground, by indiscrimi-
nately crossing walls, and finally by gaining free access by means of a boat
service.[10] The *Cork Evening Echo* correspondent acknowledged these objections, but, with regard to spectators watching from the slopes overlooking
the ground, said that the only alternative to this would have been to erect a
grandstand at that end of the ground to obscure the view for those on the
slopes.

Cork teams also lost out financially because of the difficulty of enforc-
ing payment of admission fees. In January 1934, Cork FC defeated Cork
Bohemians in the replay of their Free State Cup game. For the previous
Sunday's first game between the two sides, the official attendance had been

announced as being 5,168, giving total gross receipts of £229 0s 6d. The soccer writer for the *Cork Evening Echo*, 'Linesman', made the following remarks on these official figures:

> This is an astounding figure and seems hard to credit. Nevertheless, they are the turnstile figures. Certainly, a much bigger estimate of the crowd present is more believable, but as I have remarked before, many are the ways of getting into the ground. Our old friends, the boat excursionists, came in full force on Sunday, and heaven knows how many succeeded in getting in by other devious and hazardous means. From the gross receipts, have to be deducted all expenses, including tax, which in itself amounts to approximately £40, before the clubs get their share. By the time rent and the association's share is paid, the clubs have good reason to complain of lack of finances.

Cork soccer historian Sylvester O'Sullivan also identified this non-payment of admission fees as being a crucial factor in the financial difficulties of Cork soccer clubs in the 1930s. Beside a photograph of spectators watching a match from outside the Mardyke ground, standing on a nearby bridge, O'Sullivan commented, 'Fans like these would not pay the modest "tanner" admission charge to the Dyke when they had a "buckshee" grand stand view from Wellington Bridge.'[11] Along with these difficulties, Cork soccer teams met with little or no success in the 1937/38 season, and the crowds that had attended games the previous season were no longer turning up to watch. For the 1938/39 season, Cork City FC had an average gate of 4,000.

SPECTATORS

Even when the game of soccer was in its infancy, in the years before the First World War, it often brought out large attendances. As early as 1897, Cork team Barrackton Utd travelled to Tipperary to play Tipperary Wanderers. The attendance, which included many followers of the Cork team, had to endure what the *Cork Examiner* called a 'severe storm', but there was such interest in the outcome of the match 'that with drenched garments the majority of the spectators followed various incidents of the game from start to finish'.[12] When Freebooters from Cork played a team called Rockwell in the third division of the Munster League, the *Cork Sportsman* commented on how 'inclement' the weather was, but nevertheless a 'huge crowd patronised the match'.[13] Yet, good weather was still considered to be a major factor in determining the number of spectators who would attend a match. In January 1910, the *Cork Sportsman* predicted a large attendance for an upcoming Saturday match in Turner's Cross in the second division of the Munster League, between Cork Celtic and Church of Ireland.[14]

As will be seen later, the majority of matches before the First World War involved army or navy teams, yet such matches attracted civilians as well as members of the defence forces. When HMS *Skipjack* played the Army Ordnance Corps in the sixth division of the Munster League in December 1908, there was a 'very large number of spectators, which included a very large portion of civilians'.[15] There was considerable interest in an all-army match played in Kinsale in December 1911, between the East Surrey Regiment stationed there and the visiting King's Own Yorkshire Light Infantry, stationed at Cork Barracks. Though the weather was cold, it was otherwise dry, and the attendance 'reached very large proportions'.[16] Also, as regards travelling to matches, in February 1915, a party of Cork supporters made the long journey to Sligo the day before the match between Sligo and Cork, although Sligo won by five goals to one.

However, it was in the 1920s that large-scale crowds began to attend soccer matches in Cork. This was due in large part to the Fordsons team, based at the Ford plant, gaining league status in the Free State Cup. In March 1934, Fordsons were drawn to play St James Gate from Dublin at the rugby grounds of the university at the Mardyke in the semi-final of the Free State Cup. It was estimated that between 12,000 and 15,000 attended the game. The *Cork Examiner*, commenting on the large attendance, said, 'This is probably the largest number of people that ever attended a soccer match in Cork, certainly the biggest since the re-organising of the game in Munster, a few years ago.'[17] Fordsons triumphed in this semi-final and played the final at Dalymount Park on St Patrick's Day 1924. It was estimated that half an hour before the kick-off there were 14,000 people present, and the spectators were still coming in. Fordsons had brought many of the spectators in an excursion train and their colours were sported by many in the crowd. When the teams came on to the field they were given a great reception.

It was a similar situation two years later, when Fordsons played in the Free State Cup and were drawn at home to play Shelbourne. In January 1926, the game was held in the Mardyke and despite continuous rain, there was still a crowd of 6,000 to 7,000 present. This game was a draw and in much better weather conditions the following week, the crowd at the kick-off of the replay was of 'large dimensions'.[18] The excitement of the cup tie was reflected in the behaviour of the spectators and, according to the *Cork Examiner*, the excitement went too far, resulting in derisive remarks being made against the player who sometimes, under pressure, had to kick the ball into touch. The good cup run of Fordsons that year led them to the semi-final, where they defeated Bray Unknowns at Victoria Cross, before a crowd of 10,000. The final was played on St Patrick's Day 1926, in Dalymount Park, when the official attendance was 26,000 who paid total receipts of £1,600. Fordsons were playing Shamrock Rovers, and a player named Barry, for Fordsons, scored the winning goal. When the game finished, both he and O'Hagan, the Fordsons goalkeeper, were carried shoulder high to the dressing rooms as the Cork supporters swarmed over the barriers.

Towards the end of the 1920s, large crowds continued to come to games in Cork, for cup matches in particular, and it seems that clashes between Dublin and Cork teams added an extra interest. In 1928, for the Free State Cup semi-final between Fordsons and Drumondra, a record crowd of 18,000 attended the game. On 15 February 1930, Fordsons played Shamrock Rovers at the Mardyke. To accommodate the anticipated crowds, the Munster Football Association had intended to put in sideline seating, though sideline seats had been banned by the Free State Football Association. The Munster Football Association appealed its case and was granted permission to install the seating. For the match, 4,000 Shamrock Rovers followers travelled to Cork and there was a record attendance of 20,000, with record receipts of £900. Again, those who did not pay admission watched the game from the heights of Shanakiel, with others climbing on to the corrugated roof of the stand (on this occasion, one spectator almost fell off while attempting to catch a ball which landed on the roof).

In the 1930s, league games between Dublin and Cork sides attracted large attendances. Twelve thousand spectators, including hundreds of Shelbourne supporters, watched Fordsons versus Shelbourne in February 1931, with Shelbourne winning the game and therefore the championship. There was extra tension at this match because if Cork had won, they would have also kept alive their championship chances. What also aroused great interest and attracted large attendances was the fact that, in the 1930s, there were two Free State league teams in Cork, Cork FC and Cork Bohemians, with Cork FC being the successor to Fordsons. For their match in January 1931, there were 15,000 spectators.

Yet, it was the cup runs of Cork teams that continued to attract larger and larger crowds. In the semi-final of the Free State Cup in February 1934, between Cork FC and Dundalk, an estimated 30,000 were in attendance, a record for the Mardyke ground, 'while the gate receipts at popular prices were £1,100'.[19]

CONTESTS AND MATCHES AS EVENTS

To a large degree, the crowds that attended the matches at the Mardyke came because of the intense rivalries involved, especially in the cup fixtures between Cork and Dublin's soccer teams. The main representative team for Cork in the 1920s was that of Fordsons, which went from being a work team to a Free State League team. In the 1930s, the successor to Fordsons were Cork FC, though another Free State team had also been founded in Cork – Cork Bohemians. The local rivalry between Cork FC and Cork Bohemians evoked keen interest in Cork in the 1930s when they met in either the Free State League or the Free State Cup.

When these Cork rivals met in January 1931, there were 15,000 spectators present, which, the *Cork Evening Echo* remarked, had been 'occasioned by the old-standing rivalry between the two clubs' and led to an 'air of intense excitement'.[20] The Butter Exchange Band played the National Anthem before the game and, according to the match report, 'the players took their task so seriously that one could imagine the order "no quarter", had been given [but] Notwithstanding this, a cleaner game has never been played in Cork.'

Evidence of the continued interest in their games was reflected in the 15,000 spectators who came to watch their league game at the Cork Showgrounds, where Cork Bohemians played their home matches. The Barrack Street Band heightened the sense of occasion by playing at the match, while there was traffic congestion on the Blackrock Road leading to the venue, caused by buses, private cars, hackney and sidecars.

The clubs met again in the Free State Cup in January 1934 and the *Cork Evening Echo* summed up the sense of anticipation, saying that, 'although great interest is shown in cup ties, as a whole, the real interest as far as Cork is concerned lies in the local derby. Can Bohs win? By how much will Cork win?'[21] Ten thousand attended the game, which ended in a draw, a match described as 'Cup football at its best', and, despite the rivalry, the players 'conducted themselves in a manner which reflected the greatest credit on them'.[22]

Junior soccer games also attracted a large degree of attention. When Cork City played Barrackton in the Munster Senior League at Ballintemple, the game aroused 'considerable interest', since both teams had already played a draw in a preliminary round, and the attendance was 'the largest seen in Ballintemple for a considerable time'.[23] Earlier, in January of that year, Bohemians from Cork played Parnell Rovers, also in the Munster Senior

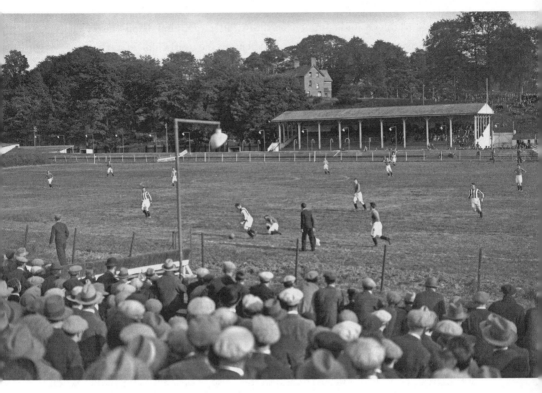

Interested spectators at a soccer match. (Image courtesy of *Irish Examiner*)

League, at Victoria Cross, a match which was played before a 'good-sized attendance'.[24] In March 1936, the *Cork Evening Echo* predicted a large attendance for an upcoming match between two selected teams representing Leinster and Munster junior league soccer clubs.[25]

The impact of soccer matches, as regards their sense of occasion and excitement, is best exemplified by contemporary accounts of the scenes before and after matches, especially those of celebration. The greatest occasions were almost invariably cup matches. This is how the *Cork Examiner* described the pre-match-day build-up to the Free State Cup semi-final between Fordsons and Bray Unknowns at the Mardyke, in February 1926, 'For over two hours before the kick-off spectators streamed into the ground, and the interval of walking was whiled away in pleasing fashion by the Greenmount Industrial School Band, which discoursed an entertaining selection of music.'[26] There was a very similar scene before the cup tie between Cork and Drumcondra at the Mardyke, in March 1936:

The trek to the ground commenced shortly after 1p.m. and despite heavy rain and a strong prevailing wind, the crowd kept up the usual Cup-tie spirit, enlivened by the strains of the Cork Butter Exchange Band. Everywhere were to be seen the green and white colours of Cork on the men and women, boys and girls. Women and girls formed a large proportion of the incoming crowds.[27]

Bands were part of the joyous celebrations that followed Cork victories in the Free State Cup in the 1920s and 1930s. When the Fordsons team won the Free State Cup in 1926, fans who returned that night at around midnight were greeted at Glanmire Station by bands. The following night, the victorious team returned to blazing barrels and the players were carried shoulder high to waiting cars, which brought them to Patrick Street. There they entered the Victoria Hotel, and the players went to the upstairs windows to acknowledge the crowds. A victory ball was held in the Arcadia Ballroom, where Jack Kelly, on behalf of the Fordsons team, presented the match ball to Mr Edward Grace, Managing Director of the Henry Ford Company.

There were similar scenes following the victory of Cork FC in the Free State Cup in 1934. It was estimated that 10,000 people crowded the Glanmire terminus and the streets of Cork to welcome back the victorious team. Tar barrels were set alight and four bands played to add to the sense of occasion. The players, when they arrived, were presented individually to the Lord Mayor, who in turn was cheered by the team and everyone else on the platform. The players then boarded a wagonette and, headed by the Erin's Own Pipe Band, the procession passed through the various streets until it arrived at the club rooms at Princes Street, this street being so packed that it took a considerable time for the players to reach the club premises. Though each player was called upon to make a speech, which they attempted, they could not hear even themselves, because of the cheering.

In the following Friday's edition of the *Cork Evening Echo*, the soccer writer 'Linesman' said that the reception accorded the victorious Cork team eclipsed any he had seen before and he felt that it was a mystery how so many people packed themselves into Princes Street to welcome the team. He also recorded the thanks of the Cork team to Conway's Yard for their supply of the wagonette which brought them through the city that night.

There was also a great sense of occasion when the first soccer international to be held outside Dublin was played in Cork on 19 March 1939. Sideline seats were installed and new banking had been speedily completed, while one-way traffic was arranged for the grounds around the Mardyke. The Hungarian team arrived in Cork on a Saturday afternoon and the

Greemount band were part of the welcoming party. The team were accorded a civic reception by the Lord Mayor, and an official attendance of 16,000 paying £1,100 in receipts, watched the game.

NEWSPAPER COVERAGE

The coverage soccer received in the local press fell into a number of categories. There was, for instance, the focus on individual games and how they were previewed, with the press coverage adding to a sense of excitement and anticipation. There was then the review of games and the praise or criticism levelled at teams and individual players. Finally, there was more general comment on the administration of the game in the country as a whole, with a certain perceptible bias towards the Cork case as regards where and when matches should be held.

Newspapers, as we have already seen, created a sense of excitement by telling readers about the arrangements for entry, and advising them to come early and to have the correct amount of money for the stilemen. This sense of anticipation was heightened by the way matches were previewed. For example, this is how the writer 'Centre Half' previewed the tie between two Free State League teams, Cork Bohemians and Bohemians from Dublin, before their meeting in a cup match, 'There will be rare gathering to see the meeting of Bohs and Cork Bohs tomorrow ... Cork Bohs play what is regarded as the more traditional Cup style, with the ball flung about widely, in an effort to catch their opponents off their balance.'[28]

The excitement was conveyed even more strongly in a piece in the *Cork Evening Echo*, on Friday 17 April 1936, as the paper looked forward to the cup final on the following Sunday between Cork FC and Shamrock Rovers to be played in Dalymount Park. The first paragraph of the article said the match was likely to prove a 'classical exposition of Association Football'.[29] The writer then went on to describe what he felt would be the atmosphere of the day for the spectators from Cork who were travelling:

On Sunday morning Kingsbridge station will deliver up a nice proportion of Cork people, unmistakably garbed in blue and white, and knowing nothing of any other attraction – but the Cup Final. It will be a pilgrimage with the match as centrepiece to a day brimful of events. Nearly all Dublin must be seen on foot or car before their gay caps and berets droop to submissive angles and effort is made to reach the homeward trains. There is nothing like it in the Free State's Football calendar for enthusiasm and sheer love of a great game, as a cup final to soccer followers is worth a hundred league games and the same number of any other outstanding fixtures.

When it came to commenting on the performance of the Cork teams, the local press was not slow in giving critical opinions on individual players. For a drawn game in the Free State Cup between Shelbourne and Fordsons in January 1926, the *Cork Examiner* noted that both wing forwards for Fordsons were 'poor', but that 'Roberts, Kelly and Buckle were hard workers'.[30] The paper reserved its greatest praise for the Fordson defenders, to whom 'all the honour of the game' belonged and who 'worked like Trojans'.

In January 1931, Cork FC lost to Bohemians in the first round replay of a Free State Cup match in Dublin after drawing the original game in the Mardyke. The *Cork Evening Echo* described the failure in the replay as a 'tragedy', while, for not winning the first day at the Mardyke, the Cork team were 'deserving of the greatest censure'. However, the writer did add that he had 'the greatest sympathy with them in their defeat'.[31] This still did not prevent the writer from penning this criticism in the same article in referring to the cup replay in Dublin, 'Let me say here and now that I don't intend to offer a word of criticism to any individual members of the team beyond saying that one played hopelessly, three poorly, two fairly well and the balance splendidly. On that meagre information, readers may speculate to their hearts' content.'

The local press was similarly quick to give advice to players on how to correct faults in their play. 'Offside', in his soccer notes in the *Cork Evening Echo* of 11 January 1935, focused on a recent display by the Cork goalkeeper, of whom he said, 'but once again to my grief, I must impress upon him the great danger of leaving his charge'.[32] In March 1936, though Cork FC had won through to the final of the Free State Cup after defeating Shelbourne in Cork, the reporter included a piece under the subtitle 'Lessons to Learn'.[33] It included this advice, 'A better understanding is badly needed between the two fulls … both O' Reilly and Percy should bear in mind that a centre which reached the goalkeeper is a centre wasted.'

The Cork team was unsuccessful against Shamrock Rovers in the final and again certain individuals came under the spotlight for their inadequate displays, 'Percy rarely got away with any confidence and was often beaten to the centre. King and Madden, the inside forwards, played too far back, and were not mobile enough to join forces with Turnbull at the right time.'[34]

The local press in Cork also voiced displeasure that more games were not played in Cork as opposed to Dublin. For example, in 1934, 'Linesman', in his column, referred to how a Munster delegate at a meeting of the Free State Football Association had advocated the playing of one of that year's Free State Cup semi-finals in Cork, since receipts would be increased substantially. 'Linesman' agreed, saying that playing one of the semi-finals in Cork would have meant an increase of at least £500 in gate receipts, while the last semi-final to be played in Cork had yielded a record gate of £750.[35] In summary, the Cork Evening Echo wrote that, 'the angle from which the subject was originally debated provides cause for just resentment on the part of Southern supporters'. The same paper, in 1935, in a comment on the cup draw for that year, suggested that there should be a way of devising the cup draw so that each of the provincial centres of Cork, Dundalk, Sligo and Waterford could secure a match, though it acknowledged that Dublin clubs might have some grievance over this.[36]

One final aspect of press coverage which should not be overlooked was that, similar to GAA writers and columnists, those who covered soccer were not slow to highlight what they regarded as poor sportsmanship on behalf of players and spectators. In 1910, when Celtic Strollers came to Cork to play HLI Reserves, the Cork Sportsman noted how the Celtic team, who were from Belfast, kept sending the ball into touch when under pressure. The writer said such practice was 'not in accordance with ... the true idea of sportsmanship'.[37] It was also noted that the Belfast team did not retire the proper distance from free kicks and if the match referee had been from Munster, the offending players would have been sent off.

At a match the following week, the Cork Sportsman directed criticism at what it felt was unacceptable behaviour during the match between the 43rd Company RGA and Barrackton Utd played at Spike Island. The newspaper complained about the shouting that took place between the players, a practice it described as not 'playing the game'.[38] The piece said that it was the business of the captain to control the team and that one captain was enough for any team — the spectators paid their admittance to see a game of football between twenty-two men and not a 'howling match'. In 1935, the Cork Evening Echo's 'Centre-Half' referred to a junior cup tie between Distillers of Dublin and Butchers of Cork, which was going to be replayed. The writer hoped that there would be none of the unpleasantness that had attended the first game, which played in Cork, since 'Spectators must learn to control themselves even if disappointed.'[39]

ORIGINS OF RUGBY IN CORK

There is evidence of rugby activity in Cork as far back as the 1870s. Charlie Mulqueen, in his history of Munster rugby, refers to a minute book of a rugby club in Queen's College, Cork, dating from 1872.[40] The IRFU was founded in December 1874, while on 5 December 1874, a team called Queenstown FC fielded a rugby side.[41] In a piece entitled 'History of Rugby in Munster', the *Cork Examiner* of 4 April 1914, referred to how rugby was first played in the province at Midleton College in the early 1870s. In 1879, the Irish Football Union, based in Dublin, and the National Football Union in Belfast came together, leading to a demand from clubs in Cork and Limerick, as well as other Munster clubs, that they would have more say in the running of the game nationally.[42] In terms of playing games, Munster defeated Leinster in a game played in Cork in 1880, while in the same year, Munster sent a touring party to Wales.

The 1880s saw the founding of more clubs in Cork, along with a greater level of organisation of the game, this being part of the development of the game in Munster generally. On 12 January 1886, at a meeting at the Victoria Hotel in Cork, the rules and regulations for a new competition, the Munster Senior Challenge Cup, were drawn up. The final of the competition was played in April 1886, between Bandon and Garryowen. In 1880, there were officially six rugby clubs in existence in Cork, cited by Van Esbeck in the IRFU Annual of that year, these being Queen's College, Midleton College, Cork Bankers, Blackrock and Cork FC.[43] Van Esbeck also notes that few clubs were officially registered in the 1880s and 1890s. One Cork club that appeared in the early 1880s and which subsequently became a major force in Munster Rugby was Cork Constitution. It originally comprised of those working on the newspaper of the same name; because the newspaper was not published on a Sunday, staff were free to play sport on the Saturday. The newspaper staff also had their own cricket team.

Meanwhile, in Queenstown, a number of splinter clubs had been founded. For example, in 1887, two teams, League of the Cross (a temperance society team) and Queenstown Catholic Young Men's Society, played each other. In 1888, a team was formed from these two teams, going under the name Cove National Football Club. Some of the players on the team had already played in the GAA games, while others had been banned from those games for not playing football under the GAA rules. Here, we see how in the early years of both rugby and Gaelic football, both codes were sometimes being mixed and players were often playing both games. The aforementioned Cove National Football Club played Nils Desperandum from Blackrock, a club which at the time fielded both rugby and GAA sides. Around the same period, another team from the Cobh area, Queenstown Green Rovers, held a tournament in which teams such as Ballintemple and Shamrocks from Cork took part. The *Cork Examiner* of 23 January 1893 reported how the home team had an easy win in the tournament but noted that it was Gaelic football it was playing.

Such occurrences were symptomatic of the haphazard development of rugby in Cork in the early decades. The Cobh Pirates historian notes that there were no cups or leagues organised in the early years of the various rugby clubs in Cobh, with challenge matches sufficing, and players were often borrowed from other clubs. For example, a side from one part of Cobh, called Rushbrooke, borrowed players from Queenstown FC. The Queenstown FC club disbanded in 1890 and a new club called Pirates took its place. However, in the early 1890s, players from the Pirates were also playing with Cork FC. Van Esbeck also notes that it was difficult to get referees or touch judges for games in the 1890s.

Because of the lack of a competitive structure, clubs such as Cork Constitution advertised for matches against other junior clubs. For example, in 1894, Constitution issued a challenge to the Pirates team from Queenstown. In turn, the Pirates team played other teams from the city with such names as The Favourites, Wellingtons, Wanderers and Queen's College, Cork. These names indicate that the teams had been formed in an *ad hoc* way and were probably not registered with the official rugby authorities. As we have read, there were a number of teams being established in the town of Queenstown. One of these, Queenstown Corinthians, formed in 1898, were in the fortunate position of being able to play navy sides due to the British military presence in Cork Harbour. Earlier in the decade, some of the British military had joined the Pirates team in Queenstown, and for the 1892/93 season a Lieutenant Newbeginge was captain of the team.

Despite the haphazard development of the game, by the 1890s there were signs that the game was beginning to put down roots in the city and in towns such as Cobh. Even if many of the clubs were not officially registered, Van Esbeck estimates that there were approximately forty junior or minor clubs in existence, mostly in and around Cork City in the early 1890s. A sign of greater organisation was the meeting of city clubs in December 1895 to inaugurate a cup competition for junior clubs. When the competition was held in 1896, eight clubs were involved. In 1897, a city and county schools competition was begun, while the city schools of Presentation College and Christian Brothers College were encouraging the playing of the game.

From an individual club point of view, Cork Constitution were expanding their membership base by opening it up to non-newspaper staff in the 1895/96 season. In 1897, Constitution acquired the playing fields on lease at Turner's Cross, and in that year the club fielded three teams. In Cobh there was a trend of formation, disbandment and reformation of clubs throughout the 1890s and the early 1900s. When Queenstown FC disbanded in 1890, a new club called the Pirates was formed. A club called Queenstown Harriers made a brief appearance for a few months in 1892. Meanwhile, the Pirates side was still active, and indeed in 1898, fielded a juvenile team in the 1897/98 season. A secondary school in Cobh, Presentation College, had an association with Queenstown Corinthians. Three years after the turn of the century there was no rugby team in Cobh, though another Corinthians side was in existence for a brief period before fading away by 1905. In 1909, Queenstown FC affiliated, but again had faded before the outbreak of the First World War. The beginning of the modern club occurred in 1924 with the formation of the Queenstown Pirates, who adopted the emblem of the white skull and crossbones.

ORGANISATIONAL ISSUES

Following the formation of clubs, the most important organisational issue facing players and officials was the procurement of playing facilities. As we shall see, some clubs fared better than others in this regard. In the case of the various clubs that were founded in Cobh, acquiring playing fields seems to have been a disorganised affair. When one such Cobh club began activity in mid-1888, it used a field near Cobh Cathedral, which was then under construction. However, it was the generosity of individuals upon which clubs such as Cobh most depended. As early as 1886, the club used a field across the mouth of Cork Harbour in Monkstown, which had been given by a local butcher who was also a town commissioner. For the 1892/93 season the Pirates had the use of a field put at their disposal by the MP Arthur Hugh Smith-Barry. However, no permanent venue for the playing of rugby in Cobh was acquired for the new century. In the early 1930s, the playing season for a Cobh rugby team began late owing to the team's inability to procure a ground.

Cork Constitution also used a number of different venues in its early years. In 1897, the club acquired Turner's Cross on lease, but in 1899, while keeping the lease on the Turner's Cross ground, the club moved to a field in Ballintemple, this site having the useful advantage of being near the tramway line. This was not to remain a permanent ground for the club, however, and shortly after the move to Ballintemple, grounds adjacent to the Lough in the South Parish came to be used. During the first decade of the 1900s, the Lough grounds became unavailable, after which the club played junior and minor matches at a venue on the Blackrock Road.

However, Constitution had acquired a major interest in the development of the major rugby venue in Cork, namely the Mardyke. When a Leinster delegate to the IRFU, at a meeting to discuss the proposed development of the Mardyke, asked if the grounds belonged to a syndicate, a Mr John Reece from the Cork County rugby club replied that they were leased from a Captain Jennings, in the names of an Alderman Meade, a patron of Constitution, and F.M. Morrogh and Reece himself. He further informed the Leinster delegate that the running of the grounds had been entrusted to a six-man committee, consisting of three members each from Constitution and Cork County. These developments took place in the early 1900s, as the Mardyke was being discussed by the IRFU with a view to holding an international there.

COMPETITIVE STRUCTURE OF RUGBY IN CORK

The early years of rugby in Cork saw little organised competitive activity under the auspices of the IRFU. The Cobh Pirates historian notes that in the 1870s and early 1880s there were no organised leagues or cups, and that clubs in Cobh organised challenge matches.[44] In 1894, Cobh Pirates played Constitution when Constitution issued a challenge to them. Cobh rugby teams such as Corinthians played various navy sides, such as that of the ship the *Black Prince*. The only formal type of competition in which Cobh teams played was a junior cup in 1887 and a tournament hosted by Queenstown Green Rovers in the early 1890s.

Similarly, in the case of Cork Constitution, club matches were organised on an *ad hoc* basis; in the 1890s Constitution advertised for matches against other junior clubs, such as the challenge they issued to Cobh. Constitution took part in a junior cup competition organised in the mid-1890s and, for example, on Good Friday 1896, played in a junior competition at a stud farm in Douglas, owned by a Mr John Reece. We have made reference to such junior competitions already in discussing the growth and expansion of rugby in Cork. In the first decade of the new century, new competitions were inaugurated, such as the Cork Charity Cup, which was to provide funds for both the North and South infirmary hospitals. Also, at the same time, the Cork Tramway and Electric Light Company presented a cup for minor competition.

As with the GAA, rugby teams played games to raise funds for charitable causes. In 1910, a Queenstown team played a match for the Queenstown Hospital Fancy Dress Fund. At the 1933 AGM of Cobh Pirates it was decided to play Sunday's Well for the Cobh Coal Fund, but the match was never played, and a sum of 11s was donated to the fund instead. There is reference to the newly formed Cobh Corinthians playing in a charity match for the Cobh Coal Fund in December 1939. Finally, in November 1914, following the outbreak of the First World War, Constitution played Dolphin in a match to raise funds for the Munster Fusiliers Fund.

ADVERTISING

There are references in the minutes of Cork Bankers to attempts by the club to advertise their fixtures. At a committee meeting on Monday 27 November 1927, the secretary reported that a Mr Musgrave from Constitution had placed a boarding outside the Metropole Hotel on the way to Glanmire Station. This boarding was to be used to advertise rugby matches, as long as they were not Sunday matches, and the Constitution club was to have first claim on its use. The secretary of Bankers was instructed to find out how to apply for the use of the advertising board so that the Bankers could place a poster on it for their upcoming Munster junior cup match against UCC on Wednesday 24 November and to make the necessary application. When the club attempted to revive its fortunes in October 1930, it decided to try and give as much publicity as possible to its opening match against Dolphin and it was suggested to put the team in the paper or to get a piece written on the club's revival in the weekly rugby notes.

In order to ensure that team members and supporters were aware of upcoming matches, the club took the step of inserting the season fixture list on membership cards. At the beginning of the 1929 season, fixture cards were sent to the printers and the club envisaged having between seventy-five and one hundred printed, depending on the cost.

CLUB RULES

Due to the lack of primary sources from other clubs, other than Bankers, there is little or no coverage in club histories of club constitutions and associated rules. There were, of course, the rules and constitution of the governing body of rugby in Cork, this being the Munster branch of the IRFU. There is in existence a rule book from Queen's College Cork, dating back to 1872. On 12 January 1886, a meeting at the Victoria Hotel, Cork was convened to draw up the rules and regulations for the Munster Senior Challenge Cup.

The authority of the Munster branch was at times referred to, such as sometime between 1911 and 1914, when UCC defeated Constitution in the Munster Senior Cup. Constitution objected to the result on the basis that one of the university players had not been resident in Munster for twenty-eight days before 1 February, though this objection was not upheld. At club level, for example, Constitution opened their membership up to those other than employees of the *Cork Constitution* newspaper, though this led to allegations that the club poached players from other clubs.

The Bankers club was particularly strident in attempting to prevent what they perceived as illegal transfers to other clubs, although there is evidence that conscientious individuals did not want to infringe on such regulations. At a committee meeting towards the end of 1922, the minutes record that the club committee was of the opinion that a player who begins playing with one club should not be 'plucked out' of that club in the same season. This followed a request from another club, not mentioned in the minutes, for a Mr Hanrahan from Bankers, to play with this club in the Munster junior cup, a request which was refused by the Bankers committee.[45] A committee meeting on 2 January, reveals that the club in contact with Hanrahan was Dolphin, at which the Bankers committee decided to write to Dolphin in connection to his being picked for the Dolphin Munster junior cup team.

Another instance of clashing loyalties occurred in November 1930. A Mr Hanrahan and Mr Delaney had been asked to attend a committee meeting with regard to appointing a selection committee for the Bankers team. Addressing the meeting, Mr Hanrahan said that Mr Delaney could not see his way to act on the selection committee. The minutes then go on to state that Mr Delaney had refused to attend the meeting, since he was afraid that his services might eventually be needed by Constitution, even though Bankers had pointed out to him that 'such were not our intentions'. After some discussion, it was agreed that an independent selection committee would be beneficial to the club, the committee to be made up of five members. Relations with other clubs on the matter of conflicting loyalties were not always so strained. For example, at a Bankers committee meeting on 3 December 1928, a letter was received from Constitution, thanking Bankers for allowing an A. Archer to play with the latter in their match against Lansdowne.

The Bankers club had also to draw up its own rules on transfers, since it seems that from time to time players wanted to leave Bankers for other clubs in the city. There seems little that Bankers could do to prevent such transfers going through eventually, but they did their best to minimise the damage. At a committee meeting on 30 November 1924, the Bankers secretary read a letter from a Mr Whyte asking for a transfer. This was to be refused until such time as he had fulfilled his obligations to the club. On Friday 25 August, at the beginning of a new season, the club decided to grant a transfer request from a member who wanted to join Dolphin. However, the same meeting asked the secretary to ascertain whether the subscriptions of those who transferred from the club had been paid for the previous year. In October 1926, it was decided to write to a W.D. Rourke of Cobh, asking him to remit 7s 6d for the previous year's subscription before his transfer, which was fixed provisionally for 9 April 1927.

Cork Constitution player breaks away: note the large crowd in the stand. (Image courtesy of *Irish Examiner*)

The club drew up other internal rules relating to membership and play-ers. At the beginning of the 1924 season, membership cards were distributed to everyone on the committee for distribution to members, with the deci-sion being taken that no card should be handed out without payment. At the AGM of the club in September 1927, the unanimously elected chair-man, McDonald, referred to the minutes of the previous year's AGM, at which it was decided that only playing members of the club could play in the Charity Cup, which he referred to as being a 'very wise judgement' and a 'great sign' of the club. A motion at the same AGM, that two members of the junior team should get honour caps, was rescinded by a two-thirds majority. Another reference to rules relating to membership was made at the club's AGM on Tuesday 27 August 1929. A Mr T.M. MacDonald asked whether the rule regarding playing members being members of the Irish Bank Officials' Association was not passed at the previous year's AGM, to which he was assured that this was indeed the case and the minutes were then signed.

So what is worth noting about the membership of clubs in Cork for which histories are available? There are some references that point to the sources for membership of such clubs. In the late 1870s, when the first club was in existence in Cobh, its player base was drawn, in the main, from fami-lies who owned small businesses in the town, especially vintners' and drapers' businesses. As well as playing against British naval teams, the Cobh teams of the early 1890s sometimes drew members from them, the majority of such members being from the HMS *Triumph*.

In a much later period, when a new club, Cobh Corinthians, was formed, an individual already involved with the sailing club encouraged young mem-bers of the club to join the rugby club. A more controversial membership issue had arisen earlier in the decade, when a rugby club, under the auspices of the local Catholic Young Men's Society, had been established. As well as being president of the society, a Revd Mr J. Bowler was president of the rugby club, and the team jerseys were white with a yellow sash to repre-sent the papacy. Fr Bowler insisted, however, that only Catholics should be allowed play with the team and this demand lead to friction because the secretary of the club was a Protestant. As a result, the name of the club was changed to Cove RFC, though the Fr Bowler remained president.

With regard to Cork Constitution, Van Esbeck hints at the make-up of the membership at the time of the club's formation. Van Esbeck describes the tone of the newspaper, from among whose employees the club was formed, as being 'Unionist in tone with content geared towards the better-off citizens of Cork'.[46] As we have already noted, by the 1895/96 season, Constitution had opened up its membership to those not employed by the paper, though as Van Esbeck notes, this led to accusations of poaching. Just as players left Bankers for clubs such as Dolphin, Dolphin players went to Constititution. Van Esbeck mentions a Constitution player, John Wren, who played in the team's pack in the early 1920s, and who was a 'recruit' from Dolphin.

The places of work of players and members provide a significant background to the activities of Cork rugby clubs. In Cobh, the occupations of some prominent members in the late 1880s are mentioned. There was, for example, a General J.J. Piatt, prominent in the club, who was a former American Consul to Ireland who lived in Cobh from 1882 to 1892. Other prominent members were a Mr Hayes-Allen, a prominent solicitor in the town, and a Joshua T. Head, a surveyor for the Lloyds insurance company. The treasurer around this period, Mr J. Gallie, owned a plumbing business.

More significantly, employment (or the absence of it) frequently meant that a club, such as Cobh, lost players. In 1938, the British forces stationed at Cobh moved out, which caused an economic slump, and so there were insufficient players for the 1938/39 season.

The Constitution club history refers to Captain Patrick Hennessy, a club member after the First World War, whose playing career was disrupted by the call of business, but who 'rose to eminence' with the Henry Ford Company and was later honoured with a knighthood.[47] The club was very fortunate in having as a member one Henry Tivy, whose regular subscription of financial aid, according to Van Esbeck, amounted to many thousands of pounds. A very important work-related factor for Constitution was that in the club's early years, when players worked for the newspaper, they had Saturdays free to play matches or practise, since the paper did not publish on a Sunday.

SCHOOLS AND RUGBY TEAMS IN CORK CITY AND ENVIRONS

We have already seen the way GAA clubs forged links with neighbouring schools, especially in the hurling strongholds of Farranferris and the North Monastery, thereby ensuring that a strong player base was maintained for the mutual benefit of both school and club. As rugby took hold in Cork, certain schools embraced it and became synonymous with the game, a tradition which has continued into modern times.

Recorded personal memories and club histories point to the 1890s as the decade when certain schools embraced the game. Van Esbeck refers to the playing of rugby in the 1890s in the schools of Presentation Brothers College, Christian Brothers College and North Monastery. Also, Midleton College was one of eight teams who played in the first competition of the Munster junior cup in 1896, while Cork Grammar School attended the first meeting to set up the competition in December 1895. It was around this time, according to Van Esbeck, that Presentation Brothers College and Christian Brothers College were beginning to take to the game and as he notes, 'These two great nurseries of the game in Cork had started the production line so to speak, and Constitution, as so many other clubs were [sic] to derive untold benefits.'

Interestingly, a past pupil of Christian Brothers College, in recalling his school days of the 1890s, does not remember games playing a major part of school life, except for the game of handball which was played in an old court. He also remembers cycle races at the school, which were 'all the rage' in Cork at the time.[48] Those who played rugby at the school sometimes went on to play rugby in Queen's College (later University College) Cork in the pre-First World War years. Rugby links with schools were not just a feature of city-based teams. In 1898, Cobh's Queenstown Corinthians fielded a team, its players emanating from the local Presentation Brothers College in the town, which by this time had been ten years in existence. This particular link with the local school was still evident in the 1930s, with staff at the school encouraging boys to take up the game. One past pupil from that time recalls being handed a note on a Saturday, informing him that he was playing the following Sunday. In the 1937/38 season the local Cobh team experienced an influx of new members from the local Presentation Secondary School, which had been having a particularly successful season.

Both Presentation College and Christian Brothers College played non-school teams at the turn of the century. In March 1900, the *Cork Examiner* reported that Presentation College had defeated a boys team from the *Black Prince* ship by a score of three tries to nil, while the paper also mentioned an upcoming fixture between CBC and GPO. In 1918, Presentation College won the Munster Senior Schools Cup and some members of the team went on to play with Constitution.

The recorded memories of former pupils of these rugby-playing schools gives an insight into the ethos of both the schools themselves and the way rugby was incorporated. One past pupil of Christian Brothers College recalls a Brother Moloney, who was the most popular of all the brothers in the school, with his 'ruddy complexion', who trained both the junior and senior teams of the school. The same Brother Moloney was also in charge of the library, where such titles as *Clive of Clare College* and *The Fifth Form of St Dominics* were to be found, and which, no doubt, reinforced the game's ethos in the boys of the school. They also had a moral influence, as the writer says that such publications, 'Very definitely and completely cured me of the pernicious habit of reading the "Magnet", the "Gem", "Sexton Blake" and all the other penny dreadfuls which for years I was wont to hide under my pillow.'[49] The same person recalls the rivalry with Presentation College:

> These inter-college conflicts were desperate affrays. Temperatures and pulse rates were unduly elevated for days beforehand, and on the day of the match, emotions were at fever pitch. Twickenham, Murrayfield, Ravenhill and – most of all – Lansdowne Road, have had their thrills, but the tries scored by Billy Duggan on the Mardyke sometime before the First World War put them all 'in the half-penny place'.

Senior boys in the school who had achieved sporting fame were eulogised in rugby schools like Christian Brothers College, such as two Irish internationals from before the First World War, Harry Jack and Vincent McNamara. They were:

> …spoken of with hushed reverence by all CBC boys. They were Christian Rugger internationals, and we young shavers gawked at the photographs in the Hall featuring the curly-headed Harry Jack and the well-groomed Vincent McNamara, who had played for Christians before they wore the green jersey to represent their country.

The memories of another CBC past pupil enforce this image of the older boys as role models to the younger boys. Walter Harley wrote these recollections in the centenary souvenir of the founding of the Christian Brothers College, 'It is characteristic of young schoolboys to try and imitate the habits of older boys. I was no exception and the activities of the senior boys as the annual Rugby match with the Presentation College drew near were a thrill.'[50] Another memory of Walter Harley is that of seeing Bertie Flynn, who had subsequently achieved a high position in the British navy:

> …being led off the pitch, blood smeared and in an apparent state of total collapse. To our youthful minds his condition indicated permanent debility, if not early demise. But to our amazement a short time afterwards he re-commenced

playing and his injuries did not affect his play. [We] were astounded at his stamina ... I well remember how we followed the team's activities, cheered our young lungs out when they appeared on the playing pitch and prayed that their efforts would bring victory and a lesson-free day for us and a view of the cup which would be displayed in the big classroom.

Harley had a premature end to his rugby career when he broke his wrist in a game against North Monastery and had to go to the North Infirmary to have the broken bone set. The match itself was a 'needle affair', but after his injury Harley was 'somewhat of a hero' in his class.

In a 1950s publication to celebrate the centenary of Presentation Brothers College, a past pupil gives some insight into how rugby became a central part of school life. The writer, Dr D.C. Kelleher, recalls that in the intermediate grade, he and his classmates began to 'play football seriously'.[51] Brother Curtain, who was involved with the school teams, would tell the young players to remember the school motto, 'Semper Victores' and 'to play our best, and not come off the field with our heads bowed'. Another past pupil, Frank Gallagher, remembers how he was the 'poet laureate for the important matches, writing the yearly song and putting the words with cartoons of the players on the main notice board a week or so before the final'.[52]

The same writer tells of his memories of match days; memories of those pupils who watched the games and how, 'A rush by Christians or North Mon towards our lines was white agony along the whole line of tense faces.' Gallagher remarks on how he never had enough money to pay for a seat on the outside cars 'which rode back from the Mardyke or Turner's Cross with the triumphant teams and their wealthy comrades, but we ran alongside quite a bit of the way'. The author mingles such sporting memories with others which are reminiscent of the links between Christian morality and sport that are to be found in the English public schools. For example, the same individual, in addition to his sporting memories, remembers how Presentation School 'helped to shape us and strengthened in us a sense of duty and honour, which, for me, at least marked out the course of a turbulent and unyielding life'.

GEOGRAPHICAL SPREAD OF RUGBY CLUBS IN CORK

Club histories and, to a certain extent, newspapers, do give some indication of where clubs were located and where their player bases were. We have already noted the influence of work as a source of playing members, such as Bankers, GPO and the *Cork Constitution* newspaper. In the first years of the rugby club in Cobh, there was a team on the outskirts of the town, in the Rushbrook area, which borrowed players from Queenstown FC in the town itself. The Queenstown Pirates team of the 1880s and 1890s included players from Monkstown and Glenbrook, both situated across Cork Harbour from Cobh.

The Cobh Pirates' history refers to the geographical location of teams in Cork. For example, at a tournament hosted by Queenstown Green Rovers around 1890, a number of city teams were listed as taking part, such as Celtic Ramblers, Ballintemple and Shamrocks. Ballintemple was overtly named after an area of the city, this being a suburb in the direction of Blackrock and Douglas. However, in the 1890s, Queenstown Pirates played teams from the city such as: The Favourites from Berkeley Hall, Wellingtons, Wanderers, Queen's College, and Cork Constitution. Another team from the city with whom some Queenstown Pirates played were simply known as Cork FC.

SPECTATORS AND GAMES

As was the case with Gaelic games and soccer, grounds were procured wherever possible, even if this sometimes meant some degree of travelling to games, even for the home team. For example, in the 1870s, the original Cobh Pirates team had to cross Cork Harbour by ferry to Monkstown to play their matches. In 1889, the Queenstown rugby team played Cork FC at Cork Park, which was to eventually become the Cork Athletic Grounds. Two years earlier the same venue had hosted a match between Queen's College and Limerick County in the Munster Challenge Cup, before a crowd of 3,000 spectators.

It is worth noting here that rugby clubs (along with the representatives of other sports in the city) took part in a meeting with the Agricultural Society, who had expressed a wish to sell the grounds in the vicinity of Cork Park. Turner's Cross also accommodated rugby, alongside Gaelic games and soccer. In 1900, the *Cork Examiner* gave notice of a match to take place there on a Tuesday at 4p.m between GPO and Christian College.[53]

On 1 April 1901, Cork Constitution played Queen's College in the final of the Munster Senior Cup, at which there was a 'huge attendance' even though there was strong criticism of the doubling of the admission price at the venue.[54] A team called Cork County had, according to the *Cork Sportsman* in 1911, procured a new ground at Victoria Cross, to the west of the city, where a match between the hosts and Limerick team, Garryowen, was played in October 1911.[55] The way in which clubs improvised in terms of facilities can be seen in the case of Cobh Pirates, who, when reformed in 1920, played their first match against a navy team in a field marked off by coats, with sticks held by spectators to mark the goals and crossbars.

However, the central venue for rugby in Cork, around which the game grew, was the Mardyke grounds, to the west of the city, which opened in 1904. According to the *Cork Examiner* in September of that year, trustees had taken over a large field along Mardyke Walk and were sparing no expense in making it a properly equipped arena.[56] Already at this time, Cork Constitution and Cork County had laid out practice pitches at the site, but by the end of the following season it was envisaged that there would be six playing pitches there. A match pitch had already been laid out and was described as, 'undoubtedly the best laid-out and best drained Rugby ground in Ireland'.

From the point of view of spectators, there were to be no fewer than four entrances to the ground and penny trains coming out from the city centre. A spacious building, 'unequalled in this country as a football pavilion', was to be erected at a cost of £1,000. The two-storey building was to consist of dressing rooms, bathrooms and a large kitchen, plus a large hall capable of holding 400 people, which was to be used for 'meetings, concerts and other reunions – all luxuries of the football world hitherto unknown to Southern players'. 'Retirement rooms and comfortable tea-rooms' were to be on the second storey, where there would a 'fine view' of the match pitch.

Further details on the grounds were to be found in the report in the *Cork Examiner* of 12 September 1904, which recorded a meeting of the IRFU in Dublin on the previous Saturday evening, the purpose of which was to discuss an application from the Munster branch to hold an international in Cork. The chairman, in addressing the meeting, said that in recent years the Cork clubs had been playing on grounds totally unsuited to rugby, but now they had 'without a doubt, one of the best Rugby football grounds in Ireland'.[57] The grounds comprised a total of nineteen acres and also had the hoarding used at the last Cork Exhibition. The chairman did mention that there had been opposition to the grounds being procured for rugby, and that there had also been opposition to the use of hoarding by those who had wanted it removed, but 'through the enterprise and liberality of certain Cork citizens that the Cork clubs were enabled to procure the Western Road grounds, at great expense'. He continued by saying that £1,400 had been already spent on developing the grounds and gave his support to playing an international in Munster, since it would encourage the game in the province.

An Ulster delegate's remarks at the meeting provided further details on the new rugby ground. The delegate said that he had been to the ground, along with another Ulster delegate and a Leinster delegate, within the previous forty-eight hours, and he had noted how electric tramways could carry visitors to the entrance of the ground and that there was also an approach for those coming by carriage and by foot. In addition, there was an approach by ferry for those on the opposite side of the river. With regard to the pitch itself, he told the meeting that the subsoil was sandy, which would allow any moisture to drain away, while the pavilion was 'even better than the best that they had in Ireland'. After some further discussion, it was decided unanimously to hold the game in Cork.

GAMES AS CONTESTS AND EVENTS

No less than Gaelic games and soccer, the growth of rugby-playing activity was marked by rivalries and a sense of heightened atmosphere around some of the games. One such rivalry, which developed in the late nineteenth century, was that between Queenstown and a team referred to by the Cobh Pirates historian simply as 'Cork'. He refers to a piece in the *Cork Constitution* that said, 'Queenstown has been very militant for some weeks back and meets Cork on home territory tomorrow, when an opportunity will be afforded of judging whether the visitors' loud talk is justified.'[58]

This game was played in November and won by Cork, and the same teams met again in December 1889. Queenstown were again defeated by Cork Constitution, with the Queenstown style of play being described by the *Cork Constitution* as 'more vigorous than telling'. The newspaper added that the match was marked by 'many and useless wrangles, of which Queenstown provoked more than their fair share'. Queenstown were no doubt anxious to even the score with Cork and these matches were also played against the background of a sense of grievance on behalf of the Queenstown team, who had felt that more of their members should have been picked for the Munster team of that time.

Heightened feelings were also evident after the match played between Presentation College and Blackrock in April 1895. The original report of the match, in the Monday 29 April 1894 *Cork Examiner*, stated that Presentation

College had won the game by one try to nil. The atmosphere at the game was such that 'the excitement of the players and the enthusiasm of the spectators reached a climax, as the ball was dangerously near the Presentation line'.[59] However, an indignant letter was printed in the following day's *Cork Examiner* from the captain of the Blackrock team, which claimed that the match had actually ended in a draw. The writer went on to challenge Presentation College to another match on the following Saturday. He also added that the Presentation team was made up of players from other clubs rather than pupils at the college.[60] As in Gaelic games, replayed games sometimes led to incidents of indiscipline. In the 1899/1900 season, Queenstown Corinthians played Skibbereen in a replay of a junior cup match. There were many disorderly scenes and a Skibbereen player was sent off. These incidents disillusioned the younger Queenstown players; they returned to playing soccer and so the Corinthians team broke up.

It is also worth noting that the latter game was also a cup tie, which, judging from contemporary reports, was notable more for the commitment shown than for any great method in the playing of the game. When the *Cork Examiner* was describing the game between Queen's College and Cork Constitution, it remarked that the play 'degenerated into that usually seen in Cup matches'.[61] A match in March 1905 between Cork County and Queen's College was described as a 'typical junior cup tie'.[62] Other parts of the report describe the play like so, 'it resolved itself into a series of mauls fiercely contested … In parts it was splendid, but generally speaking it was not football … The science of the game was but little displayed on either side'.

Cup matches involving schools could be just as keenly contested. The senior schools cup match involving Christian College was a 'hard game' which, 'to say the least, was not of the kid glove order'.[63]

Other games played were of a more friendly nature, often played to mark a specific occasion. At Christmas 1898, Cork Constitution hosted a game between themselves and Old Wesley from Dublin – this being the first match between Constitution and a team outside Munster. The occasion was marked by an after-match banquet to honour the visitors. Some months later, in February 1899, Cork Constitution reciprocated the fixture at Donnybrook in Dublin, travelling the evening before. At Easter 1903, Cork Constitution invited the Welsh club Treherbert to come and play them in Cork, and while guaranteeing the Welsh club's expenses, Constitution also made a profit on the venture. Another visiting Welsh team, Glamorgan, was the guest side in a match to mark the opening of the new Mardyke ground on 24 September 1904.

Finally, there was the attraction of matches involving the navy and army teams. In the early 1890s, a team from Queenstown played a garrison team from Fermoy. 'A number of ladies' were present for the match, the attraction for these spectators being attributed to the fact that an army team was playing.[64] Also at Cobh, this time in the 1930s, there was the spectacle of the local rugby team playing the crew of the navy ship HMS *Westcott*; present in the attendance were the crews of other British ships, as well as a French protection ship and a Spanish trawler.

THE SOCIAL DIMENSION OF RUGBY IN CORK

The social dimension to rugby in Cork had a number of aspects. There was, for example, the way in which clubs organised social activities for their members, such as annual dances, like that organised by the Cork Bankers Club. In the earliest years of the club, it was decided to organise a dance for the members of Cork Bankers under the auspices of the club. A committee meeting held on 13 November 1923 decided that a dance would be held provided Harrison's Band were available to play. A dance committee was formed to organise the event.

A committee meeting of the club on 18 October 1928 gives more detail of the proposed arrangements for that year's dance. One of the committee members, Mr Clarke, reported to the meeting how he had interviewed Mr Prendergast, the proprietor of the Arcadia Ballroom, and had provisionally booked the hall there for Friday 30 November. A number of conditions were agreed on how the dance should be held. The Bankers Club would advertise the dance and a club member was to be on the cash box. The Arcadia management was to supply the supper in the form of a running buffet and get a percentage of the price of each ticket. Messrs Cassidy and Clarke were authorised to engage the venue for 30 November 1928.

In addition, there was the practice of entertaining opposing teams to refreshments after games, which no doubt helped to foster a social scene for rugby players and supporters. This made up a significant part of organising games. A meeting of Cork Bankers on 22 February 1926 picked a team to play Mallow, who were due to play Bankers in Cork. It was decided to entertain the Mallow team to tea, and the secretary of Bankers was to make the necessary arrangements, including confirming the hotel that would be available. Similarly, in February 1927, Bankers acceded to a request from Macroom for a friendly match and again the secretary was deputed to make arrangements for the 'entertainment' of Macroom.

If the opposing team were not going to supply refreshments to Bankers, then the club ensured such arrangements themselves. For a match to be played in Mallow on 8 January 1927, the secretary of Bankers was asked to write to a hotel in Mallow to supply tea and sandwiches on the day of the match. However, such a practice could impose financial strain on a club. A committee meeting on 5 September 1928 discussed a possible future fixture with 'some Dublin club' during the forthcoming season, but it was pointed out that entertaining the visiting team would entail considerable expense, with the result that nothing definite was decided. One possible solution to such a problem was the practice in Cobh, whereby all visiting teams were given a meal, with each Cobh player paying for his opposite opponent. A number of venues in the town were used for such entertainment.

POLITICAL ISSUES

Compared, for example, to the GAA's turbulent 1880s, there is much less evidence of episodes where politics and rugby clashed. There are, however, some pointers as to where the political allegiances of clubs lay. We have already noted how the Cork Constitution club was founded by the staff of that newspaper, a publication which was described by Van Esbeck as 'Unionist in tone with the content geared towards the better-off citizens of Cork'.

Echoes of Constitution's past are evident in Van Esbeck's allusions to the fact its players took part in the First World War, 'so many who had fought out great battles on the field of rugby competition were now destined to fight out battles of a different dimension as war broke out'.[65] For the duration of the war, the Munster branch, like other branches of the IRFU, had suspended competitive activity, with the exception of charity fixtures. The Constitution club formed a committee to raise money to help people with relatives in the armed forces and in November 1914 they played Dolphin to raise money for the Munster Fusiliers Fund. Van Esbeck refers to how members of the club had lost friends in the conflict and that Henry Magarth, a player who had captained a club team, died in the war. Similar to GAA activity, rugby was disrupted during the 1919/20 season. Charlie Mulqueen, in his history of Munster Rugby, notes also how the club activity was suspended during the Great War and how, in 1920, four clubs – Limerick, UCC, Dolphin and Garryowen – took part in the first Munster Cup after the war.[66]

The intrusion of politics into rugby does emerge in the history of Cobh Pirates, however. The author refers to a game of rugby played between League of the Cross (a temperance society) and Queenstown Catholic Young Men's Society. Why the players on these teams did not play with the already-established team in the town is explained by the author, 'Many, while they enjoyed the game, must have felt uneasy about playing for the Queenstown FC side, having a different tradition and social background.'[67] The same author refers to another newly formed club in 1888, Cove National Football Club; some of its members had played Gaelic games while others had been banned from the GAA for not playing football under Gaelic rules. This particular club played against Nils Desperandum from Blackrock, who at the time fielded both rugby and GAA sides. In 1898, Queenstown Corinthians was formed, made up of students of the town's Presentation College. The club historian stresses how such players were of a different generation from those who played with Pirates, the latter having an 'unpleasant association' with the British military.

The beginning of association football in Cork was very much linked with the British garrisons in the city and the navy presence in Cobh. However, even at this early stage in the development of the game, civilians were attending games and civilian teams were taking part in leagues alongside army teams. While acknowledging the importance of the garrison teams in helping to spread the popularity of the game, it would seem that there was an enthusiasm for the game among civilian-sports followers in Cork, who came to games in the 1900s, it being the 'garrison game'. Also, when the Munster Football Association reorganised itself in 1922, it witnessed an increase in civilian teams. The political trauma of this period did not seem to adversely affect the playing of the game in Cork and if anything the game prospered, as witnessed by the large crowds who came to see Free State League and Cup matches in the 1920s when Fordsons became Cork's representatives in the Free State League.

Similar to the GAA, local rivalries were an important predicator of interest in the games, as witnessed by the interest in matches between Cork FC and Cork Bohemians when both played in the Free State League. The point has already been made that local junior and minor soccer games attracted more interest than Free State League games, but knockout games had the greatest impact on those who followed the sport in Cork. This was shown by the large crowds who turned up for Free State cup games and the numbers who travelled for cup finals, as well as the large crowds who turned up for the homecoming of victorious teams.

The *Cork Evening Echo* gave much coverage to association football. Historian Maura Cronin has referred to how it was known as the 'working man's paper'. This may therefore point to association football being primarily followed Cork's working class. Similarly, its greatest readership was within the city, indicating that the game was primarily followed there, not forgetting the area around Cork Harbour where the British military presence was strong.

Further observations can be made on the development of rugby in Cork City and its environs. It was certainly not as well organised in the 1880s and 1890s as the GAA teams seem to have been. Teams came together on an *ad hoc* basis, while teams like Constitution, which was to become a major force in the game in Cork, had to advertise for matches in the 1890s.

Work teams, which were a prominent feature of soccer and to a lesser extent the GAA, hardly figured in Cork's rugby story. While Cork Constitution did originate among staff, they soon accepted players not directly linked with the paper. One can see from the minute book of the Bankers Club that the first loyalty of those who worked in banks and played rugby was to the clubs they played with, and efforts to have a senior team from all bank workers who played rugby failed. Work-based clubs such as Bankers were also adversely affected by the efforts of club teams to take their players.

The association of rugby with a certain religion or class can be gauged by some of the tensions that raised themselves, particularly in relation to the club in Cobh, and it is noteworthy that members of the Constitution club fought in the First World War and indeed lost some members as a result.

Finally, one is struck by the manner in which rugby permeated and simultaneously reinforced the ethos of the schools where it was played. The rivalries with other rugby-playing schools and the way in which students supported school teams is very redolent of the public schools in Britain, which was a major part of the beginnings of organised sport in Britain.

III

CRICKET

While it is difficult to ascertain exactly when organised cricket began in Cork, the minutes of the Cork County Cricket Club give some indication. The earliest entries from the minute books contain a letter from a Mr Sharman Crawford, in which he outlines the aim of the new club. Along with those who were willing to pay a life subscription of £10, it was envisaged that there would be both playing and non-playing members, who would pay sums of £2 and £1 respectively. The letter itself was dated 25 November 1873 and went as follows:

Sir,

Messrs Anderson Cooper, Thomas Hewitt, and myself, having undertaken to form a New Cricket Club in Cork, which shall be a credit to the County as well as the City, I beg to give you our ideas of what should be done ... If we succeed in getting a sufficient number of Life Members to enable us to build a suitable Pavilion, and obtain a lease of ground, we think that the Ordinary Members' Subscriptions would suffice for current expenses, including the pay of a Professional Bowler.

We hope that you will become an Original Life Member, and allow us to add yours to the subjoined list of names of those approving of our plans,

I remain your Obedient Servant,
W.H. Sharman Crawford.

After a number of months, a meeting was held in the Imperial Hotel, Cork, on 4 April 1874, for those interested in forming a new cricket club in response to the circular of Mr Crawford. With Sir Thomas Tobin in the chair, a list of those present was drawn up totalling fourteen, including the Right Honourable J.B. Roche, Standish Barry, Anderson Cooper and Thomas Hewitt.

At the same meeting, the 'following Corkmen and gentlemen' were proposed and seconded as original life members: the Earl of Cork, the Earl of Bandon, Sir John Arnott, A.H. Smith-Barry, Captain Piggott Beamish, and Captain H. Crawford. Other names noted as members at this meeting were Mayor E.A. Shaldam, Arthur Stewart and W.J.J. Hunt. Also drawn up was a list of playing members (those who were to become members on paying their respective contributions). The same meeting decided that Messrs Sharman Crawford, Anderson Cooper and Thomas Hewitt were to be trustees of the club and were to be empowered to take a lease of the 'Club Ground' on the best terms procurable.

Anderson Cooper was proposed and seconded as the honorary treasurer, while Thomas Hewitt was proposed and seconded as honorary secretary. A president and vice-president were also appointed for the season. As regards the cost of membership of the new club, it was to be an instruction to the committee that the annual subscription for playing members be £2, excepting in the case of college students in attendance at lectures and others resident twenty miles from the club ground, in which case it was to be £1, the same to apply to non-playing members. The new committee was to draw up rules 'on this subject especially'.

In the immediate years following the founding of the club, steps were taken to put it on sound financial footing. On 26 February 1875, thirteen members were listed as being present at a meeting of the club, with a Mr G. Purdon in the chair. It was proposed, seconded and carried unanimously that the sum of £21 11s 3d, which had been the remaining balance in the hands of the treasurer of the old club, be handed over to the County of Cork Cricket Club. Other resolutions passed at the same meeting included a request to the trustees to get a lease of the 'present cricket ground at the Mardyke on the best procurable terms' and that the club committee be given full powers to build a pavilion and house for a caretaker. Furthermore, the committee were to have full power to fence the ground and 'otherwise to improve it in any way they shall see fit and proper'.

The club committee seems to have gone about these tasks with considerable success, since at a meeting of the club on 3 April 1875, a vote of thanks was passed to the trustees for the improvement to the field and the erection of a pavilion. There was, however, the financial cost of such work, and on 13 November 1875, Mr Cooper submitted the accounts for the years 1874 and

1875, which had been 'duly annotated' by Messrs Crawford and Dunscombe. Mr Cooper informed the meeting that there was a balance due to him of £82 17s 10d in the pavilion account fund as well as £8 18s 3d in the ordinary account, the total being £91 16s 1d. It was then resolved that a 'whip should be made … with a view to clearing off the debt if possible'. It was also resolved that because of the indebtedness of the club, no professional should be employed for the 1876 season. The proposed circular referred to is included in the minute books of the club, which noted:

> …the support which this club has hitherto received and trust that each individual member use his best endeavours during the coming season to enlist members into the fold of our Institution which, with proper support, must prove of advantage to the County and City of Cork.
>
> Anderson Cooper, 7/7/77.[1]

At the Imperial Hotel on 7 April 1877, at what seems to have been the AGM, Anderson Cooper was moved to the chair, with twelve club members present. The following club members were listed: president, Sir George C. Colthurst; vice-presidents, the Earl of Bandon, W.H. Crawford, A.H. Smith Barry and M.D.H. Herriot; honorary treasurer, H. Sharman Crawford, and honorary secretary, Mr Dunscombe (who was given the power to appoint an assistant). Both treasurers were absent and, as a result, the chairman produced the club accounts, which showed that the sum of £5 6s 19d was owed to the treasurer, Mr Crawford, which he declined charging to the club but intimated that he would receive a subscription from the members to reduce the amount. Messrs Hewitt, Cooper, Lambkin, Dunscombe and Pike were among those who had already contributed their subscriptions.

At the following year's AGM, held in April 1878, Mr Crawford, the honorary treasurer, reported that the accounts were in satisfactory condition, while the secretary, Mr Dunscombe, told the meeting of the club's playing record during the season just past. The club had won thirteen matches, lost five and drawn two. Mr Crawford and Mr Dunscombe were both re-elected to their respective positions, while the secretary was to have the power to appoint an assistant, who was to be a free member.

On Sunday 19 April 1886, a club committee meeting was held at the pavilion at the club's ground, at which it was decided that future committee meetings would be held at 58 South Mall, at two o'clock on Thursday afternoons. The treasurer was to order a bat, one bag of match balls, a pair of wicket-keeping gloves and a landing net, while a forthcoming match against Leinster was to be advertised by poster. Those present at the meeting were Capt. Bainbridge RN, Jack Cronin, N. Dunlea, J. Gray and the club secretary.

A brief perusal of details in the minute books dealing with some of the club's AGMs reveals the personalities who were either active in the club or were the club patrons. Such meetings were also notable for addressing the issue of membership, in particular who could join and on what terms. The 1888 AGM was not held until 1 June of that year, when there were approximately seven members present. The president of the club that year was the Right Honourable Earl of Bandon. A Professor Jack proposed some individuals as college members, and others joined as ordinary members. It was decided that officers of the navy and army who lived in excess of ten miles from Cork were to pay subscriptions of £1. It was also recorded in the minutes of this meeting that a particular regiment had not joined the club. Finally the same meeting elected six members to serve on the match committee for 1888.

At the AGM the following year, Mr W.S. Crawford was proposed as the new club president, to succeed A.W.H. Crawford, who had died. The meeting is also notable for the fact that two assistant secretaries were appointed, one of whom, along with the treasurer and secretary, was assigned the duty of arranging matches. A cycling club had requested permission to lay down a cinder track around the cricket ground, but the cricket club secretary was to write back explaining that the cricket club had no lease on the ground and could not grant permission for the laying of the track.

On 12 April 1891, with Sir George Colthurst in the chair and eleven present at the AGM, Mr A.F. Sharman Crawford was elected to the club as a member and it was also proposed and seconded that ten life members be 'brought in also', to pay off existing liabilities.[2] Lt-Gen. Colthurst and Professor Jack were elected as joint secretaries and it was decided that the ground be opened for practice on 21 April.

At the AGM on 8 April 1892, it was proposed and seconded that the 43rd Regiment become members on paying the sum of £8. The ground was to open on 10 April and a Mr P. Wren was appointed assistant secretary, while the same committee as the previous year was to be retained. It was also proposed and seconded that the east side of the Mardyke be drained, with the club and adjoining occupier sharing the costs.[3] At an AGM some years later, on 3 April 1897, the club decided to engage the services of a professional, to be fixed at '£1 minimum', and the ground was to open on 12 April. A sum of £65 was paid to relay the grounds, with six inches of ashes and six inches of mould over this, and sods were to be replaced. Significantly, it was unanimously decided to admit twenty members from Queen's College for a fee of £8, and it was resolved that Queen's College were to have use of the grounds for their annual sports for £10.

These gleanings from the minute books of Cork County Cricket Club, as well as outlining the origins of the club and the beginnings of cricket in Cork, refer to issues which will now be discussed in greater detail, such as aspects of membership, grounds, committee structure, rules, competitive structures, finances, and equipment and cricket activity among school goers and juveniles.

MEMBERSHIP ISSUES

In discussing the origins of the Cork County Cricket Club, it was noted how various forms of membership were adopted, such as life, playing and non-playing memberships. There were also special rates for college students, for example. The cost of such memberships, as already noted, was outlined in the earliest minutes of the Cork Club from 1873. The cost was £10, £2 and £1 for life subscription, playing membership and non-playing members, respectively. At the AGM on 11 April 1878, it was unanimously agreed that paying life members give an annual subscription of £1. Years later, there is reference to the cost of membership of the club, when it was decided that all members of Her Majesty's Services were to be charged the same subscriptions as ordinary members (£2).

Throughout the latter decades of the nineteenth and early decades of the twentieth century, the club made a number of attempts to increase its membership. We have already noted how, at a meeting of the club on 13 November 1875, it was resolved that 'each individual member use his best endeavours during the coming season to enlist members into the field of our Institution'. At the club's AGM in April 1902, it was proposed and seconded that in order to improve the popularity and standard of the game in Cork, the committee should be allowed to admit as members at a nominal subscription any member of any other playing club in Cork or County 'whose services in their opinion would prove of benefit' to the club, although said members would not be entitled to vote at a general meeting.[4] The motion was passed unanimously.

At a committee meeting on 23 October 1902, it was resolved that steps be taken to increase the income of the club. For example, to increase non-playing membership, the club was to send a circular to the leading and most likely parties in the city and county, asking them to become members. In 1908, again with a view to improving the financial position of the club and decreasing its debts, it was proposed and seconded at the AGM that a subscription list be opened with the aim of collecting the sum of £30, and the secretary was to send out a circular to obtain further subscriptions.

Who, then, took up membership of the club? This can be ascertained by studying the prevalence of certain occupations among the membership, and the individual names and addresses of those who joined. What is striking from the outset is the prominence of British army regiments who joined as individual regiments. In one of the earliest minutes from Cork County Cricket Club, a list of life members recorded on 4 April 1874 included a Captain Beamish and Captain Henry Crawford. A meeting on 23 May 1874 took the decision to allow any regiment stationed in Cork to join the club for the season for the fee of £10, with the option of joining up to 1 August for the reduced fee of £5. In the following years there are various references in the club minutes to regiments joining the club or to the club's asking for subscriptions from various regiments. At the club's AGM on 6 September 1898 at the Imperial Hotel, members of the Hampshire and Leicester Regiments were present. The Hampshire Regiment promised to join the club at the usual regiment subscription rate of £10, while the Leicester Regiment would pay £5 for a half-year subscription. There is also a reference to the club asking the 17th Lancers about their intentions of joining.

At the following year's AGM, the club decided to write to regiments with membership terms for the following season. An entire regiment could become members and have use of the ground (when vacant) for the sum of £10. Alternatively, if a regiment decided not to join as a whole, individual officers could join for £1 as playing members or pay a 10s subscription to be non-playing members. Officers were also to have the services of a professional for 10s.

At a club committee meeting held at Mr Pike's office on 29 March 1904, a letter was received from the president of the Gordon Highlanders thanking the club for its courtesy in inviting officers of the regiment to become members. The letter to the club said the regiment would have 'much pleasure' in joining and the subscription of £10 would be forwarded on 15 April.[5] At a club general committee meeting held at 96 South Mall on 13 December 1913, the issue of the Leinster Regiment not settling their account was discussed, as well as several other subscriptions that had not been collected. As a result, it was suggested that Harman discuss with the treasurer what steps could be taken to 'get in' the subscriptions.[6]

At a committee meeting on 24 November 1916, the club recorded how it was 'deeply indebted' to the officers of the 3rd Leinster Regiment and the 3rd Royal Dublin Fusiliers for their 'very generous subscriptions'.[7] In the 1920s, all members of the British army and navy were to be charged £2, the same as ordinary members.

There was also a strong link between the club and employees of banks. At an extraordinary meeting on 1 July 1881, it was recorded that a motion 'that thirty-four Bankers be accepted for the season for the sum of £10' was defeated.[8] At a committee meeting on 16 April 1925, among the new members elected was a Mr T.M. Graham, with an address at the Bank of Ireland.

The club minutes give details of names and addresses of individual members who joined. In the earliest club minutes there is a list of those who attended the original meetings and those who became life members. A meeting held on 4 April 1874 was attended by those interested in founding a new club. Those listed in the minutes as being present at this meeting in the Imperial Hotel were: R.U. Penrose Fitzgerald, Right Hon. Alan J.B. Roche, Mr Standish Barry, Anderson Cooper, Tomas Hewitt, Parker Dunscombe, Alexander Jack, W.O. Wrench, James Lambkin, A.J. Tucker, Mr B. Leslie, Jerome Murphy, and Thomas Gillman. Those who were to become original life members were: the Earl of Cork, the Earl of Bandon, Sir John Arnott, A.H. Smith-Barry, Capt. Piggot Beamish, Captain Crawford, R.U. Penrose Fitzgerald, Robert Hall, Henry Hewitt, George Humphreys, Mayor E.A. Shuldham, Arthur Stewart, and W.J.J. Hunt.

At the club's AGM on 7 April 1877, it was recorded that among those who had already contributed their membership were Messrs Hewitt, Cooper, Lambkin, Dunsombe and Pike. The minutes of the club record a detailed list of names and addresses of club members, again including a number of members belonging to the military. There were two addresses of Carlisle Fort and Camden Fort, the individuals being members of the Royal Artillery. Also recorded in the same minute were the names of a Captain W. Murphy and Captain Willis. Cork City addresses recorded include the Mardyke (which is mentioned a number of times), Sunday's Well, Woodhill, Cara's Court Room, and Great George's Street West. A county address of a playing member was followed by the initials RIC and based at Youghal. All the aforementioned addresses were those of playing members.

Captains Murphy and Willis, both non-playing members, gave addresses respectively as Richmond and simply 'County Cork'. The city addresses given for other non-playing members were Patrick's Hill, Lee View, South Mall, St Luke's and Belgrave Place and Mt Verdon. What is again notable is the presence of British army officers and soldiers. For example, there was a Captain Augustan with an address at 'The Barracks', another two members with an address of Cork Barracks, and a Colonel of Fort House, also being part of Cork Barracks. Two other elected playing members had addresses on Patrick Street.

When members were proposed and seconded for membership at the club's AGM on 23 April 1903, nearly all the addresses of these individuals were in Cork City. These included Lower Glanmire Road, Beechmount, Lafalgan and Cleve Hill. There were also, among the addresses, large individual houses such as Frankfield House, Charlemont House, and Ballintemple House in Blackrock. One of the new members gave his address as 'care of Beamish & Crawford' and another address was from the South Mall, which was quite possibly a business address. Rushbrook, near Cobh, was the address of another new member, and reflecting the continued interest of the military in the game, a Major Maher of the County Club was another member proposed and seconded for membership.

At the following year's AGM, addresses recorded for those members admitted to the club included Western Road, Douglas, Blackrock, Silver Springs, and Camden Quay. The military was represented by a Captain P. Henry from Ballincollig, where an army barracks was situated, as well as by the Gordon Highlanders from Victoria Barracks. Another member admitted at the meeting lived at The Lodge, St Anne's, Blarney, some miles from Cork City, and from the west of the city, there was a new member from Bandon.

A list of new members recorded in the minutes of the AGM on 2 May 1910 indicates their social backgrounds. Those who joined included: Brig.-Gen. Barry Copley, GB; Captain Higgin; Professor Alexander; Maj.-Gen. Medcalf, and Revd M.L. Bradshaw. A club committee meeting minute on 16 April 1925 included a list of new members with addresses outside Cork City, such as Queenstown and Charleville.

And so, we can deduce that those who joined Cork County Cricket Club were mainly from Cork City. There were a few members from nearby towns such as Queenstown and Blarney and those further afield, such as Charleville and Bandon. The list of members also shows the preponderance of the military among the membership, together with those from Anglo-Irish backgrounds.

THE GROUNDS OF CORK COUNTY CRICKET CLUB

Early details regarding the grounds used by Cork County Cricket Club indicate the way in which they were acquired for the sport, and how they were to be used in future years both for cricket and for non-cricketing activities. At one of the first meetings of the club, held on 26 February 1875, one of the resolutions passed dealt with the cricket ground. This resolution went as follows, 'That in terms of Rule 8 the Trustees are now requested to get a lease of the present Cricket ground at the Mardyke on the best procurable terms.'[9]

The following year, the question of giving the grounds for other sports arose. At the AGM on 3 April 1875, it was originally proposed and seconded that no athletic sports be held on the grounds for a year. An amendment was then proposed, seconded and subsequently carried, that it be at the discretion of the club committee to decide if the grounds could be granted for athletic sports, the amendment being carried on a vote of twelve to four. However, a further amendment, that the application of an athletic club for use of the ground on 21 and 22 April be granted, was rejected, again on a vote of twelve to four.

At a committee meeting on 23 July 1881, the club committee unanimously carried the motion that the Rifle Brigade have the use of the cricket field on 25 August for their athletic sports, the field to be given free. At the AGM of the club on 10 April 1886, the club heard an application from the 'Cyclists' Touring Club to lay down a bicycle track around the ground, but the application was refused because it was felt that the ground was too small for it. However, the same meeting did decide to grant the ground to Queen's College (later University College) and also to grant the ground to Cork AAC for their respective sports at a cost of £5 per day, but under the condition that these clubs not be given use of the pavilion. Other examples of the club granting its ground for non-cricket activities will be discussed later.

From the point of view of availability of facilities for cricket, there was a shortage of grounds in Cork, particularly at the turn of the century. The *Cork Sportsman* was particularly strident in highlighting the lack of grounds for playing cricket, sometimes in a sarcastic tone. For example, the issue of the paper on 18 July 1897 discussed the plight of Constitution Cricket Club, which had arranged a match at the Mardyke only to be 'tersely informed' that Cork County were playing cricket there on the following day, while the alternative, the Camp Field was also not available. The piece continued:

In desperation we approached the proprietors of the only other ground available, and they, in a true sportsmanlike manner, refused us, although they admitted that the ground was not otherwise appointed. Of course, we guaranteed any expenses, but still it was of no use; this sporting club adopted the dog-in-the-manger policy. We are not surprised.

In the following years, the same paper highlighted this problem of ground availability for those who played cricket. In June 1908, the *Cork Sportsman* commented on the lack of cricket activity and noted how it had been a 'comparatively blank week in Cork Cricket'.[10] It also noted how, in Cork and 'the neighbourhood', there was a 'terrible scarcity of cricket grounds'. The writer pointed out how, in the previous year, there had been grounds available in Douglas Village and Blackrock, and while neither ground had been ideal, clubs at 'least had something', but neither had been available in the current year. However, on a more hopeful note, the writer remarked that a team from Presentation Brothers College were about to begin playing, if they could secure a field, while the Incorporated Church of Ireland Cork Young Men's Association (ICICYMA) were making a start in getting a ground.

The writer of this same piece also proposed that, 'The Football Club would do well for Cork Cricket and for themselves if they were to let out the grounds for cricket during the season.' With at least six affiliated clubs using the ground and 'with proper arrangements the gate receipts should amply provide for the cost'. In the following week's notes, under the heading 'Constitution Cricket Club Notes', it was reported that it had been 'another blank week for the Cons', this being mainly due to a lack of grounds.[11] On the sixth of that month, Constitution had been due to play Cork County, but Cork County had been obliged to hand over their ground for croquet. Constitution were also due to play ICICYMA, but could not do so for want of a ground. The Camp Field was available but the military authorities had been unwilling to allow two civilian teams to use it, a course of action which the correspondent endorsed and hoped that a club would be enterprising enough to 'annex' a ground. In the same issue, there was reference to a ground at the Cross Douglas Road, at which a game was played between Bohemians and Bankers.

However, the minute books of Cork County Cricket Club do reveal a willingness on the part of the club to make their grounds available for other cricket clubs for a fee. At a committee meeting of Cork County Cricket Club, held at the pavilion on 29 April 1898, it was recorded that the ground was to be granted to 'Legal C.C.' on any two evenings a week, plus use of the nets after six o'clock in the evening for the fee of four guineas, and a fee of £1 was to be paid to Kenny, the club professional, for overtime. Other conditions were that there were to be no more than fifteen on the ground and that use of the pavilion was not to be granted.[12]

An application from Constitution Cricket Club was also granted for use of the ground on one evening a week for a fee of 3 guineas and 10s to be paid to Kenny. At the club's AGM on 6 September 1898, the club heard an application from Constitution Cricket Club to practice one evening a week on the Mardyke Ground with the 'price to be settled afterwards'.[13] Yet it was decided to offer the ground first to 'Legal' Cricket Club as they had paid in excess of £3 for use of the pitch on two evenings a week and paid Kenny 30s.

At the following year's AGM the same 'Legal C.C.' were again granted use of the Mardyke for practice for the upcoming season, for a fee of £4 4s and 10s to the groundsman. However, this was on condition that a balance of £1 4s due from the previous year was paid. The Ordnance Survey Cricket Club were also granted use of the Mardyke for the same fee of £4 4s. In addition to Constitution Cricket Club applying for use of the ground, at the 1904 AGM of Cork County Cricket Club there were similar applications from Queen's College Cricket Club and Church of Ireland Young Men's Cricket Club. While the Constitution and Church of Ireland clubs paid the usual fee of £4 4s, Queen's College were to pay £10 for use of the ground on every night of the week.

The association between cricket and places of work is evident when one examines the continuing practice by which Cork County Cricket Club allowed other cricket clubs to rent its ground. In the first decade of the twentieth century, bank employees had formed their own club and used the Mardyke grounds. At the club's adjourned AGM in 1910, Cork County considered a verbal application from Bankers Cricket Club for a reduction of the rent payable by them, which at the time was the sum of £10, entitling Bankers to use of the ground for practice on six nights a week as well as playing their matches there when the ground was available. Cork County were unanimously of the opinion that such a reduction should not be granted.

At a committee meeting on 28 April 1916, the club secretary was directed to send invitations to all military and naval clubs in and around Cork, giving such clubs free use of the ground and pavilion for the upcoming season. Of course, the previously mentioned Constitution Club (like its rugby counterparts) had its origins in the newspaper of the same name. The club had obviously disbanded for a while, since an application from what was called the 'newly formed' Constitution Cricket Club for use of the Mardyke ground was heard at a committee meeting of Cork County in May 1926. In order to encourage cricket, Cork County would grant use of the ground to Constitution on Tuesdays and Fridays for the 'nominal sum' of £1.[14] The same minute refers to how the usual charge of £15 for use of the grounds on two nights weekly and one Saturday per month was being waived on this occasion. However, if the new club was a success, then Cork County reserved the right to charge the usual fee with regard to future applications from Constitution.

In February 1931, Cork County heard applications for use of the Mardyke from St Lukes Cricket Club and Purcells Cricket Club, the latter being a work-based club. When the committee of Cork County met in April 1933, also in attendance were representatives of the other clubs using the ground. Work-based teams with representatives at the meeting were Purcells, Furlongs and Cork Milling Company. The yearly rent charged to such clubs was increased from £10 to £12 10s, and there was an additional charge for use of the ground for matches, which varied depending on whether a Cork team was playing another local team or a visiting team from outside Cork.

The cricket club was also let out to younger sports players. The AGM of Cork County Cricket Club in May 1911 decided that the use of the ground was to be granted to the university cricket club for the sum of £8. In May 1916, Cork County granted an application from Cork Grammar School for use of the ground for practice for their school sports, for which the school had offered the sum of £10.

Occasionally, Cork County experienced problems when letting their ground, the most outstanding and specific issue concerning the apparent unwillingness of Cork Bohemians to pay the sum due for their use of the Mardyke. In April 1925, Cork County discussed how Bohemians Cricket Club had not paid the half-year's rent for use of the ground for the previous season, and Cork County's secretary was instructed to write and inform Bohemians that any application for use of the Mardyke for the upcoming season would not be entertained unless the outstanding amount was paid.

While the outcome of this particular impasse is not clear from the minutes of Cork County Cricket Club, relations between both clubs continued, and in September 1928, Bohemians sent a letter to Cork County thanking the club for their kindness to them during the season. Yet there were still problems in the 1930s for Cork County, as they attempted to collect the rent due from Bohemians. At Cork County's AGM on 16 April 1935, the matter was raised of Bohemians not having paid the previous season's rent and it was decided that they be written to and told that if the outstanding amount was not paid then the ground would not be open to them from 1 July 1935. In May 1939, Bohemians made a suggestion to Cork County that the charge of 11s to local clubs for use of the Mardyke when playing visiting teams be discontinued, but Cork County refused the request.

We have already noted how, in the 1880s, Cork County granted the use of the ground for sports other than cricket (such as for the sports of Queen's College and to the Rifle Brigade for use in 1881). This practice continued and the club remained open to giving the ground for non-sporting activities such as band promenades. It seems to have been a practice to grant the ground on an annual basis to the university for its athletic sports. At the Cork County's AGM on 26 March 1896, it was agreed that the cricket field be let to Queen's College for its sports, as the cost of £10 with a £3 deposit.

Croquet was another sport played on the Mardyke grounds. A Cork County Cricket Club committee meeting in February 1903 had a letter read from a Mr Murphy, secretary for croquet tournaments, asking for use of the grounds for a number of weeks beginning on 17 August for a fee of £10 and an additional fee of £5 if the weather was fine. In October of that year, a letter was read from the same Mr Murphy asking for remission of the rent paid for croquet tournaments, since several members of the cricket club had gained free admission to the tournament. Cork County resolved that a remission of £1 be permitted for those who organised the tournament, but a cheque of £19 was still due to the cricket club. It was then unanimously agreed that an amount of £20 rent be charged for use of the cricket club for the following year for the croquet tournament, it being distinctly understood that all members of the cricket club would have free admission.

The same year, the Cork County Club considered a proposal from the Greater Cork International Exhibition for use of the cricket ground. The cricket club agreed to give the ground for sports being held in association with the Exhibition, but such sports were not to include the sports held by the university and Presentation School, which had always been held under the auspices of Cork County Cricket Club.

As previously mentioned, Cork County also let out their ground for general entertainment events, particularly band promenades. At the club's AGM in 1897, the club resolved to give the grounds solely for band promenades in the month of May, on every Thursday, with the objective of paying off a debt incurred due to improvements made to the grounds. At the following year's AGM, Cork County decided to grant the ground to Catholic Young Men's Society for band promenades, again with the aim of reducing the club deficit. Cork County resolved at the same meeting to let the grounds for other sports to solvent clubs, cash to be paid beforehand. The issue of the application from Catholic Young Men's Society to hold band promenades on the ground was again discussed at a committee meeting of Cork County on 29 April 1898. The society was to have permission to hold four promenades at a cost of £25, these to be held after six o'clock in the evening. If these terms were acceptable to the applicants, one of the promenades was to be held free of charge for the distress fund.

In April 1915, the Cork County committee were in receipt of a letter from the secretary of Catholic Young Men's Society, asking the cricket club for the terms under which the society could have use of the cricket ground either on a weekly or monthly basis. The letter further added that the society would sign any agreement to defray any expenses incurred when they occupied the ground. The Cork County committee instructed its secretary to write back for further particulars as to how many evenings the society would require the ground and to inform the society that the cost of the ground per evening would be £5. The following month, the Catholic Young Men's Society, based at Castle Street, offered Cork County the sum of £3 per night for twenty nights, after 7p.m. The society also promised that no sports would be held on the evenings on which the society had the grounds and guaranteed Cork County against any damage to the ground or property thereon, the whole offer being acceptable to the cricket club. In May 1927, the St Vincent de Paul Society applied for use of the ground for an evening band promenade, the charge to the organisation to be the same as for sports and cricket clubs, while Cork County would consider giving a subscription to the charity.

Cork County did not always give use of the ground to organisations or groups who made such requests. In May 1916, the committee of the Barrack Street Band made an application to Cork County for use of the ground on a Sunday in June to hold an open-air dance. The Cork County Club's committee instructed its secretary to tell the Barrack Street Band committee that it was not in the power of Cork County's committee to grant such a request and suggested that the band committee apply for the field on some holiday afternoon.

The granting of the grounds for other activities is indicated by a Cork County committee meeting held at the office of Dr Dunlea in April 1926. The committee discussed a letter from a Ms Sweetman, applying for the use of the Mardyke from 4p.m. to 6p.m. on 1 June, a request which was granted with no money to be charged. At the same meeting, the committee granted a portion of the ground to Duffy's Circus for 19 May. The club also granted a request from the committee of the Drapers' Club for use of the ground at the usual fee of £15 and a £5 deposit in case of damage. Some years previously, Cork County had billed the Drapers' Club for damage to the property during sports held under the auspices of the Drapers' Club. Cork County had held a special committee meeting to consider damage to the pavilion on 24 June, when the plumbing had been damaged due to a drain being plugged with broken bottles, cardboard and coarse paper. The Drapers' Club was to be sent the bill when the cricket club had received same.

Cork County Cricket Club, on certain occasions, gave their cricket ground to some organisations for nominal rent, probably reflecting sympathy with the aims of such organisations. At a committee meeting in June 1915, a letter was read from W.H. Seymour, honorary secretary of the Cork City Volunteer Training Corps, applying for use of the ground, when available, for training. Permission was granted on condition that such letting was subject to 'all engagements, cricket or otherwise'.[15] A nominal rent 'of say' £1 per annum would be charged and the club secretary was instructed to give this reply. At the same meeting it was agreed that Bohemians and Church of Ireland be allowed use of the ground for practices and matches at a reduced rate of £3 per club for the season. This reduced rate may have been due to the impact of the war and the difficulty in arranging matches.

Another occasion on which a nominal fee was charged by Cork County for use of the ground occurred in July 1931, when A.W. Langford of the Cork Boy Scouts Association asked for permission to put up a hut as a headquarters at one end of the ground. Permission was granted and a nominal fee was to be charged.

Cork County also looked sympathetically on the case of the Cork Catholic Young Men's Society. At a Cork County committee meeting on 16 July 1915, a deputation was in attendance from the Catholic Young Men's Society, including Revd Fr R. O'Sullivan, John Sisk, the society's vice-president, and Frank Barnes, the society's secretary. They had attended this particular meeting to discuss the open-air cinematography which had been held on the Mardyke ground under the auspices of the society. The venture thus far had been unsuccessful from a financial point of view and, at that time, the society owed the cricket club £20. The society declared that it would be thankful if it were granted use of the ground for a number of evenings in August at a reduced tariff, and that they 'would of course' pay the £20 owed.[16] The cricket club's committee would grant the society the ground four evenings in August free of cost, so as to allow them to recoup their losses in some measure.

The cricket ground of Cork County was also the subject of a dispute between the cricket club and the corporation over the issue of the requisitioning of the ground under the Food Order Scheme during the First World War. Cork County held a special committee meeting in April 1917. The meeting had been called due to a misunderstanding about a proposed offer by the club to the corporation of the eastern end of the cricket field for allotment under the Food Order Scheme. Mr Tuke explained that any offer made was subject to the landlord's consent, the offer being purely patriotic to help the country in time of need. Mr Beamish accepted Mr Tuke's explanation and said that as landlord, he would not be a party to handing the ground over to the corporation. If the allotment was to be granted at all, he would put his own employees on the allotment. However, the minute of the meeting noted that the cricket club should understand that it was quite probable that the ground would be required under the scheme and if so, the club would be required to leave the ground when it had received due notice.

CRICKET COMPETITIONS AND MATCHES

At a local level, Cork County Cricket Club, probably similar to other such clubs in Cork and surrounding districts, relied to a large extent on the presence of army and navy teams for fixtures. A club committee meeting in November 1916, which reviewed the past season's cricket, noted that, owing to the fine summer and number of military cricketers stationed in the district, over forty matches had been played and the game was kept 'well alive … in wartimes'.[17] At a club AGM in April 1924, it was decided to write to troops stationed in Cork Harbour with a view to arranging matches, though it was also decided to write to 'national troops' at Michael Collins Barracks.[18] This trend continued in the 1930s. At a meeting in May 1937, home and away fixtures were confirmed against Spike in June and September respectively. At the club's AGM in April 1938, the club secretary was instructed to write to W.A. Pearson, Chaplain at the Berehaven Rectory, for the purpose of arranging matches, both home and away, against the Bere Island garrison.

There was also a local cricket league in which Cork County took part. At a club AGM in March 1927, correspondence was read suggesting the formation of a cricket league. The club secretary was instructed to write and state that the club approved and would give whatever assistance it could. The club felt it necessary to hold a number of meetings in 1929 to discuss whether it would enter the Cork and County District League. At a committee meeting in September, it was resolved to have an extraordinary meeting in October to determine the position of the club with regard to the Cork and District League. A committee meeting was held prior to this extraordinary general meeting at which the rules suggested for the running of the Cork and District League were discussed, before being put to the general meeting. This extraordinary meeting was of the opinion that the conditions for running the Cork and District League should be approved.

There was a reference to a junior league in 1939, when Mr D. Coffee told the AGM of Cork County Cricket Club that an effort was being made to start a junior league during the forthcoming season. Christian Brothers College was among the teams mentioned as intending taking part, as well as Presentation College, Bohemians, Constitution and Church of Ireland. Mr Coffee had asked what facilities such teams could have available at the Mardyke, whereupon it was decided that each club entering the junior league pay an entrance fee of £1 to be paid to Cork County Cricket Club. Those clubs wishing to play their home matches at the Mardyke were to pay a fee of £3. It would seem from these proceedings that Cork County may have been in charge of the league, when one considers that the entrance fee was to be paid to the club.

Away matches played by the club usually took place in Dublin or Ulster, though, as we shall see, cost was often an inhibiting factor. It was in the 1920s that references to these matches were most common, suggesting that before this the club was not in a position to travel. However, there is a reference to Cork County being invited to a match in Dublin by Phoenix Cricket Club. At the club's AGM in April 1906, a vote of thanks was passed to the Phoenix Club for inviting Cork County to their ground in Dublin on the following June and for the Dublin club's hospitality in inviting the Cork team to be their guests for the occasion. The occasion was to be Phoenix Cricket Club's match against the North of Ireland.

An indication of the problems in attempting to play away fixtures is revealed at an emergency meeting of Cork County in July 1925. The meeting discussed the projected fare for travelling to Dublin, and the 'extreme doubt' about getting the team to travel.[19] No final decision was to be taken until the following Friday, but it was finally decided to cancel the engagement. In the meantime, every endeavour was to be made to get an eleven to travel on a Sunday to fulfil the engagement. When the dates for the following year's inter-provincials were being fixed in December 1925, the hope was expressed at the meeting that other matches could be arranged along with the inter-provincials that would involve Cork County. On the following February, it was decided to play Trinity on 13 and 14 June, before the inter-provincial matches. Cork County would also endeavour to play North Down and Cliftonville Cricket Clubs, if a sufficient number of players could remain on in Belfast after the inter-provincial matches.

Mention was again made of these fixtures against Trinity and North Down, with the Trinity game to be played in Cork at the end of June. Cork County were also confirmed to play Limerick on 17 June at Limerick. However, problems arose with the fixtures against North Down and North of Ireland Cricket Clubs. These extra fixtures had to be cancelled due to an insufficient number of players being able to guarantee that they would be present to play. Instead, a fixture against Trinity was to be played. In September 1926, the club committee heard how it had been arranged that inter-provincials were to be played every third year, commencing with a fixture in Cork on the following year.

The same meeting also decided on some fixtures for a proposed week-long mini-tour to Dublin. For Trinity Week, Cork County would open with a fixture against Trinity and follow this with fixtures against Leinster Cricket Club and one other match, to be arranged at a later date. Again it was proposed that inter-provincial matches be arranged to coincide with these club matches and that they be fixed as near as possible to mid-June. The following year's AGM included a review of the previous year's fixtures in which the club had played. The secretary reported on a tour to Dublin and Belfast (which was notably the first time that a Cork team had ever played in Belfast). In the match against Trinity a ground record had been set for an individual score, the previous record having been set by a lieutenant of the Infantry Regiment.

Perhaps more significant occasions, from a social as well as a cricketing point of view, were the matches played against visiting teams, especially from other countries, such matches being especially popular around the turn of the century. One of the first references to such an event was when a bat was presented to the club by 'R.A. Ireland' as a memento of 'their pleasant match', and it was decided that the bat would then be awarded to the individual who scored the highest innings for the forthcoming 1898 season.[20]

One of the major occasions in the history of Cork cricket occurred in 1903, when a team from London, including the famous cricketer W.G. Grace, visited the Mardyke for an exhibition game. In February 1903, a committee meeting noted a letter from Sir J. Kennedy, Bart, asking if Cork County, in conjunction with the Cork Exhibition Committee, would guarantee £100 towards the expenses of a game between the 'Gentlemen of Ireland' and a team from London including W.G. Grace. Cork County's committee resolved that Mr Chirnside from the club should correspond with the Exhibition organisers, with a view to ascertaining their feelings on the matter, and then to communicate with Sir J. Kennedy.

At the subsequent committee meeting, the question of guaranteeing the sum of £100 towards the game was discussed. The club secretary reported that the committee of the Cork Exhibition had agreed to put forward the sum of £25 towards expenses incurred in staging the match. The meeting unanimously agreed to undertake to pay the balance of the money needed, since it was of the opinion that there would be 'no difficulty to get the requisite number of people in Cork to come forward'.[21] At the club's AGM in April, Chirnside confirmed that, in conjunction with the Cork Exhibition Committee, it had been arranged for a match to take place between London County and the 'Gentlemen of Ireland' and that the committee of Cork County had guaranteed £100 towards expenses incurred in hosting the match.

As well as London County, Cork County Cricket Club was also involved in arranging an invitation match involving South Africa and the 'Gentlemen of Ireland'. At a committee meeting in 1903, club member Chirnside put before the meeting the proposal that South Africa's cricketers should visit Cork. After some discussion, it was resolved that Mr Chirnside should attend a meeting in Dublin with the authority to undertake the fixture. The club would guarantee £100 or, in lieu thereof, half the gross gate or the whole gate less expenses. The expenses were to include those of the 'Gentlemen of Ireland'. The following March, the committee resolved that a printed circular should be sent to the likely guarantors for the South Africa match. In April, at the club's AGM, the secretary reported on the proposed match between 'Gentlemen of Ireland' and South Africa, the fixture to be held on Thursday, Friday and Saturday, 30 June and 1 and 2 July 1904.

Team selection for cricket matches in the 1920s involving Cork County was a source of discord within the club, especially the issue of non-club players being picked. This issue was discussed at a committee meeting in April 1926, when it was resolved that members of Cork County Cricket Club were to be given first preference as players in all county fixtures. Outside players were to be invited to play only when 'absolutely necessary' to complete teams.[22] At a meeting in July 1927, Captain Harte, who, as has already been noted had resigned as secretary and been seconded to the club committee, raised the matter of team selection. At the committee meeting held at J. Hall's office on the South Mall, a letter was read from Captain Harte in which he refused to go on to the committee. The letter, containing 'strong' and 'objectionable' language, protested at the inclusion of two officers from Spike Island who were not members of the club but who had played in the county side versus the Cambridge Crusaders from England.[23] Not alone had Captain Harte refused to go on to the committee, but he had also tendered his resignation from the end of the season.

In reply, the secretary told the meeting that both officers referred to by Mr Harte had joined the club in the meantime. At the same meeting the selection committee explained its actions. A Captain Ferguson had been selected to keep wicket since he had a reputation for being 'a good bat and wicket-keeper'.[24] The other officer, Captain Morton, was a 'good bowler' and had captured four wickets against Cambridge Crusaders, whereas the other members of Cork County had only taken two wickets each. The selection committee offered a number of other reasons for the selection of the two officers. For example, according to the selection committee, no Cork County members had entered their names to play in the match against Cambridge Crusaders. In addition, both Captain Norton and Ferguson had travelled to Limerick with four other players to make up a Cork county side after the secretary had failed to find three other county members willing to travel. The secretary referred to how Captain Norton had captured five wickets for twelve runs in that particular match.

Captain Harte then appeared before the committee, saying that he was writing entirely on his own behalf and initiative. He withdrew his reference to the action of the selection committee, describing his behaviour as an act of 'gross impertinence'. In the discussion that followed, from which it seems Captain Harte was now absent, it was noted that Captain Harte was 'technically right'. However, it was also pointed out that if good teams were to come to Cork then the home team would have to 'put up the best show possible'. The action of the selection committee in selecting the two officers had to be seen in the light of defeats of previous years. It was then proposed and seconded that a letter be sent to Captain Harte accepting his resignation with 'much regret', and the selection committee also tendered its resignation.

GAMES AS EVENTS

Detailed observations on the role of players and spectators are hard to find in the contemporary accounts of cricket matches in Cork in the late nineteenth and early twentieth centuries. When a team called Na Shulers played Cork

Garrison in August 1886, the correspondent in the *Cork Examiner*, referring to Na Shulers, noted that the team 'could hardly be called representative', as it was composed of both Cork county and military players.[25] The *Cork Sportsman*, in August 1908, referred to the players of Bohemians Cricket Club. The correspondent for the team described a match they had played against Cork County, who had included two professionals in their side, and the correspondent found their inclusion difficult to understand. The correspondent claimed in the same piece that Bohemians had not been able to field their best team against Constitution, noting that 'several of our players having found the need of a holiday after the strenuous work of this cricket season'.[26]

Any references to the spectators at cricket matches tend to focus on how fashionable the attendance was, as well as the presence of ladies at matches. At a match between Cork County and Spike Island in June 1894, the *Cork Examiner* remarked on the 'presence of a large and fashionable attendance of onlookers'.[27] It is also interesting that the same piece described how, when the score had reached 208 for Cork County, 'it was found that train time was near, and stumps were drawn'. There was a similar description of the attendance at a game between Na Shulers and Cork County in the summer of 1898, the match beginning on a Saturday morning. The weather throughout the day had been 'delightfully fine' and the attendance of spectators within the pavilion during the afternoon was 'large and fashionable'.[28]

Cricket matches were social occasions for both spectators and players. When two military teams, the Manchester Regiment and 2nd Berkshire Regiment, played a match in June 1891, a 'very fine band' from the Berkshire Regiment attended in the evening.[29] A newspaper report noted that, 'its beautiful playing was much admired by the large company present on the grounds as well as by a very appreciative audience in the Mardyke'.[30]

The article listed the pieces played by the band, though the writer did seem to contradict himself somewhat when remarking that 'the playing was not of a very high standard, still it was interesting'. After-match hospitality was another aspect of cricket matches. When the Bankers travelled to Castlemartyr to play the local team, the visitors were 'hospitably entertained' after the match.[31] The presence of ladies at cricket matches was also noted, as in the *Cork Sportsman* of September 1908, where, when reporting a match between Bohemians and Constitution, it was noted how, 'the attendance was good, and but two of the fairer sex regular and enthusiastic "followers" of the fortunes of the "Beaux" braved the elements'.[32]

It is also interesting to observe from match reports how some games were

Cricketers at the Mardyke, under the shadow of Sunday's Well. (Image courtesy of *Irish Examiner*)

played during weekdays, so presumably the players could afford to, or were able to, take time off. In June 1908, in its report of a match between Cork County and Royal Artillery of Ireland, the *Cork Sportsman* noted that the match had been played on the previous Friday and Saturday. In the following month, Cork County had played Dublin University, this time on a Monday. However, it may only have been Cork County players who could play during the week. When Bohemians played Bankers at the Cross Douglas Road in the summer of 1908, the game was played on a Saturday.

There was also a social aspect to entertaining visiting teams both during and after a match. Such a social aspect of cricket was given a more flowery description in the account of a match between a Midleton Eleven and a Mr A. Williams Eleven, though the piece was under the heading of the 'Constitution CC

Notes'. After describing some of the game itself, the article continued, 'We now sat down to a well-served luncheon when having satisfied the "inner man" and smoked the pipe of peace, we started to annex that 105 but we didn't get them'.[33]

NEWSPAPER COVERAGE

A cursory look at the newspaper coverage of local cricket matches in Cork reveals that correspondents were particularly exercised with the issue of sportsmanship and adopted a very strict position on the issue. One particular subject that drew the ire of cricket writers was that of criticising umpires and appealing to umpires for favourable decisions. Under the heading 'An Onlooker's Observations', a writer in the *Cork Sportsman* had this to say of a match involving Bankers and Bohemians:

> The umpire's decision was questioned from the pavilion during the Bohemians' batting. This is not good taste, and teams should recollect that it's not a pleasure to anyone to take up the job, and that the umpire is the best judge whether a ball goes to the boundary or sticks in the long grass, at all events, he is sent to watch these things and should know … Such remarks as 'Is that a boundary umpire?' are unnecessary.[34]

There was a similar instance of such newspaper criticism, again in the *Cork Sportsman*, in August 1908, when the writer spoke in particular of one player and what the newspaper perceived as unsporting behaviour:

> This trundler, however, is too fond of appealing to [the] umpire. In fact almost every ball caught by the wicket keeper elicited an appeal, and even after the decision was given the appeal was re-iterated. It may be due to the bowler's excitement on this particular occasion, but it is not 'Play the Game'.[35]

Later that month the *Cork Sportsman* had reason to comment on what it perceived to be unsportsmanlike behaviour of some cricket players:

> …some players have a bad habit of appealing about once an over or so without an ostensible reason. This is a habit that the umpire should sternly repress, either by ignoring the appeal or by giving his decision in a tone of voice not calculated to encourage a repetition of the offence.[36]

The writer was also critical of the umpires for not consulting each other enough and for calling 'out' too quickly. In addition, umpires were criticised for not being able to distinguish between a throwing and a bowling action:

> ...the rare occasions on which a bowler is 'no-balled' for this offence by amateur umpires prove how few of the latter have the courage of their convictions. That many bowlers do occasionally 'throw' instead of 'bowl' is fact beyond dispute; otherwise there would be no necessity for the M.C.C. law on the point.[37]

Newspaper writers were concerned that the game should be played in the proper spirit, even if technically the rules were being adhered to. In a piece in the *Cork Sportsman* entitled 'Notes by an Observer' the cricket writer witnessed what he felt was a breach of etiquette in the way a certain player was dismissed, though his innings were an 'excellent effort':

> The manner in which he was sent back to the pavilion was loudly condemned all round. It might be according to M.C.C. Laws, but it is not in accord with the traditions of the Mardyke, and savours too much of 'talent money' and professionalism to ever become popular here. The action of the Con skipper inviting Sedall back to try and complete his century showed very good taste, but of course could not be availed of by the batsman, who had everybody's sympathy in being dismissed in such a manner. [38]

In a similar fashion to other sports already chronicled, cricket writers showed frustration at the lack of punctuality in starting games. For example, a league cricket match on a Saturday in August 1908 should have commenced at 3p.m., but did not do so until 4p.m. The writer was of this view, 'We have exhausted all the known adjectives in our vocabulary against this unpunctuality, and we do not wish to chronicle the language of some of the spectators as time went by and only half-dozen of the twenty-two players were present – their anger was justified.'[39]

On another occasion, a cricket writer was annoyed with the lack of match reports, which should have been forthcoming from the teams themselves, 'It is the business of the home team to supply the press with accounts of matches. This and other small things constitute the ethicate of cricket, a thing to be cultivated as much as the game itself, if a club would look after its reputation.'[40]

Local Cork newspapers also carried news from international cricket. In February 1909, the *Cork Examiner* referred to the Australian team's visit to

England and how for the purpose of the tour there had been a first trial match between an Australian XI and the Rest of Australia. In January 1934, there was a similar reference to an upcoming Australian tour of England, and how one player named Lonergan had made a 'bold bid' for the trip to England, having formed a 'bright partnership with Richardson'.[41]

Finally, newspapers were used to advertise cricket equipment and dress. The following was advertised in the *Cork Constitution* in September 1886 under the heading 'Cricket':

Thoroughly Seasoned Bats
by
Corbett/Warsop/Ayres/Bussey/Slazenger
And All The Leading Makers

Complete Outfits For The Game
Balls/Guards/Boots/Gloves & Co.

Elephant House
78 Patrick Street Cork

Also Dublin & London[42]

In June 1908, the following advertisement appeared in the *Cork Sportsman*:

Well-seasoned bats by leading makers
Leg Guards Batting Gloves Wicket-Keeping Gloves

Balls at all prices
Special Terms to Clubs
Robert Day & Sons Ltd, Cork.[43]

SCHOOLS AND JUVENILE CRICKET

According to a *Cork Sportsman* of August 1908, there had recently been founded a juvenile club under the auspices of Cork County. The writer praised the new team, saying that 'they showed good cricket and "played the game" for all it was worth'.[44] In the same month the Cork County juveniles played a game, the teams being made up of those members inside the county boundaries versus those outside, and Cork County 'with its usual hospitality, provided an excellent lunch and tea for its juveniles'.[45]

A little earlier in the summer, the cricket writer on the *Cork Sportsman* expressed regret at the lack of organised junior cricket activity:

> More should be done for junior cricket in Cork. There is no nursery for young cricketers; and the best teams must rely largely upon casual importation for recruits. This is especially noticeable with the Cork County itself … Could not a junior league be established? The numerous schools in Cork would furnish a team well worth developing.[46]

The writer noted how junior cricket had been adversely affected by intermediate examinations, though he did add that there were still three months cricket left after June. He also hoped to see an inter-school competition 'attracting as much interest as the rugby competition does. All that is needed is the ground'.

FINANCES OF CORK COUNTY CRICKET CLUB

The more interesting financial aspect of the running of Cork County was how the club negotiated with the bank for overdraft facilities. However, before we focus on that facet of the club's financial affairs, let us first look at a number of other aspects of the club's finances that can be garnered from the minute books.

For example, at the club's 1886 AGM, when the club had been approximately ten years in existence, members heard how the club had an income of £160 for that year and expenses of £180. These would have been fairly considerable sums in that period. The balance sheet of the club's expenses, as discussed at a club committee meeting in November 1916, showed that the main sources of income were subscriptions, hire of the ground and bar/ telephone receipts. Subscriptions were the largest source of income, coming to over £100. The greatest expense was £50 paid in wages, and just over £42 was expended on purchases for the bar. Mr L. Whyte, the honorary auditor, had examined the accounts for the club.

The club had to deal with debts that accumulated, and the ways in which the problem was addressed are worth noting. One way in which the club continued to operate despite a deficit, was asking the bank for an overdraft based on guarantees from the members. For example, at a committee meeting in

December 1904, a Mr Chirnside was instructed to ask for an overdraft of £50 to meet the accounts due. It was envisaged that the increase would be met by sums outstanding due the club, while the revenue of the following year was there 'to look forward to'.[47]

At the club's AGM in May 1907, the secretary reported that the Munster and Leinster Bank had written to the club requesting a further guarantee by the committee of £50, making this a total guarantee of £150. It was agreed by the meeting that the guarantee should be given and the committee signed their names thereto. It was then proposed and seconded that the meeting would indemnify the committee of the club for any sum or sums guaranteed to the Munster and Leinster Bank, providing that 'said sum or sums do not exceed £50'.[48]

When the adjourned AGM of 2 May 1910 was resumed on 18 May 1910, the secretary, in submitting his statement of accounts, told the meeting that all liabilities had been paid with the exception of old standing liabilities which amounted to £297 9s 5d and also a balance due to the Munster and Leinster Bank of £474 13s 10d. There then followed a discussion as to whether the debts should be consolidated as one to the bank, after which the following course of action was decided upon. The treasurer was to approach the bank to procure the further sum of £120 or a guarantee of the purpose of paying off club liabilities. Some of the members estimated the figures they could guarantee: £25 was guaranteed by Sir George Colthurst, J. Murphy, R. Harman and G.C. Chirnside, and J. Dunlea and Godfrey Pike guaranteed £10. The amount owed to the Munster and Leinster Bank did decrease over the following years. At the AGM in May 1911, the amount owed to the Munster and Leinster Bank was £160, while at a general committee meeting in December 1912, the amount owed to the bank was listed as £109 16s 4d and the overall financial situation was described as 'very satisfactory'.[49]

The club also relied on the voluntary contributions of members to help clear club debts. At a committee meeting in April 1908, the financial state of the club was discussed. The amount of liabilities, excluding anything which would come under capital expenditure, was £389 12s. The committee discussed the best means of eventually liquidating the debt. It was resolved that a voluntary subscription list be opened to 'procure a sum necessary to meet immediate claim sum of £30 promised at the meeting'.[50] The finances of the club were to be placed before the AGM, which was due to be held on 9 April at 4p.m. It was decided that after that meeting, circulars should be sent out to club members requesting their support.

At that same AGM, a discussion was held on how the club debt could be liquidated. It was proposed and seconded that a subscription list should be opened and an amount of £30 was intimated. The secretary was to send out a circular to obtain further subscriptions.[51] At the following year's AGM, in May 1909, it was proposed and seconded that the sum of £25 be taken out of funds towards the further liquidation of old debts.

RULES OF CORK COUNTY CRICKET CLUB

At the meeting of those interested in forming a cricket club in Cork, held at the Imperial Hotel in April 1874, the newly appointed committee was authorised to draw up rules for adoption by the club. The early implementation of rules dealt with two major issues, namely subscriptions and discipline. These subjects were to dominate the discussion of rules at the club in the subsequent decades.

As early as 1875, one of the club rules was altered as follows, 'All Annual Subscriptions shall be payable on 1 April in advance and any member, or subscriber whose subscription is not paid before 1 July shall cease to be a member … until his subscription be paid, shall he be entitled to play in a match.'[52]

At a meeting in April 1880, a resolution was passed whereby 'every Member who can show that he has not been in the County of Cork during any one Cricket Season be not required to pay his subscription for that Season'.[53]

Other references to rules on membership in the minutes of Cork County in the following decades relate either to punitive measures designed to get members to pay, or to the way in which the club decided to charge membership for those who lived a certain distance from Cork. The club also had to make rulings on the issue of membership for members of the British forces stationed in Cork who wanted to play the game.

The following are a number of examples of how the club tried, by its rules, to get members or aspiring members to pay their subscriptions. At the club's AGM in April 1884, a motion was carried to the effect that no one would be admitted to the club unless they had paid the subscription for the previous year, and the secretary was to write to the people in question to this effect. At the club's AGM in March 1896 it was resolved that members who did not pay their membership by 1 July were to be struck off the list. At a meeting in December 1925, the club committee decided to remove the names of members owing subscriptions of two years or over.

An entry from the minute book from 1925 seemed to show that the club was accepting that some subscriptions would never be forthcoming. In April 1925, the committee decided that subscriptions and accounts outstanding were to be left to the discretion of the treasurer and secretary 'to write off as they considered proper'.[54] Some entries from the minute book of Cork County for the 1926 season show how the club ruled on the subscriptions due for various types of member. In April, as the new season began, the committee ruled that members living outside a twenty-mile radius should be charged a fee of £1. In May, the committee agreed that members of other clubs who wished to join Cork County could be admitted to the club on payment of £1 subscription. Also, all members of HM Services were to be charged the same annual subscription as ordinary members (£2).

DISCIPLINE

Club rules on disciplinary matters related mostly to the use of alcohol. As early as 1885, the club's AGM resolved that a member who appeared on the field under the influence of drink would be cautioned the first time and if the behaviour was repeated, then the member would be 'deprived of the proceedings of the club'.[55] A committee meeting in May 1924 took the decision to print a card in large type saying that only members were to be supplied with alcoholic drinks. The following year the club secretary was deputed to issue an order that the bar shut no later than 9.30p.m. on Saturday and 10p.m. sharp on other week evenings, in accordance with the new licensing act. The bar was not to be opened on Sundays.

The club committee did deal with other matters of indiscipline. In May 1881, the club secretary was instructed to write to a D.F. O'Neill, telling him that his conduct had been brought to the notice of the committee. If the offending behaviour was repeated the committee would feel obliged to bring his conduct before a general meeting of the club.

In July 1925, the committee discussed the behaviour of a certain player. The committee was to call up the player to get an apology from him and this decision was to be intimated to the player in question by a gentleman appointed to do so. Later that month, at an emergency committee meeting which discussed the question of travelling to Dublin to fulfil a fixture, a letter of apology was read from the player discussed at the previous meeting. As a result, the committee felt that the apology was sufficient and the incident was considered closed.

Finally the club had to draw up some rules to govern the hire of the grounds by other clubs. After an incident involving the boundary fence of the club grounds, in July 1924 the committee decided that for all sports meetings a fee and deposit was to be paid, five clear days in advance of the fixture. Thus far the Drapers' Club had been the only organisation who had complied with these terms.

The reference to Cork County Club asking the national troops if they were interested in joining the club is tantalising, though how serious was the intention and how sanguine were the committee one cannot know. The minutes are silent on any further correspondence and there is no evidence of Free State Troops being part of the cricket world of Cork. However, for as long as the British naval bases remained in Cork Harbour, those stationed there continued as part of the sporting world of Cork cricket.

For the Cork bourgeoisie, the troubles in 'rebel Cork' and the bitter Civil War do not seem to have impinged in any way on Cork County Cricket Club. While the First World War had drained the club of members and filled their story with sad memories, the events of the Great War and the Civil War seem, if the records are anything to go by, to have had virtually no impact on the social and leisure world of those who played cricket in Cork. There is no mention of damage to property, there is no mention of menace to members, there is no reference to serious disruption of fixtures and facilities. It is as if the members of Cork County Cricket Club inhabited a social space utterly removed from the world of conflict and the guerrilla warfare that dominated the historical narrative of rebel Cork in these years.

IV

GOLF

It is in the last decades of the nineteenth century and the early decades of the twentieth century that one sees the roots of golf take hold in Cork City and county. The exact year in which golf was established is unclear, and historians such as Menton and Gibson refer to various second-hand sources to give a general indication as to when golf was first played in Cork.

In his book *Early Irish Golf, The First Courses, Clubs and Pioneers*, William Gibson refers to golf being played at Kinsale as early as 1883. A British army regiment, the King's Own Borderers, arrived in the town from Fermoy in 1883, and had several golfers within its ranks. Gibson cites a publication called *The Field*, dated 16 June 1883, which described how there was a golf links situated at the Musketry Camp, four miles from Kinsale, adding, 'There are eight holes and the course is fairly good ... There are caddies in plenty to be had'.[1] *The Field* carried an account of matches, mentioning several officers of the local British army regiment, which subsequently departed Kinsale in 1884.

There is evidence that Kinsale was not the only location for golf in Cork in 1883, judging by a piece in the *Belfast Newsletter* of 1 November 1886, 'Since November, 1881 when the Belfast Golf Club was instituted ... no less than three additional courses have been laid down in different parts of the country. The second was at Fota Island ... one of our contemporaries noticing an opening game there in 1883.'[2]

Citing further evidence that golf was being played in and around Cork in the 1880s, Gibson refers to another article in *The Field* in the autumn of 1888, which described how the then Governor of Malta, Sir Henry Torrens, had stated his intention of introducing the game of golf in the island, saying that he had already introduced the game in Cork when commanding there. However, Gibson is of the opinion that the earliest golf club in Cork was that of Rushbrooke, near Cobh, founded in 1892, while the *Golfing Annual* of 1895/96 records how Cork Golf Club was founded on 1 November 1894. Menton's history lists ten Cork clubs which were founded and affiliated in the years from 1901 to 1915, covering various areas of the county as well as the city environs. This growth can be seen in the wider context, in which 163 clubs were affiliated to the Golfing Union of Ireland by 1911.

However, the focus for this study is on clubs in the more immediate environs of Cork City. Similar to the aforementioned clubs in the other parts of the county, the exact dates on which these clubs were founded has not always been easy to ascertain. In listing the various clubs which opened for play in the latter decades of the nineteenth century and the early years of the twentieth, Menton alludes to the opening of Cork clubs at Fota Island in 1883, Cork Golf Club in 1888 and Rushbrooke in 1905. Though founded in 1888, Cork Golf Club did not affiliate to the Golfing Union of Ireland until 1900. Fota and Cork Golf Clubs were located immediately to the east of the city, while Rushbrooke was situated on the western outskirts of Cobh. Gibson cites contemporary newspaper accounts that refer to the Fota course. The *Belfast Newsletter* of 1 November 1886 noted, 'one of our London contemporaries noticing an opening game there in 1883'.[3] *The Irish Times* of 6 January 1906 reported 'New Links at Fota'.[4] The reference to the new links leads Gibson to deduce that the earlier links at Fota had not survived, and that the club had been revived in the new century.

While the club at Kinsale was possibly the earliest golf course founded in the county, Gibson says that a more modern course was instituted there in 1897; the club formally affiliated to the Golfing Union of Ireland in 1912 (Gibson's source being the *Sportsman's Holiday Guide* of 1897). The link with the British military was still in evidence; the secretary of the more modern club was a Captain Shattock of the Royal Artillery based at Charles Fort on the outskirts of the town.

However, it is with the clubs of Muskerry, Monkstown, and in particular Douglas, that this study will particularly be concerned. Muskerry, situated outside the city in the direction of Iniscarra, had its origins in an earlier club called St Anns. St Ann's Hill was situated on land owned by a Dr Barter, on which a hydropathy establishment was also situated. Before this course had been established, those who wished to play golf had been transported to a farm in Dripsey also owned by Dr Barter, but the playing of the game was then transferring to St Ann's Hill. This was the precursor to the Muskerry Club, which began in the 1900s. However, Gibson cites *The Irish Times* of 18

September 1897, referring to a newly established Muskerry Golf and Lawn Tennis Club.

Gibson notes that the *Golfing Annual* of 1895/96 gives the founding date of Cork Golf Club as 1 November 1894. The *Golfers Guide* for 1897 confirms the existence of a course at Killahora at Queenstown Junction Station. Gibson, like Menton, refers to a club at Rushbrooke called Queenstown Golf Club, which existed before 1895 and which was still in existence in 1909. In mentioning the club at Rushbrooke, Gibson also alludes to a club at Rochestown, which, like that at Rushbrooke, was in existence before 1895. In another reference to the club at Rochestown, Gibson says that it was in fact established 1895, according to the *Golfing Annual* 1895/96, and two named officers of the club were a Miss L.C. Parke, Ballinlough, and a H. Humphreys of Ballintemple. Gibson states that there was no further mention of this club in any golf publications after 1910. The official address of the club was Blackrock, Rochestown, Co. Cork. This address, and the addresses of the officials, would indicate that the club had its origins in the suburb of Blackrock, though the course itself was situated further outside the city in Rochestown.

In discussing the origins of Cork Golf Club, situated now at Little Island, Gibson notes a difficulty in ascertaining exactly when it was founded, since the club records were burned in 1945. He does, however, cite other publications with regard to founding dates. The *Golfing Annual* of 1895/96 records that the club was founded on 1 November 1894. This date was confirmed in the *Golfers Guide* of 1897, which noted the location of the club at the Queenstown Junction Station. In October 1898, Cork Golf Club moved to its present location, and in the years from 1910 to 1916 the course was extended to eighteen holes. J.P. Sharman-Crawford, who had links with other sports in Cork, is credited along with a Mr H.H. Maudsley with discovering the location for the new course.

A golf club for which greater detail will be provided later was Douglas Golf Club, situated in the south-eastern suburbs of Cork. Referring to the early years of the club, Gibson cites the *Irish Field* of 25 September 1909, which reported how good progress had been made on the new links and clubhouse at Douglas. It was hoped that nine holes would be ready for Christmas and that an eighteen-hole course would be completed by the spring, the architect of the course being the renowned Harry Vardon, who had laid out the course the previous July. The *Golfing Annual* of 1909/10 also recorded the foundation of the club as being in July 1909, with a membership of 261. The entrance fee was 4 guineas, while the annual subscription was £4 for men and £2 for women.

MEMBERSHIP AND SUBSCRIPTIONS TO GOLF CLUBS

In the early years of golf in Ireland, very few had access to golfing facilities. By 1900, when the first constitution of the Golfing Union of Ireland was drawn up, golf had been established in over 200 areas (since the founding of the Royal Belfast Golf Club), however, some of these locations were on private estates and not open for membership.

The previous reference to Douglas having a membership of 261 in the year 1909 is only one of a few references to the actual membership figures for golf clubs in Cork. For example, the *Golfers Guide* of 1897 indicated that Mallow Golf Club had a membership of seventy in 1897. The *Irish Golfers Guide* of 1910 gave the membership of Muskerry Golf Club as 300. A history of Monkstown Golf Club does provide membership figures, from the club's earliest years to the inter-war period. The *Golfing Annual* of 1908 recorded that the Monkstown club had 350 members, including ladies. In the inter-war period, the membership varied from 100 to 200 men, while the membership figures for ladies were between 20 and 30. A club member in this period, one Ted Whitaker, recalled how, when he joined in early 1920, the club had from eighty to one hundred members. He also recollected how, in the late 1920s, the club had 'a small membership of well-behaved members well versed in the rules which were strictly adhered to'. At the same time, a club such as Douglas would seem to have had a larger membership, since a general committee meeting of the club in February 1927 decided to admit forty new members from the 1 to 21 May of that year.

From the earliest years, golf clubs were charging membership and entrance fees for the privilege of playing on the various courses. In 1896 *The Irish Times* reported on the institution of a club in Trabolgan in East Cork; the annual subscription was fixed at 2 guineas, although a limited number of members would be permitted to play without paying an entrance fee. The *Golfers Guide* of 1897 noted that the subscription fee for Mallow Golf Club was £1 for men and 12s 6d for ladies. At the turn of the century, the course at St Ann's Hill (which preceded the Muskerry club) was available for the use of visitors and open to officers of the army, navy and RIC, at an annual subscription of half a guinea. At the first AGM of

Muskerry Golf Club in 1908, an entrance fee was fixed at 1 guinea. The *Irish Golfers Guide* of 1910 gave a detailed list of the various charges for different types of members and visitors to the Muskerry Club. The entrance fee was £1 1s and the annual membership fees were as follows: men, £1 11s 6d; ladies, 15s 6d; visitors, 1s per day, 5s per week, 10s per month, and 2s 6d on Saturdays and Sundays.

In 1912, the entrance fee for Monkstown Golf Club was £1 1s. The annual membership was then fixed as £2 2s for men and £1 1s for ladies, while there were varying charges fixed for visitors who wanted to play on the course. For one day's play, the fee was 1s for weekdays and 2s 6d at weekends. A week's play cost 5s, and the fee for a month's play was 10s. When, in December 1914, a Lieutenant Newport asked the committee of Monkstown Golf Club if both he and other officers could play on the club's golf links, the club secretary replied that the subscriptions due would be 1s per day or 21s for six months. By May 1921, a family subscription was £5 5s, a year's subscription for gentlemen was £3 3s and for ladies £2 2s, and non-playing members paid a sum of £1 5s. These fees applied to local members – the definition for such members being those members who lived in the postal districts of Monkstown, Passage West, Queenstown and Ringaskiddy. In the 1920s, the annual subscription fee at Monkstown was £2 5s. By 1934, there were various categories of membership, for example, for a local member the subscription fee was £3 3s, a non-local member paid £2 2s, and the fee for ladies was £2 2s. There was also a family rate of £5 5s.

The way in which subscription and entrance fees could vary, and the factors that influenced such changes, can be studied in some detail when one looks at the minute books of Douglas Golf Club, which cover the period from 1921 to 1939. The *Golfing Annual* of 1909/10 noted that in 1909 the club had an entrance fee of 4 guineas and an annual subscription of £4 for men and £2 for ladies. When the club held its AGM in January 1922, subscriptions for the New Year were set at £5 for gentlemen and £2 10s for ladies, while locker rents were 6s and 5s respectively. In 1925, the club committee took a number of decisions on what sums were payable by the various types of member. In May of that year, it was decided that on or after 1 July of that year, the entrance fee would be £5 5s, while past members who 'asked to join' would be admitted without an entrance fee being charged.[5] This allowance for former members was confirmed at a meeting in April 1926. A meeting of the club committee in July 1925 passed a motion that on or after 12 August, intending lady members were to be charged an entrance fee of £2 2s. The club committee reserved the right to change the entrance fee during the course of a year. A general committee meeting on 10 May 1927 agreed that the period for which an entrance fee of £2 2s was being charged should be extended to 30 June, this in fact being a reduced entrance fee. In what was possibly a reference to visitors fees, the committee discussed reducing the 'club's fees' from 2s 6d to 1s 'per entrance', the matter being referred to a general meeting.[6] At a special general committee meeting on 15 February 1930, it was recommended to the newly elected committee that the entrance fee should be abolished, as the total roll of membership had showed a falling off in the preceding years.

EXEMPTIONS FOR MEMBERS

Until the turn of the century, the course at St Ann's Hill was available for play to visitors and open to members of the army, navy and Royal Irish Constabulary, though information available does not make clear if some fee was expected from these players. Some time around 1908, when the first general meeting of the Muskerry Golf Club was held, an exemption from paying the entrance fee of 1 guinea was granted to officers of the army, navy and RIC on full pay. Those also granted such a privilege included bank officials, since they were liable to be transferred, as well as clergymen. The *Cork Examiner* of 1 September 1906 referred to how Cork Golf Club had unanimously resolved that officers of the navy fleet be made honorary members of the club during their stay in Cork City. It was also proposed that on the following Thursday a match be played between twelve members of the home club and twelve of the fleet.

Over the following decades such exemptions continued to be granted to these same professions. In 1934, at the Monkstown Club, an entrance fee of £1 1s was set, but exemption was agreed for 'officers serving in the Army, Navy or Civic Guard, and persons not permanently resident in the County or City of Cork who are approved by the Committee'.[7] These people could be elected as associate members, with the membership fee being waived. Bank officials did not have to pay and in fact they dominated club membership during this period, with many employees of the Munster and Leinster Bank assuming captaincy of the club.

County members were also granted exemptions from paying certain fees.

For example, a committee meeting of Douglas Golf Club in 1923 decided that the entrance fees of county members for 1923 were to be refunded, with a J. Lambkin dissenting. The same committee meeting heard a letter read from a correspondent who wanted a concession made on his outstanding subscription, but the committee unanimously agreed that no concession could be made. This was only one instance of how members of golf clubs in Cork often requested exemptions from paying membership fees, citing various reasons for such requests. For instance, the minute book of Monkstown Golf Club from 12 May 1912 includes a letter from Mrs Phipps asking to be put on the Absentee List. The Secretary was directed to write and say, 'As she had gone to reside in Dublin, she would be placed on the Absentee List, but on the understanding that once she visited anywhere in Munster, she would be liable for her subscription.'[8]

As well as the many requests for exemptions from paying fees, there were frequent appeals for part or total refunds on their membership subscriptions. A committee meeting of the club on 20 March 1925 heard a letter read from a doctor asking for a refund of his subscription, owing to his inability to play. In reply, the committee decided that half the subscription rate be charged. On 10 January 1927, the entrance and subscription fee of a T. Forde was excused, owing to this individual's inability to play due to an accident, and his election was cancelled.

A letter was read at a general committee meeting of the club on 8 January 1929 from a Revd Barry, CC, asking that, in view of his illness during nine months of the previous year, some action be taken regarding his subscription. It was decided that, in the circumstances, Revd Barry be regarded as a non-playing member and that he pay a subscription of £1 1s for the year 1928. Later that year, a letter was received from a member named Rickson, who had joined in January but had been transferred by his work to another county. It was proposed, seconded and passed that in this case half the entrance fee and the full membership fee be refunded.

There were other reasons why some members were exempt from club membership or at least from some of the membership fee. In July 1931, it was decided to grant an exemption from membership to an individual who had 'helped so much' with the club sweep.[9] Another member was to be excused his membership fee because of a change of residence and his forthcoming marriage.

COLLECTING SUBSCRIPTIONS

From the outset, the Douglas club had difficulty with some members who did not pay their subscriptions on time. As early as August 1921, the club secretary was to apply either in person, or by registered letter, for outstanding subscriptions due to the club. On 19 September 1924, the club decided that members whose subscriptions were outstanding should be written to by registered post. However, at the club AGM in February 1925, the secretary was informed that subscription notices had not been received by many of the members and he was asked to give an explanation for this state of affairs at the next meeting.

During the 1920s and 1930s, the club resorted to a number of harsher measures in order to acquire subscription fees due. A general club meeting held at the club on 11 May 1926, took the decision that if subscriptions from members were not paid, such members would not be permitted to take part in competitions, the notice to be posted up in the club house. Another example of the actions taken in this matter was a decision made at a meeting of the committtee on 8 September 1931, when a special letter was to be sent to a Mr J. Hegarty regarding his outstanding subscriptions for 1930 and 1931, which also included money due from a bar account. The committee did not want to take extreme measures to collect the amount due and so the secretary was now asking him to settle his account within seven days. In November 1930, it was proposed to send a draft letter to all members in default, pointing out that their names would be posted if their subscriptions were not paid by the New Year. In December 1932, a list of subscription defaulters was drawn up and it was felt that a sum of £20 was recoverable from these.

ADDRESSES OF MEMBERS OF DOUGLAS GOLF CLUB

In 1913, Monkstown Golf Club changed its rules, which henceforth enabled individuals not resident in Cork City and county to become members of the club at a fee of £1 1s (the fee for ladies being 12s 6d). However, detailed club records listing the addresses of members are unavailable. These would help determine whether the membership in general was from around the Monkstown area or whether it drew the majority of its members from outside the area, especially from Cork City. But the minute books of Douglas

Golf Club do provide the names and addresses of individuals who were passed for membership; so what can we deduce from such information?

There is no preponderance of individuals from the local Douglas area among those members with Cork City addresses. In fact, the vast majority of those passed for membership at various committee meetings were from the southern, western and north-eastern areas of the city. At a general committee meeting on 13 December 1927, four new members were elected. Three identifiable addresses were Western Road, Bellview Park and Lower Road. Western Road is situated on the western side of the city near the Mardyke and Lower Road is to the east of the city, on the way to Glanmire.

The addresses of those passed for membership at a general committee meeting on 8 April 1931 are notable for the names of banks given as addresses. Of the six addresses recorded, two were the Provincial Bank of Ireland and Bank of Ireland. Douglas Road, which extends from the centre of the city to the Douglas suburbs, was also listed, as was Elizabeth Place. An address for one of the newly elected members was that of Killiney, Dublin, indicating either that someone was coming to live in Cork or was securing country membership, though this is not alluded to in the minute book.

The following addresses of new members were recorded at a general committee meeting on 9 June 1931: Maynooth; Lough Villas, the Lough; Cat's Hill; Blackrock Road; Summer Hill; Pouladuff Road; Connacht Avenue; Frankfield, and Carlow. The non-Cork addresses would again indicate that people were moving to Cork and wanted to join a golf club there. Pouladuff Road and the Lough were quite near to each other, situated adjacent to the South Parish, and Connacht Avenue is situated near to the university. Summerhill is situated near St Luke's and is a north-eastern suburb, while Frankfield was then a country address near Douglas.

At a general committee meeting on 8 September 1931, there were various Cork and non-Cork addresses, as well as work addresses. Just as in previous instances, the work addresses were those of banks, in this case those of the Hibernian Bank. Non-Cork addresses included: Rangoon, India; Clontarf, Co. Dublin; Victoria Road, Belfast, and St John's Hill, Waterford. Cork addresses included Lotamore, Montenotte, College Road and Douglas, while a Cork County address mentioned was Clonakilty. That same month, a captain from Collins Barracks and an employee of the Provincial Bank in the South Mall joined, while others to join were from Summerhill, College Road and Brooke Street. The same minute notes an individual who was passed for membership with an address of St Thomas

Hospital, London. Names and addresses of those seeking membership were posted on the notice board; two of the addresses were in Dublin and the Cork addresses were Greenmount, Anglesea Terrace, Watercourse Road, and College Road.

At a general committee meeting on 9 February 1932, after receiving a letter from Revd M. McSweeney, a motion was passed that he be made an honorary member. Elected for membership at the same meeting were a Revd T.J. Duggan of College Road, a Miss O'Callaghan of Glenbrook and Miss A. Brown of Wellington Road. Glenbrook was situated near Monkstown on Cork Harbour and Wellington Road is just above McCurtain Street on the north side of the River Lee, near the city centre. On 12 April 1931, seven individuals were passed for membership. A number of the addresses were from outside Cork, including the Bank of Ireland in Armagh, Dorset Square in London, and Milltown Golf Club, Dublin. Three ladies joined, one with an address at Townsend Street, Skibbereen, another with an address at the Mental Hospital, Cork, and finally a lady with an address at Old Blackrock Road, Cork. Finally, on 9 June 1932, three individuals were passed for membership, with addresses of Mourneabbey (near Mallow), Eglington Villas and Harbour View. Clearly, locality was not the key factor in determining membership. It would appears that occupation, inclination and social rank/status were more important than 'local residence'.

ELECTIONS, LISTS AND TEMPORARY MEMBERSHIP

A limit was put on the numbers who could join golf clubs in Cork. This issue was addressed in 1908 by the Monkstown club, when the chairman of the new club committee raised the question of putting a limit on the number of members. At the time, the membership was slightly under 300 and further applications were being made, so it was decided that the membership limit be set at 325.

In Douglas Golf Club, for which more detailed records exist, there are a number of references to individuals being 'elected' for membership. At a general committee meeting on 13 December 1927, four new members were 'elected by ballot'.[10] Similarly, at a general committee meeting on 21 August 1928, new members were elected. Election would always seem to have been by ballot, since these are the words used at a meeting minute note on 9 February 1932, when three members were elected. An indication of the formal procedure is found at a meeting of the committee on 14 December 1926, when the election of a Miss Gilbride as a member was put in abeyance until 1927, since she would be abroad.

Linked with the question of membership and election of members, was the issue of those who wished to become members and were put on a waiting list. There is particular reference to such waiting lists pertaining to aspiring lady members in Douglas Golf Club. On 8 February 1924, it was proposed and seconded at a general committee meeting that a waiting list be established for intending lady members from this date. When the club committee met on 13 September 1927, it was proposed and seconded that the waiting list for five ladies be opened and closed again. Aspiring lady members had to fulfil certain conditions, and these conditions were not always met. It was proposed and seconded at a committee meeting on 19 March 1928 that the captain and secretary see a Miss Tivy; the minutes state that the circumstances regarding the election of a lady member had changed and that such an election should be withdrawn. The following month, a long discussion took place on the opening up of the ladies' membership list, at which point it was proposed and seconded that the waiting list be reopened and that the names proposed for membership should not be posted on the notice board until fourteen days before the next monthly meeting. The same issue was raised at a meeting in July of that year, when it was proposed and seconded that the ladies' membership list be opened for the admission of married couples and the wives of existing members (with locker accommodation to be provided by the husband).[11]

There were other forms of membership, such as honorary, county and temporary. When, in November 1928, a letter was read from a Mr McKnie, signalling his resignation from the club, it was unanimously agreed by the committee that he reconsider the matter and become a non-playing member. On 26 February 1929, a Dr Calnan was to be approved as a county member, his address being Inishannon, west of Cork City. On 22 June, the club committee decided to elect N. Collins as an honorary life member in recognition of special services rendered to the club, the said Collins having helped to raise £600 for club funds. Finally, there was the issue of members joining temporarily for certain periods. On 11 December 1928, the secretary was directed to enquire about the number of temporary members from Fords who were joining Douglas and to report his findings.

USE OF LINKS FOR PLAY

We have already noted that clubs granted special rates of membership to such groups as the army, the navy and bank employees. The above reference to employees of the Ford Company acquiring temporary membership is one of a number of examples whereby certain professions and associations were granted special access to the course at Douglas.

On 15 February 1924, a general committee meeting of Douglas Golf Club heard a letter from the Jewellers' Association in Dublin asking for permission to use the club links during the Easter Holidays for their annual competition. The committee granted the request. On 15 June 1925, it was proposed and seconded that the members of the Medics Psychological Association of Great Britain and Ireland be elected honorary members of the club during their visit to Cork, as per the letter from a Dr McCarthy of the Dental Hospital on 13 June 1925. A committee meeting of the club on 27 August 1925 heard a letter read on behalf of the Merchant Tailors Convention, requesting use of the club links to play competitions on 10 September 1925. It was proposed, seconded and passed that the application be granted. On 8 May 1928, the committee received a letter of thanks from Ford & Sons for use of the links for a competition. A committee meeting on 9 June 1931 had it proposed and seconded, with no objection, that the use of the pavilion and links be given to the Civil Service Club Golfing Society on any Monday suitable to them.

GOLF AND POLITICAL ISSUES IN CORK

The way in which political issues impinged on Cork golf clubs related firstly to the turbulent events from 1918 to the early 1920s, and secondly to legislation which the new Free State government introduced and its impact on the running of golf clubs. The *Irish Field* of 1 May 1926 carried a piece on Douglas Golf Club, noting that it was a limited liability company and mentioning some of its prominent personalities. The piece is notable because it refers to the clubhouse being burned during the War of Independence, adding 'It is now known that the burning of the clubhouse was the result of a blunder in interpreting an "order" but the damage was done and seemed irreparable.'[12] This reference coincides with anecdotal evidence that an order was issued for the burning of Cork Golf Club because of its links with the

British forces, but that those who carried out the burning mistook the Douglas Club for Cork Golf Club.

This episode coincides with the availability of minute books, with the first meeting listed in the minutes taking place on 27 May 1921, the venue being the Imperial Hotel. The general committee meeting discussed the burning of the pavilion and the advisability of playing on the links; it was decided to wait for the views of members at a general meeting that was to follow. A special general meeting was held on the same day, again at the Imperial Hotel, with Revd M. McSwiney in the chair. The question of resuming play on the links was discussed and various opinions were expressed. One proposal that was seconded was that the issue of resuming play be left to the committee and that a further general meeting be called if necessary by means of notice in the public press. A counter proposal was also seconded allowing play to continue in the existing conditions pending a report from the committee. The former proposal was carried by a margin of one vote after a long discussion and the individual who suggested the latter withdrew his proposal. The same meeting decided that a subcommittee should be appointed to organise a fund so that 'inside staff' be compensated for losses in the fire.

Some days later, both a general and a special general meeting were held in the Imperial Hotel. At the committee meeting, it was proposed that if a loan per gentleman member in cash did not realise the amount which the committee deemed sufficient to begin the reconstruction of the club, then the present club should be wound up voluntarily and a new club be formed from those members who were prepared to subscribe. Lady members were to hold a meeting to decide the amount they wished to contribute 'per head'.[13]

At the special general meeting that followed, it was proposed and seconded that play on the club's links be recommenced at the earliest time possible. Any suggestions forthcoming on the reconstruction of the club were to be put to the club committee, following which a circular would be sent to each member of the club. This circular would also advertise another meeting, which would then decide on replies received, and the voting at that meeting would fix on on the system to be adopted for raising the money necessary to continue the working of the club. The findings of the committee would be binding on all members of the club, this being passed unanimously. It was proposed and seconded at the same meeting that a special vote of thanks be conveyed to Monkstown and Little Island Golf Clubs for giving the members of Douglas Golf Club full use of their respective links 'during the present crisis' and this also was passed unanimously. A special vote of thanks was also proposed and seconded to J.G. Musgrave for lending three huts to the club as temporary premises pending rebuilding of the pavilion. Another reference to the Troubles occurs in the minutes of a general committee meeting, when a letter was read from the Republican Office asking the club to suspend play until such time as prisoners were released. The minute book simply records, 'No action on the matter'.[14]

PLAYING RULES

While clubs had some discretion on what rules they could introduce for their own particular circumstances, playing rules were, to a large extent, determined by the central governing body, especially in such matters as handicapping. This preoccupied the Golfing Union of Ireland at the end of the nineteenth century. At the inaugural meeting of the Golfing Union of Ireland in 12 October 1890, one of the stated aims of the new association was to establish a fixed principle of handicapping. Towards the end of nineteenth century, golfing clubs, societies and associations were organising their own methods of allowance for handicaps. In the early years of golf in Ireland, handicap scores were set according to the score of the best player in the club.

In October 1894, the Golfing Union of Ireland decided that each club should select a green score to which members should be handicapped, and a scheme for handicapping was submitted to various clubs in 1896. The Union's secretary, George Coombe, was to visit all affiliated clubs to discuss par scores with local committees and standardise the way scores were recorded. Various handicapping systems were being introduced around the turn of the century, but no real standardisation seems to have taken place until 1925, when the British Golf Union introduced what was called the Standard Scratch Score by the British Golfing Union's Advisory Committee. Achieving standardisation in golf's scoring system was made more difficult by the fact that in 1897, there were an estimated 109 courses in Ireland open for play, but only thirty-six were affiliated to the Golfing Union of Ireland.

Apart from this standardisation of regulations on handicapping, golf clubs in Cork acted independently in formulating their own rules regarding behaviour on the course and in clubhouses. In the case of Douglas Golf Club, great care was taken in drawing up the club rules and a special rules committee was formed. On 25 March 1925, a special rules committee meeting was held at

Winthrop Chambers, Winthrop Street, and a draft of the proposed alterations to the club rules were 'gone through'.[15] At a general committee meeting on 15 June of that year, it was proposed and seconded that the rules subcommittee be empowered to obtain legal advice in connection with the drafting of the club rules. A special general committee meeting held in October 1925 at the Metropole Hotel, included a discussion on the new rules. The various rules were passed for final consideration, for which a special meeting was to be called. Copies of the amended rules were to be typed and distributed to members of the committee prior to this meeting.

Playing rules were concerned with the etiquette that members and guest players of clubs were to observe while on the course. These covered care of the course and decorum *vis-à-vis* other players. The *Cork Examiner* of 18 January 1902, in a piece describing a competition played in Cork Golf Club, included the following message from the green committee of the club, 'The "Green" Committee is anxious to impress on members the necessity for replacing the turf. Through neglect of this some very bad lies are to be encountered at present, and the links rendered very unsightly.'[16] At a special general committee meeting of the Douglas Club on 21 January 1929, a discussion was held regarding the condition of the course, one of the issues arising being that of reminding members to replace divots.

Rules relating to players seem to have been passed with a view to stopping certain individuals making a profit on the sale of golf balls. A general committee meeting of 8 March 1927 ordered that the new professional, who was appointed on probation, was not to be allowed to sell new or second-hand golf balls. Another general committee meeting on 19 October 1927 decided that printed notes be obtained and posted in the club prohibiting the purchase of golf balls from a certain individual.

House rules related to the kind of access that was allowed to certain members within club pavilions and dealt with the matter of access to the bar. An entry from the minute book of the Monkstown Golf Club from the 25 October 1923 read, 'It was decided that the room over the kitchen in the Castle be reserved solely as a smoke room for new members of the Club.'[18] Other rules related to the use and sale of alcohol in the club premises. It was proposed and seconded at a special general meeting that club members have the privilege of inviting guests for lunch on a Saturday or Sunday. It was proposed and seconded at the same meeting that the steward be reminded that visitors to the club could not be supplied with excisable liquor, except on the invitation or in the company of a member.

In October the club committee were concerned about a practice among members whereby the victors of competitions bought bottles of whiskey in the bar to celebrate. At a general meeting on 12 October 1926, it was directed that members be informed that it was the committee's wish that such practices should cease and that any liquors obtained over the counter should be on single orders. The next committee meeting proposed and seconded that a notice be posted on the door of the secretary's office indicating the committee's request that any member of the club winning a prize should not purchase bottles of whiskey, and that the steward be instructed accordingly.

MATTERS OF DISCIPLINE

Issues of discipline at the Douglas Club embraced matters pertaining to players and members, as well as to employees of the club. For players and members, offences for which they were notified and admonished related to play on the course and to behaviour in the club premises. The club's general committee, when meeting on 8 November 1921, considered the past services and trustworthiness of a J. Power and decided to allow him his own conditions of play. It seems to be the same individual, however, who was in question when the committee asked him to furnish them with an explanation as to why he played on Friday 4 November contrary to the committee's orders.

On 10 July, the Green Committee, when discussing the recently played Captain's Prize, heard a suggestion that views of absent members be ascertained in relation to the disqualification of W. Henchion and C. Joy for their non-compliance with Rule B regarding card competitions. It was then proposed and seconded that they be disqualified subject to the above.

The general committee meeting of the club on 10 July 1930 dealt with a number of discipline-related incidents. The chairman raised an incident between a W.C. Hosford and the secretary. It was proposed and seconded that Hosford be approached and informed that an apology was expected, or else the secretary would write to him in relation to a complaint from a W. O' Reilly where players in a four-ball match acted without due courtesy. A motion was then passed that a letter be written to these players citing the rule on the subject.

The same meeting discussed an incident between a H. Whelan and M. McCarthy at Lahinch. A letter was read from Whelan explaining his position and he also explained his position verbally at the meeting. It was decided to write to McCarthy informing him that another meeting would be called in three days time and giving him notice to attend. On 17 July, a special general committee meeting was called to discuss the matter. Letters from both Whelan and the club secretary to McCarthy were read out, as was McCarthy's reply. It was proposed and seconded that the committee accept McCarthy's apology closing the incident and that both individuals involved should consider the matter closed.

A general committee meeting on 23 April 1928 had been summoned to discuss the case of J.H. McCarthy, who had driven a motor car over a number of greens on the evening of 18 April. A letter had been sent to Mr McCarthy and a reply had been received. It was then proposed and seconded that he be expelled, with three voting in favour and ten against and with one person abstaining. It was then proposed and seconded that he be suspended for six weeks and seriously admonished and warned as to his future conduct. This was passed with eight for and four against. A three-month suspension had also been proposed and seconded but had not been carried. The secretary was then to convey to McCarthy his six-week suspension along with a serious admonishment and warning.[19] The matter was still not closed, however, as at a general committee meeting on 8 May 1928, a letter was read from Mr McCarthy on the matter of his suspension. It was then proposed and seconded that his suspension should cease on 31 May. Seven voted for this course of action and two others proposed that the original suspension stand. In what may have been a related matter, letters were read from three club members and one committee member offering their resignations, following which it was proposed and seconded that all be asked to reconsider their decisions.

Other matters of indiscipline related to the misbehaviour of members resulting in damage to the links or the clubhouse facilities. The club committee on 13 April 1926 drafted a letter to two club members asking them for whatever knowledge they had relating to damage to the lavatories. On 11 May 1926, a general committee meeting received letters from Messrs Dunne and Sullivan denying all knowledge of damage to the lavatory and the committee was to send a suitable letter of acknowledgement. At a general committee meeting on 30 October 1924, the secretary was deputed to write to a member in relation to his language in the presence of some female staff of the club, and to warn that if such behaviour reoccurred, then the committee would have to take definite action on the matter.

In addition to dealing with the behaviour of players and members, the club committee also addressed the conduct of employees, be they caddies or staff working in the clubhouse. One such issue pertained to the sale of golf balls by staff to members. A special general committee meeting heard a letter from J.J. O'Sullivan, outlining how on one occasion he had purchased second-hand golf balls from Sheridan, after which it was decided that a letter be drafted to Sheridan asking for a further explanation on the matter. A general committee meeting of 9 November 1926 discussed the issue and the secretary reported Sheridan's reply, in which he denied the sale of second-hand balls, but his written denial was deemed to be unsatisfactory. The same issue arose at a general committee meeting on 11 October 1927. A Miss K. Sutton reported that she had bought golf balls from an individual who had previously worked as a caddie. This had occurred on the fifth fairway, and it was proposed and seconded that the wrongdoer be interviewed.

Caddies seem to have been suspected of wrongdoing in another incident reported to a general committee meeting on 3 September 1929. The meeting heard of the loss of 11s taken from someone working in the clubhouse, whose clothes were hanging in the engine room. It was stated at the meeting that every effort had been made to trace the culprit from among the caddies who had been present at the time, but without any result. It was then proposed and seconded that the caddy master should prepare a list of undesirable caddies or those deemed unsatisfactory and, as opportunities might arise, the secretary should dismiss them.

The behaviour of the steward on the premises was also a cause for concern. The committee heard of an incident involving the steward in the bar on 9 October 1927, and it was decided that a special general committee was to be held in connection with matter, with the steward being asked to attend. Similarly, a special general meeting on 16 October 1929 dealt with the suspension of the steward for intemperance on a Sunday. He was to be suspended from Monday morning to Wednesday night. This action had been taken after many warnings about the steward's intemperance, especially on the previous weekend and in the previous six months. The committee had decided to give the steward one month's notice rather than one week, so as to allow time to secure accommodation for himself and his family.

LADIES AND JUVENILES IN GOLF CLUBS

From the earliest days of golf in Britain and Ireland, ladies had been to the fore. For example, the Irish Ladies Golf Union was formed in 1893. In the early days of both the Golf Union of Ireland and the Ladies Golf Union, men ran both organisations. Ladies had to form themselves into a branch before applying to affiliate to the Ladies Golf Union of Ireland. Noting competition results, Menton refers to the situation at the turn of the century, when the wives, daughters and sisters of members in golf clubs were playing the game.

At the turn of the century in Cork there is evidence of such golfing activity by women. The *Cork Examiner* of 15 May 1902 referred to the Ladies Monthly Medal Competition at Cork Golf Club, noting in particular the performance of a Miss Hilda Curry, 'Considering the short time Miss Curry is at the games this is an excellent performance, and promises well for greater prowess.'[20]

On 24 February 1902, the *Cork Examiner* included a description of 'Mixed Foursomes', in this case one of the best ever held on the links.[21] Fifteen women had taken part in the first round of the competition and the prize-giving ceremony was described thus, 'The prizes were very handsome ones, presented by a lady member herself, a keen and capable golfer, and the conditions under which handicaps were made were distinctively novel. Both circumstances contributed to making the competition one of more than average interest.' Similarly, the *Cork Sportsman* carried details of the first ladies medal at Muskerry Golf Club for which thirteen ladies entered.

The minute books of the Douglas Club illustrate the role of women in that organisation. A ladies' special general committee meeting had been held subsequent to the general committee meeting of the club on 3 June 1921. Eleven ladies were present and it was decided to collect money for a fund for the 'inside staff'.[22] A letter was read from a Mrs Grey at a general committee meeting on 11 January 1924, recommending alterations in the running of the ladies' section, but it was decided 'to adhere to existing conditions'.[23] When the ladies' branch of the club put a request to a general committee meeting on 30 April 1924 that Magee the greenkeeper would 'start off' their opening meeting, the request was refused.[24]

The Douglas Club allowed membership and use of the links to juvenile players as well. On 1 May 1925, the committee decided that the use of the links be offered to juvenile players – twenty-five places each to both sexes. Their hours of play on the course were to be restricted, to finish at 6p.m. in summer and 5p.m. in winter, with no rights to the pavilion after these hours and with no recourse to the locker room. However, at a meeting on 11 May, it was proposed and agreed that the conditions for juvenile members set at the previous meeting be rescinded. Instead it was proposed that twenty-three juvenile members of each sex be admitted on similar terms as the ladies. The annual subscription for boys was to be £2 2s and for girls, £1 1s. The age limit was to be from fifteen to twenty.

On 28 May, the question of conditions governing juvenile membership was again raised. It was proposed that any of the four juvenile members already proposed who decided to be accepted as full members could join without paying an entrance fee. However, if a juvenile section should be created at a future general meeting of members, then those who had become full members could revert to the juvenile section under the rules governing that section and be refunded any extra subscriptions paid. However, this motion was not seconded and so not pursued. It was then proposed, seconded and passed that the rules committee make provision for rules governing juvenile members, these to be brought before the committee at a general meeting.

ADVERTISING AND TRAVEL

Advertising and travel were closely related from the early days of golf in Ireland, since clubs advertised their links in relation to how they could be accessed by train. Menton refers to the fact that the course at Portrush advertised itself in February 1892, saying that it had been pronounced by prominent players as being one of the best in the United Kingdom. The same advertisement then went on to give details of the price of hotels and travel tickets for those intending using the course. Menton also cites an advertisement from 9 April 1892, which went as follows, 'To golfers and friends commencing on Saturday, 2 April, a fast train will leave Belfast every Saturday at 2.00p.m. for Newcastle, return tickets 3s first class, 2s 6d second class, and 2s third class.' Further south, the Great Southern and Western Railway was granting a special concession to golfers from Dublin to Lahinch 'for one guinea first class return'.

Menton makes the important point that in the early days of golf, courses were laid out not far from railway stations and the early pioneers of golf were seen in red coats at railway stations going to the nearby courses. This was reflected in Cork, where, in the early years of the twentieth century, there was a strong link between the availability of rail facilities and the location of golf courses. When the course at St Ann's Hill, Blarney was referred to in the *Golfing Annual* of 1902/03, it was mentioned that it was situated a quarter of a mile from St Ann's Hill Station on the Muskerry Light Railway.

During the period 1919-1923, there was some disruption to the service on the Cork, Blackrock and Passage Railway, and the Monkstown Club made their links available to members of Cork Golf Club due to the lack of travelling facilities to Little Island. The Monkstown Club used the same railway service, the journey time from the city centre to the course being twenty-five minutes, and specials were run to coincide with important competitions. An entry from the minute book of the Monkstown Club from 10 May 1924 reads, 'The vice-president announced that the Cork Blackrock and Passage Railway Company Ltd had consented to re-issue Golfing Tickets on this line at single fares.'

Similar to advertisements in the North of Ireland regarding Portrush, courses in Cork also promoted their facilities in various publications. The golf links in Clonakilty were mentioned in the *Sportsman's Holiday Guide* of 1897 as being situated within half a mile of the Imperial Hotel in the town.

Golf clubs also used the press to advertise special functions. The *Cork Evening Echo* of Friday 19 January 1934 carried an advertisement for a whist drive in the Arcadia, which was being held by the ladies' branch of Muskerry Golf Club. A dance was to follow, a combined ticket costing 5s. A ticket for the dance only was 2s 6d. Prizes for the night were on view at M. Roache's, Jeweller, on Patrick Street, where tickets could also be obtained.

Another method of advertising was that employed by Douglas Golf Club, as agreed at a general committee meeting on 3 December 1931. Here, it was proposed and seconded that a notice card giving details of the club's green fees be distributed to hotels and clubs in the city. In addition, there was a market for golf accessories and various retailers in the city advertised what they had available for those taking up the game. The *Cork Constitution* of 27 November 1894 carried the following advertisement:

High-class Goods at Moderate Prices

Just Received One Case of Golf Capes
Bought Under Price, Selling at Cost
5s 11d to 27s 6d.

D. Mullane
Ladies and Children's Outfitters
58 Patrick Street, Cork.[25]

The *Cork Examiner* of 10 April 1914 carried an advertisement from J.W. Elvery & Co. Ltd, who were giving special terms to golf clubs on items such as waterproofs and rainproofs.

COMMITTEE ISSUES

Members of Douglas Golf Club were elected by ballot to the club's general and subcommittees. At the AGM at the Imperial Hotel on 27 January 1922, the general committee of ten was elected by ballot. Sixteen individuals were then proposed for election to the green committee, with six being eventually elected. At the AGM of the club on 29 January 1924, six members were elected to the general committee, with five spoiled voting papers. Six more members were elected to the green committee and thanks were given to Williams and Heffernan with great applause. At the AGM on 28 January 1925, eight names were proposed for the 'A' committee and sixteen names for the 'B' committee, after which a list of names was compiled of those who were elected.

The question of whether committee meetings should be held monthly or fortnightly was also raised. After several members had given their views, the meeting recommended that general committee meetings be held fortnightly rather than monthly. At the AGM on 14 February 1928, there was a suggestion that nominations for the committee be posted in the clubhouse by the end of each year, so that more members might be put forward for election. There was also a precedent for co-opting members to the committee. On 11 August 1925, at a general committee meeting, it was proposed that R. McKnie be co-opted as member of the general committee. It was also proposed and seconded that M. English be elected as secretary and that Cussen be asked to accept the position of honorary assistant secretary, to be present at all committee meetings but without the power to vote.

As well as the general committee, there were a number of other subcommittees within golf clubs to deal with matters delegated to them. A writer on the Monkstown Club cites the following proposal from the club minute book, 'That a subcommittee be formed to deal with entertainments in the Castle and that no intoxicative liquors be sold by the club at these entertainments'.[26] Similarly, Douglas appointed subcommittees to deal with the annual dance. It was decided at a special general committee meeting on 6 October 1925 that a subcommittee be formed to carry out arrangements for the dance, the committee to include two ladies nominated by the ladies' committee.

The green committee had an important role within the Douglas Club, since it had responsibility for competitions, cups and the setting of handicaps. The green committee that met on 19 September 1924 discussed a circular sent from the secretary of the Munster Branch of the Golfing Union of Ireland on the adjusting of handicaps. The committee discussed how other clubs had acted on the circular and decided that if all handicaps were scrutinised and adjusted according to the ability of members, instead of by the Hon. Secretary, then the interests of the game would be better safeguarded. Accordingly, the handicaps were adjusted and the revised list posted in the pavilion. When the general committee met on 8 February 1927 and discussed a club championship cup, it accepted the recommendation of the green committee that a specimen cup to the value of £15 be obtained for selection at the next meeting.

There could also be problems with members of the committee. According to the club president, a general committee meeting on 7 April 1931 was summoned because of investigations he had made. These investigations showed that the secretary had been 'very lax' in his duties, had not made the arrangements for the general meeting, and that nothing had been done towards the arranging of the books for 1930. At a general committee meeting on 8 April 1931, the president again referred to things being 'in a very chaotic condition', owing to the neglect by the secretary of his duties.[27] The secretary had not given a satisfactory explanation and it was decided to circularise suppliers to send in all their accounts for audit purposes to 31 December 1930. At another meeting on 20 April 1931, the club president was authorised to act on behalf of the committee until a new secretary was appointed. It was then proposed that a paid secretary be appointed and that this selection be left to the 1931 general committee.

FINANCES OF GOLF CLUBS

A look at the finances of golf clubs in Cork necessitates examining the sources of income of those clubs, especially in the context of initial set-up costs. It also involves looking at the various ways in which clubs raised money and at their ordinary expenses. The example of Douglas Golf Club will receive particular attention, but there are references in the literature of other clubs that give some detail on their expenses and how these were met.

When the Monkstown Club was formally opened in 1908, the committee had spent 'just' £300 on setting up the club and links.[28] Ted Whitaker, recalling his membership in the 1920s, said the club always seemed to be in debt, though there was a bank manager on the club committee. When the club wanted to replace a horse-drawn gang mower with a new gang mower and tractor, 'a number of us', according to Whitaker, were able to buy the new equipment for £130, though he also notes that the committee could not agree on how to raise the money, and that it 'was on our personal guarantee' that the money was raised.

The minute books of the Douglas Club provide detailed records of how the club put in place the financial arrangements to rebuild the clubhouse following its burning during the Troubles. As we have read, at one of the first meetings of the club's general committee in the Imperial Hotel on 31 May 1921, it was proposed and seconded that if a proposed loan per gentleman in cash did not raise the amount which the committee should deem sufficient to begin the reconstruction of the club, then the existing club would be wound up voluntarily and a new club formed from those members who were prepared to subscribe.

A special general meeting was held on the same date. Here it was proposed that suggestions on the reconstruction of the club would be put to the committee, following which a circular would go to each member. This circular was also to advertise a further meeting that would decide on replies received. This meeting would then vote on which methods would be adopted to raise the necessary money.

Suggestions were then outlined to the meeting as to how the rebuilding of the clubhouse might be financed. The first suggestion was that a levy of £10 be collected from each member (ladies excepted), to be payable in cash and to be repaid in full at 5 per cent. In the interim, the claims of members leaving Cork and resigning membership were to have priority, these claims to be paid in interim out of the yearly profit of the club. A second suggestion put forward was that a loan be obtained on the best terms possible from one of the local banks. This amount was to be covered by a guarantor list signed by every member of the club. The interest on the loan was to be paid by raising the subscriptions of members 'proportionately sufficient' to meet the extra demand on the revenue of the club. There is no clear statement in the minute books as to which course was pursued. However, it does seem that the club decided to procure a loan, since at a general committee meeting on 3 June 1921, it was proposed and seconded that the club secretary ask J.G. Crosbie and J.C. Greene to go to the Munster and Leinster Bank to obtain terms of a loan, this proposal being passed unanimously.

At a green committee meeting on 17 July 1924, various estimates for building the clubhouse were discussed, varying from £4,000 to £1,000. It was decided provisionally to 'take the lowest option', pending the procurement of securities and the assent of a solicitor.[29] At the AGM at the Imperial Hotel, the repayment of loans to the club by members was discussed. It was proposed that subscriptions be raised by 10s to form a fund, but this proposal received no seconder. At a general committee meeting on 22 February 1925, it was agreed that a number of individuals, as well as the treasurer and secretary of the club, were to meet Mr Scott of the Munster and Leinster Bank to discuss an overdraft of £1,500.

For the years of the early and middle 1920s, the club's minute books detail some of the forms of expense incurred in rebuilding the clubhouse and relaying the course. At one of the meetings of the general committee in 1921, it was decided to transfer the fire policy on club premises from Guardian Assurance Company and also to renew the club's third-party liability policy. On 26 January 1922, it was proposed and seconded that the amount of the public liability policy be increased to £2,000. A general committee meeting on 19 February 1924 decided on paying an order for members' claims and furniture, a sum of £2,985 3s 6d.

At a special general committee meeting on 8 October 1924, it was agreed that the course architect, Dr McKenzie, should be asked to inspect the club links and to furnish a report, the costs not to exceed £10. The general committee of the club heard at a meeting on 22 September 1925, in regard to the cost of course reconstruction up to 17 September of that year, that the amount paid out in weekly wages was £419 9s 6d. The monthly accounts at a general committee meeting on 11 May 1926, which amounted to £159 5s 8d, included a final payment to the Bristol Golf Construction Company, less the cost of damage to tools.

Another major issue relating to the finances of Douglas Golf Club concerns attempts by the club to claim money in compensation for damage to the club premises during the Troubles. In November 1923, it was agreed that the club president, M. McSwiney, and M. English should proceed to Dublin to interview the Financial Secretary to the Treasury, relative to the compensation claim arising out of the burning of the club pavilion in May 1921, including the loss of 'personal effects' of members.[30]

On 7 March 1924, the club secretary was instructed to get advice from the club solicitor regarding payments of certain compensation claims (which had already been paid from other sources) to claimants, and to get a decision on the question of the ownership of the money not being claimed. The issue was an ongoing one, as the club secretary was to see the club solicitor on the non-payment of compensation from the treasury later that year.

The secretary of the golf club incurred expenses carrying out the duties of the post. When the first annual meeting of the Monkstown Club was held in 1908, the secretary of the club was appointed at a superannuation of £20. At a general committee meeting of Douglas on 11 December 1928, the secretary was asked to withdraw from the meeting temporarily and the meeting then decided to give him a £50 cheque as reimbursement for various expenses he incurred during the year. In turn, the secretary thanked the members 'most sincerely' for the 'kindly act'.[31]

SOCIAL ASPECT OF GOLF IN CORK

In discussing the social aspect of golf in Cork, one may consider the matter in terms of how golf was associated with a certain social class, as well as how it facilitated a social life for those who were members of clubs. There were, for example, rules regulating the mode of dress, listing what was acceptable for those who wanted to socialise within the golf club setting. As Menton, in his history of golf in Ireland, remarks in a chapter entitled 'Public Golf in Ireland':

> The origin of the game is shrouded in mystery. Undoubtedly the early expo-
> nents were the more affluent members of society. However, as the pioneers
> mostly played on commonages or other open spaces, no class of citizen was
> precluded from following this leisure pastime. This public golf must be as old
> as the game itself.[32]

Yet, despite attempts to increase the number of public courses in the early years of the twentieth century, Menton notes that there was not a mention of public golf for a further thirty years.

Those who have written histories of the game of golf in Ireland have noted its link with a particular social class. Ironically, Menton alludes to the fact that when golf was being played in the early 1880s at the Royal Belfast Club, the game of golf was regarded with ridicule by the 'entire community'.[33] Menton also notes that many of the landed gentry laid out a green on their demesnes, some of these first links remaining private courses.

In Cork there are a number of references from different sources to the links between golf and the better-off members of society. The historian of the Monkstown Golf Club notes how membership of the club in the early years was drawn from the middle and upper classes, who were generally involved in the business life of the city through banking, the legal profession or varying commercial enterprises. The Monkstown Golf historian further notes that 'quite a number' of the club's membership belonged to yachting and rowing clubs in the Cork Harbour area, such as the Cork Harbour Rowing Club and the Royal Munster Yacht Club. In the inter-war period the majority of the Monkstown members were still upper and middle class.

The matter of dress also indicated a certain social tone. In the 1920s, a member of the Monkstown Club could not enter the club bar without a collar and tie, and if a member did not conform, he could expect to be reprimanded by the committee. In the 1930s, members were not allowed to appear in the club bar dressed in sportswear; a collar, tie and jacket were expected. Douglas also decided on a club blazer and tie, but at a general committee meeting it was decided not to adopt particular colours.

In Douglas, the club dance was another part of the social life of members.

Golfers pose before the clubhouse: note the presence of women. (Image courtesy of *Irish Examiner*)

The holding of a dance in the Arcadia before Christmas was among matters discussed at a special general committee meeting on 6 October 1925. It was proposed and seconded that the matter be deferred for further consideration. Later in the meeting the issue was discussed again and it was proposed and seconded that only one public dance be held in a year. It was then proposed and seconded that a public dance be held in the club pavilion on Saturday 31 October, the charge to be 5s for gents and 3s 6d for ladies. Members were to have the privilege of inviting two guests, and dancing was to be from 9p.m. to 2.30a.m. It was also proposed and seconded that a subcommittee be formed to carry out the arrangements, this committee to include two ladies nominated by the ladies' committee.

In April 1926, the committee was informed that the club dance held on St Patrick's Eve had raised approximately £60, and it was proposed and seconded that a dance be held after the April Monthly Fixed Foursomes. In October of that same year, it was agreed that an extension of the licence should be obtained for a dance on 23 October, after the mixed foursomes competition.

FACILITIES OF GOLF CLUBS

From the earliest years of golf in Cork, care was taken to establish facilities to allow players and members to socialise, as well as to prepare for their rounds of play. The *Belfast Newsletter* of 9 July 1896 noted that at Trabolgan, East Cork, a clubroom had been secured at the course, along with board and lodging. The *Irish Field* of 25 September 1909 reported that at Douglas good progress was being made on the new links and clubhouse. Clubs also had to ensure adequate maintenance of such facilities. At one of the first meetings recorded in the minute books of Douglas in 1921, a decision was reached to purchase stoves for heating new huts in the caddy shed.

Because of the previously mentioned burning of the original Douglas clubhouse, much of the 1920s was devoted to the building and furnishing of the new club pavilion. In the interim, the members used rooms at various hotels, and at the AGM of the club on 27 January 1922, a vote of thanks was passed to J.G. Cosgrave for the use of a special room at the Metropole Hotel (although this particular meeting was held at the Imperial Hotel). On 7 March 1924, the club committee sat for a 'considerable time' in approving the draft plans for the new pavilion, and instructions were given to proceed with same. On 11 May 1925, it was proposed that the tea room be stocked and polished and that lino and/or other materials were to be purchased for the lounge, committee room and the accounts office. The same meeting resolved to get lent-wood Austrian chairs and tables on 'best terms' and to have polished tops 'of Canary or other wood'.[34] On 15 June, the club committee sought to ensure that extra accommodation be provided for the steward's family, while other extra accommodation was to include a ladies' room, a hall, kitchen and bar. In February 1927, an enquiry was to be made from a local brush manufacturer as to the cost of boot cleaners for the back and front door entrances of the clubhouse. In June of the same year, a sum of approximately £40 was to be spent on forty additional lockers. Finally, on 10 November 1931, the committee decided to put oak over the mantelpiece, with the names of the captains since 1916.

More equipment had to be acquired to maintain the links of the club; in 1921, for example, a horse was to be purchased to help maintain the links at Douglas. By the mid-1920s the club was considering the purchase of a tractor, though at a general committee meeting on 22 May 1925 a decision on the tractor was deferred, pending final approval by the committee. At an earlier meeting, a J.F. Collins had reported on new terms for a triplex mower and stated that Messrs Shanks were prepared to deliver one to Cork for £125 minus 15 per cent. The committee decided to accept this offer if they could not get better terms. The subject of the tractor purchase was discussed again at the next committee meeting, when a Mr Scott, representing Fordsons of Cork, was called into the meeting, where he gave the committee an assurance that his firm would send an instructor to teach the groundsman how to drive the tractor. The committee chairman thanked Mr Scott for his offer and suitable terms.

Similarly, in the 1920s the Monkstown Club purchased a mower. Up until then, the course had been cut with a horse-drawn gang mower. At this point, a number of members got together to purchase a new gang mower and tractor for £130. The club committee had not been able to agree on the sum, so it was on the personal guarantee of the members that the money for the purchase was raised.

EMPLOYEES OF GOLF CLUBS

As golf clubs established themselves in Cork, they employed a greater number and variety of employees to attend to the needs of members and players and the care of the course. As early as 1883, *The Field* of 16 June, in describing a golf links four miles from Kinsale, noted that 'there are caddies in plenty to be had'.[35] Caddies were just one group of employees, in addition to golf professionals, those who maintained the course, and also those who worked in catering and bar areas of club pavilions.

From the earliest decades of golf in Ireland, professionals were employed by clubs. However, when the Golfing Union of Ireland was formed, the definition of an amateur golfer as promulgated by the Royal and Ancient of St Andrews was adopted by the Irish Association. This definition went as follows:

> An amateur golfer is a golfer who has never made for sale golf clubs, balls or any other article connected with the game; who has never carried clubs for hire after attaining the age of 15 years, who has not carried clubs for hire at any time within 6 years of the date on which the competition begins; who has never received any consideration for playing in a match or for giving lessons in the game; and who, for a period of five years prior to 1 September 1886, has never received a money prize in any open competition.[36]

Menton notes that many of the larger clubs began to employ professionals as more and more people took up the game, to such an extent that the Irish Professional Golfers' Association was set up in 1911 and administered by the Golfing Union of Ireland. Menton outlines the conditions under which professionals worked when the initial scheme to employ them was introduced. Professionals would be paid £2 per week, with Sundays excluded, and tuition fees were to be retained by the club. These tuition fees were to be not less than 1s per hour. Each club would pay its own professional and the Golfing Union of Ireland would bear any deficit up to a maximum of £1 per week of engagement.

What, then, was the position of golf professionals in Cork? In 1912, the fee for a lesson with the professional in Monkstown was 1s per hour or part thereof. One member remembers that in the 1930s at Monkstown, the golf professional of the day charged the 'enormous sum' of 2s 6d for eighteen holes, which the member noted, 'in retrospect seems quite generous, as the groundsmen earned £1 per week for probably forty-five to fifty hours'.

In the 1920s, Douglas Golf Club was also preoccupied with trying to set the wages of the professional and determining what extra income he was entitled to in addition to his wage. At a club committee meeting on 4 September 1924, the secretary read a letter from the club professional asking to be given the profit from the sale of golf balls. This was granted on the condition that his wages be reduced by the amount of profit he would derive from such sales. Later that same month, J. Sheridan, the professional, wrote a letter to the committee offering a reduction of 10s per week from his wages to compensate the club for the profits he would gain from the sale of golf balls. However, the committee did not deem this sufficient, and the club secretary was instructed to notify the professional accordingly. Sheridan was to retire in 1927, but he wrote a letter to the committee, which was considered on 8 March 1927, in which he asked for the postponement of retirement for six months. However, it was confirmed that he would retire from 1 April. The meeting then discussed the appointment of the new professional. A J. Bailey was to be engaged on probation for two months, his wages to be £2 a week and his fees from lessons to be 2s 6d. Bailey's probationary period was to the satisfaction of the committee, and on 14 June 1927 it was proposed and seconded that the sale of golf balls was to be transferred to Bailey on 1 July. His wages were to be reduced to 5s a week and he was to be informed of the committee's satisfaction with his work. A formal contract was also to be drawn up. At a general committee meeting on 18 September 1931, the club granted a gratuity to the club professional of £2 2s towards his expenses at the Irish Open. Earlier in the month it was proposed and seconded that the wage rates of the professional be increased to £2 per week.

Caddies were other employees whose conditions of work exercised the minds of club committees. As early as 1915, the Monkstown Club minute book records this entry, 'In accordance with agreement come to with the professional, Mrs Hayes to be paid for all Caddies' rounds at 6d per round, no charge to be made to members for caddies' lunches.'[37]

Problems arose with rationing owing to the First World War, and in May 1917, the club committee at Monkstown decided that no one should get more than two ounces of bread at any meal, a measure that should also apply to caddies. How caddies were remunerated in this period at Monkstown is indicated by a minute-book entry on 24 March 1918, which recorded that that 'caddies in future be paid 6d for first round and 5d for each subsequent round and no lunches be given them'.

On 8 May 1930, the committee at Douglas heard a proposal that a deduction of 4d per round be made from the wages of caddies for their lunches, but it was decided that the subject be deferred so that members could 'think over it'.[38] Steps were also taken at Douglas to insure the caddies, presumably from injury, and this insurance was to be with the Guardian Insurance Company at a rate of 6d per annum per member for playing members.[39] The same meeting agreed to supply any number of caddies up to twenty to the Irish Ladies Close

Championship, the caddies to be given the railway fare, the price of lunch and to be guaranteed one round per day.

Douglas also introduced the post of caddy master to supervise and oversee the work of the caddies employed at the club. It was proposed and seconded at a general committee meeting on 27 August 1925 that the secretary interview 'M. Power's brother' to invite him to accept the post of caddy master at the wage of £1 per week.[40] On 6 October of that year, a vacancy for the post of caddy master was discussed. A large number of applications had been received by the committee. It was proposed and seconded that the applicants Moorcroft, O' Driscoll and Holmes be interviewed on Saturday 17 October at the secretary's office. Messrs Musgrave, Collins and Housely were empowered to select the 'most suitable man'.[41] It was decided that the hours of work of the caddy master were to be Sundays from 9a.m. to cessation of play, weekdays from 10a.m. to cessation of play, and Thursdays off. Also, detailed instructions with regard to the arrangement of caddies were to be given to the secretary.

When on 14 May 1929 the committee discussed matters relating to the outdoor staff at the club, a need to employ girl caddies was discussed. The principle of such a step was approved, owing to the shortage of boys. The club went ahead with the move and on 3 September the club secretary was directed to provide sanitary accommodation for girl caddies and to allow for their 'housing in hut'.[42]

A general committee meeting was held after the AGM, on 29 April 1931 at the Imperial Hotel, at which a 'lightning' strike by the caddies was discussed. People were deputed to interview the caddies and to do whatever was deemed necessary to solve the strike. On 25 May, it was put into the secretary's hands to solve the strike; one suggestion made was that caddies should have been numbered and drawn. This suggestion was adopted. In a move that seems to have been related to the strike, the meeting decided to call the attention of the members to the maximum tip of 6d, as suggested by the committee, and it was decided that this be put up on individual members' lockers. A list was then drawn up of caddies who were not to be re-employed in the future, owing to 'inattention' and 'impertinence'.[43] Another controversial note was struck with the caddies on 15 January 1931, when the committee addressed the action of Revd Fr Murphy of Douglas, who had prevented five caddies from working for the club. It was decided that no action be taken until a reply was received from Dr Sexton, the Dean.

There were also problems with ground staff who maintained the course at

Douglas. On 2 December 1923, a subcommittee was to enquire into a dispute between the groundkeeper and groundsman. However, other references to employees of golf clubs who worked on the links were usually in connection with the wages and conditions of work. During the First World War, the greenkeeper at Monkstown was given a war bonus of 3s a week. At one of the first meetings of the Douglas Club after the Troubles, the committee reduced staff wages, with one individual receiving £1 per week and another £2 per week. Another groundsman was to be dismissed; these arrangements were to come into force from the following Saturday. On the following October, an individual named McCauliffe was contracted to cut the rough at 30s per week as per the green committee's instructions.

Wage increases were given to groundsmen at Douglas during the 1920s and 1930s. A general committee meeting on 10 August 1926 accepted an application from two groundsmen for a wage increase; it was proposed and seconded that their wages be raised 3s a week each. On 21 August 1928, the wages of the two general groundsmen were to be increased by 2s. Presumably because of the summer holidays, the general committee on 10 July 1928 approved the appointment of a boy for six to seven weeks. When the green committee met on the same date, it recommended to the general committee that an extra boy be sanctioned for six weeks or 'thereabouts'.[44]

The Douglas Club also employed a steward in the clubhouse to oversee the bar and other facilities, though there were difficulties in retaining individuals in the position. At a general committee meeting on 26 May 1924, the committee dealt 'at length' with the position of Power, the steward, and other staff.[45] It would seem that there had been personal differences between Power and the house staff, because on 14 July 1924 the secretary notified the committee that the differences with Power and the house staff had been 'adjusted', and that there had been a revised list of price changes agreed for catering.[46]

The hours of work for the steward were not always attractive enough to keep the post holder in the position. A general committee meeting on 10 May 1927 heard a letter from the steward, who complained that 'the hours of working are very long and the pay is small for my turnover'.[47] His resignation was accepted, but representatives agreed to meet him if he would reconsider his position. Full plenary powers were to be given to this deputation to deal with the steward. At a special general meeting the following week, the steward had the opportunity to tell the committee in detail of his grievances, although he had, at this juncture, withdrawn his resignation. He told the committee that the staff worked fifteen hours a day and, when questioned about this, he referred to how members often left the club at 11.30p.m. He also referred to additional work, such as having to issue cards in the evening and selling clubs. In addition, people sent caddies to him to get golf balls, while he himself was liable for payment. Members were often asked for 6*d* and 'expressed themselves freely' when it was demanded.

The committee addressed the issues raised. It was decided that the inner servery, bar and kitchen be out of bounds to members. On the substantive issue of wages, however, the committee could not see its way to giving an increase and other issues raised by the steward did not warrant any changes. The committee then decided to send for the steward and to assume plenary powers to make a final arrangement with Power as regards his resignation.

The following week, again at a special general committee meeting, the steward Mr Power informed the subcommittee that he was leaving his post. It was then proposed and seconded that advertisements be placed in the *Cork Examiner, Cork Evening Echo, The Irish Times* and *Irish Independent* for a manageress for catering and also for indoor staff. Prospective applicants were to apply in writing, including testimonials, and were to state what salary they expected.

The account of the organisational structures and social dimensions of golf in Cork presented in this chapter would seem to confirm the reasonable assumptions made regarding the predominantly bourgeois character of the membership and lifestyle of the Cork golf clubs. The officers, the rules and regulations, the costs incurred and the social milieu all indicate clearly the middle-class and monied basis of this particular leisure activity. The institutional links with banks and other white-collar and business occupations are further confirmation of this social basis of golf in Cork. In this, it is likely – from the secondary historical literature on the game – that the Cork experience is consistent with the situation elsewhere in Ireland throughout this period.

V

TENNIS

In terms of information available for the study of tennis in Cork from 1880 to 1930, the minute books of the Sunday's Well Boating and Tennis Club constitute the major source, supplemented by the local press. These minute books give an insight into the workings of a tennis club in Cork for the time period and, as we shall see, reveal the tensions that could occur both internally and with outside bodies.

However, to begin, an overview of this particular club's early history can be found in a history of the Mardyke by Richard Cooke. Cooke states that the club was founded in 1899, shortly after the Sunday's Well Regatta and Water Carnival. The club was helped by the regatta committee's organisers in leasing a plot of ground alongside the Mardyke Walk. The first Sunday's Well Regatta had been held on Monday 25 July 1853 and it was subsequently held annually for the residents of Sunday's Well, and what Cooke refers to as the 'city's upper crust'.[1] Cooke also makes the point that many of the residents of Sunday's Well had boathouses and piers erected at the bottom of their gardens. The regatta had consisted of various boat and other competitions, though because the regatta was a semi-private affair, it had tended to lapse. Boating was a major activity among club members in the early days and, according to Cooke:

> A regular sight on the river was a gentleman under a straw boater dressed in white shirt and blazer, rowing his wherry (light boat) leisurely upon the water in the hush of a summer's evening as his lady companion sat at the rear under the parasol held by one hand, while the other patted the Lee.[2]

Bowling was very popular among the ladies and elder members, and from 1918 to 1953 annual club competitions were held in the sport. Visitors from cross-channel naval vessels and teams from Limerick, Dublin, Belfast and other counties participated. There were also visits from teams in garrisons stationed in the county. In relation to tennis, Cooke says that the club had five grass courts laid out after the Cork Exhibition.

TENNIS IN THE LOCAL PRESS

In the 1880s and 1890s the press in Cork began to carry details of local tournaments as well as advertising tennis attire and equipment. As early as 1886 the *Cork Examiner*, in an article under the heading 'Lawn Tennis: Captain Rushbrooke's Prize', gave details of the day's play. The gentlemen's singles were played on a Saturday and the attendance was 'as usual large'.[3] In the morning, extra chairs were placed on the grass surrounding the courts and after the arrival of trains and boats from Newport, every chair was occupied. In the evening, Ms Eileen Terry appeared in the grounds to present the prizes, after which a supper was held. The same article noted the New York press's remarks about how popular the game of tennis had become in Australia.

The same tournament (The Rushbook Lawn Tennis tournament) was given coverage in the *Cork Examiner* on 12 August 1895. The tournament had come to a close on the previous Saturday. The gentlemen's doubles had to be postponed until Monday 19 August, as the gentlemen could not attend on the Saturday. The article remarked that 'at periods throughout the day play was interrupted by the disturbed state of the elements', but 'there was a large and fashionable attendance' and the entries and attendance were up on previous records.[4]

In July 1897, the tennis section of the *Cork Examiner* referred to the Cork Lawn Tennis Tournament, describing it as the 'most important tennis tournament of the year and the most splendid social festival'.[5] In July 1906, details were given in the same newspaper of the Blackrock Tennis Tournament, which was to include the following competitions: Gents Handicap Singles, Gents Open Singles, Gents Doubles, Mixed Doubles, and Ladies Doubles. It is an indication of the growth of the game that there were various confined tournaments, such as handicap singles.

The local press also confirms the playing of the game in Cork in so far as it carried advertisements for playing equipment and attire, such as tennis shoes. In September 1889, Robert Day & Sons advertised a service whereby tennis shoes could be resoled at a cost of 5s 6d per pair, which would take two days. In July 1890, the *Cork Examiner* carried an advertisement for the summer sports of cricket and tennis by Robert Day & Son of Patrick Street, saying it had the 'Largest Stock in the South of Ireland'.[6] In June 1894, the same firm, in an advertisement under the heading 'Tennis', advertised its 'Unrivalled Challenge' Bat, describing it as the 'Best Value Made', while its practice bat was 'exceptional value', with hundreds to choose from. Under the name Robert Day & Son were the words 'club contractors' and the piece also advertised special terms for clubs. J.W. Elvery & Co. was another shop which sold tennis products at the turn of the century and it was located at Elephant House at 78 Patrick Street. The firm had hundreds of racquets to select from, such as Dowling's, E.G.M.'s, Doherty's Rivals, and Posser's (which were presumably the brand names).

Women tennis players, suitably attired. (Image courtesy of *Irish Examiner*)

MEMBERSHIP ISSUES

The question of membership of Sunday's Well Boating and Tennis Club can be studied from a number of viewpoints. First there is the question of the size of membership from the turn of the century and whether it grew during the first decades of the twentieth century. Secondly, there is the issue of who became members and the procedures adopted for accepting them. Finally, there is the question of whether they had the same difficulty as other kinds of clubs in getting subscriptions.

The AGMs of the club at the beginning of the century point to a membership of between 150 and 200 people. At the club's second AGM, on 17 January 1902, the secretary's report noted that the club had had a membership of 116 at the beginning of the previous year which rose to 185, and that it then stood at 173 due to 'withdrawals and defaulting subscribers'.[7] At the following year's AGM it was noted that, for the previous year, the number of members had increased from 173 to 181, but that at the time of the meeting there were 170 members due to withdrawal of membership and absentee members. However, twenty years later the numbers had increased substantially. In January 1922, a motion was passed at the AGM limiting the membership to 320 and decreeing that a waiting list be created. This upper limit on membership was reached in June of that year. The same meeting also decided that a printed notice be put up on the billiard room, bar and card-room notifying members that the roll of membership as fixed at the last general meeting was now full. Any other name handed into the secretary for membership, if approved and passed, was to be placed on a waiting list.

As regards admitting new members, there were procedures whereby a vote was taken by the committee to admit individuals to the club. For example, at a committee meeting on 15 September 1905, a ballot was declared, with one spoilt paper and five members elected. In January 1911, the club committee re-elected Mr Walter Purcell and, though only three voted with no spoilt papers, a ballot was declared and all proposed for membership were admitted. In April of that year, several names were handed in and the club secretary was ordered to post them up.

The question of exactly how members were to be elected was discussed at a special committee meeting on 27 January 1922. With regard to the ballot committee, it was proposed and seconded that no member of the committee or ballot committee should propose or second a candidate for membership. Four other individuals were put up for membership at the same meeting, but it was decided that these names were not to be posted pending consideration by the committee, which was to be called to discuss the name of a Frank Dooley. At the following ballot committee meeting on 7 February, it was proposed and seconded that Mr Dooley's name be put up for ballot. It was then proposed and seconded that the secretary send the names of candidates for membership to members of the ballot committee seven full days before a meeting was called. Finally, in 1923, while five names were put up on the notice board, the question of the membership of a Dr Gusani arose. Captain Harte was to hand the nomination paper to the secretary. There was also a reference to a F.W.D. Good, under which it was decided that the secretary was to write and state that there were to be no vacancies for a long time.

From a social point of view, it is interesting to note whether certain professions and occupational groups were given special exemptions and advantages by the tennis club in terms of membership. Firstly, there were instances of certain individuals being given honorary membership. At a meeting in April 1902, it was decided that Mr A. Fowler be made an honorary member of the club during his stay in Cork. Similarly, at a committee meeting in June 1904, a letter was read from Mr W.J. Lawrence, accepting honorary membership of the club. Mr Lawrence had been counsel for the club in a court case with the Cork Exhibition.

It was proposed and seconded that his letter be entered in the minutes. It read:

Charlotte Quay,
Cork.

Sincere thanks for the honour they have conferred on me. I feel they have formed far too flattering an estimate of my services and accorded to me a favour altogether exceeding my deserts.[8]

Similar to Cork County Cricket Club, the members of the British army and navy were interested in joining Sunday's Well Boating and Tennis Club. While we have already noted the procedures in place to accept applications for membership, an exception was made for the British forces, as can be seen in the May 1905 minutes of the Sunday's Well Club. At a committee meeting that month, notice of a motion was given by Mr Donegan that officers of the navy, army, and Indian and foreign colonial services temporarily residing in the Cork district be admitted without ballot. Such officers would be proposed by one member and seconded by another, and they would pay an annual subscription of £1 1s. In 1914, provision was made for members of the club who were fighting in the First World War. In December 1918, it was resolved that any member of the club who had left to join 'His Majesty's Forces' were to be put on a waiting list.[9]

As regards the medical profession, honorary membership for certain periods was granted, as instanced in June 1911. At a committee meeting on 12 June, the club secretary was instructed to write to Dr Cotter, the president of the Irish Medical Association, extending the privileges of membership of the club to members of that association during their stay in Cork. Douglas Golf Club extended similar privileges to members of the same association.

However, there seem to have been some problems with regard to bank employees joining the club, in relation to whether such employees could join together without having to pay the admission fee. At a committee meeting on 1 December 1908, a letter was read from a W. Sergeant, from a bank, on the question of fourteen members of his staff joining the club. The club secretary was ordered to write to Mr Sergeant and point out to him that, as other banks paid the entrance fee, the committee could not see their way to waive it.

In May 1915, the club secretary informed the committee that approximately fifteen members of the Munster and Leinster Bank were anxious to join the club without having to pay the entrance fee. The secretary was ordered to get the names of those wishing to join, from whom the committee would expect a cheque for the total number joining, this to be paid in a lump sum. At the end of the month, a letter was read from a W. Dixon, objecting to the admission of fifteen members of the Munster and Leinster Bank staff without payment of the entrance fee. After some discussion it was proposed and seconded that the fifteen members of the Munster and Leinster Bank be admitted without payment of the entrance fee. When a vote was taken, there were an equal number of votes both for and against the proposition, following which, a Mr W. J. Crosbie withdrew his proposition and the secretary was to convey to the applicants that the club could not forego payment of the entrance fee. Staff of banks continued to be admitted to the club, presumably with the club insisting they pay a fee. In September 1916, the question of club membership of the Provincial Bank was discussed by the committee. The secretary was to see Mr W. O'Leary and inform him that if the Provincial Bank was willing to accept the same terms as the Bank of Ireland, then the committee would be willing to accept them as members.

Similar to other clubs discussed in this study, the Sunday's Well Club had difficulty in getting subscriptions paid or renewed by new or existing members. A general meeting in August 1904, called to discuss a court action between the club and the Cork Exhibition, heard how the tennis club had outstanding subscriptions amounting to £50. At a committee meeting on 19 December 1911 the secretary read the statement of accounts and details of the balance sheet, from which the secretary noted that 37 guineas were due in subscriptions and entrance fees on 30 November.

In November 1903, the secretary was asked to write to defaulting members. This action was also necessary in the years that followed. At the end of 1904 there was a call at a committee meeting for the secretary to write to defaulting members, asking them to send in their subscriptions before the AGM, which was scheduled for 15 December. In January 1905, it was proposed and seconded that a circular be sent to members asking for their subscriptions. The following April, it was proposed and seconded at a committee meeting that a circular be sent out to members asking them to pay their subscriptions as soon as possible, so as to help the club save interest on an overdraft.

In the minute books of the club for the following July, one finds an example of how the club dealt with a member who wanted some leniency on the payment of his subscription. After this individual's letter had been read, a letter was to be sent back to the applicant, containing the following, 'to consider you liable for subscriptions for 1904/1905 and again direct me to apply for same. Under the circumstances you cannot be put up as a monthly member.'[10] It was then proposed and seconded that Mr Walter Madden be told that M. McDonnell could not be put up as a monthly member and that his name be erased from the book.

In December 1907, there was a discussion at a committee meeting on subscriptions in arrears, after which it was decided that a circular be sent out to defaulting members and that in future a circular would be sent to members quarterly. The following February, the club resolved that the secretary would be authorised to inform members in arrears that, unless their subscriptions were paid before the next meeting, then their names would be removed. Another form of sanction, which was suggested at a committee meeting in 1921, was that the names of defaulters be read out at the next meeting.

At the end of 1921, the club was again dealing with outstanding subscriptions. On 18 November, it was resolved that a detailed list of subscriptions due was to be brought before a special committee meeting the following week. By December, the club had drafted a letter to be sent to all the members, which read, 'I have been directed by my committee to apply to you for subscription as set out ... which are very much overdue. Also kindly acquaint me if it is your wish to continue with membership of the club.'[11] The club also drafted a letter to defaulting newly elected members, 'Following our notification that you are duly elected member of this club, my committee are surprised to note that your subscription entrance fee which was due at election has not yet been paid and they request me to apply for same. Much early attention would [sic] obliged.'

RULES OF THE CLUB

At the second AGM, in January 1902, there was a discussion on the new rules of the club, including a rule on the entrance fee, and another rule was amended so that the period for guest membership was to be one month rather than fourteen days. In March 1902, the club agreed to get 500 copies of the club rules printed by Messrs Guy & Co. for £2 2s 6d.

In February 1922, it was resolved that a subcommittee of three, along with the secretary, were to go into the matter of the rules, have them brought up to date, and have copies printed with the bye-laws included. In addition, a typewritten list of members was to be procured for the committee room, along with a printed list of the rules and bye-laws of the club. In July 1909, a committee meeting decided that no bye-laws of the club could be made, altered or annulled unless notice was given to the secretary, who would notify members of the committee of such a motion in the notice convening the meeting at which the motion was to be moved.

A discussion of the rules of the Sunday's Well Boating and Tennis Club relates substantially to the previously mentioned issue of membership, since the club was continually drawing up or modifying existing rules on procedures to admit new members. In general, such rules on membership related to electoral procedures. In December 1905, the club committee changed club rule fourteen to read as follows, 'In the election of members the committee shall vote by ballot, such a committee to consist of the ordinary and ex-officio members of the committee and five additional members.'[12]

The club minute books contain details of a major discussion on the club rules at the AGM in December 1913. There was notice of a motion handed in to the meeting by a Dr Pearson to change the procedure for the election of members from a committee ballot to a club ballot. The club chairman, in reply to the motion, expressed the view that a good ballot committee was, in his experience, a better means of electing members than a club ballot. In reply Dr Pearson said, 'his whole idea was to throw the question open to discussion' since he thought that it would be possible to 'improve the method at present in use' by the substitution of a club ballot, and he therefore proposed that a club ballot be adopted.[13]

A Mr Donegan contributed to the discussion, saying that as an old member of the club he was 'rather inclined to think a change undesirable'. He referred to the situation some years earlier when the club had changed from a club ballot to a committee ballot, 'and it was a good thing to let well alone'. After further discussion, Dr Pearson withdrew his proposition and it was then decided that a direction be given to the secretary. When he had any application for membership he was to summon the members of the ballot committee, along with the general committee, to decide whether the names should be put up or not.

Because the club had a bar on its premises, rules were drawn up on when it should close and who was entitled to drink. In October 1908, there was a long discussion at a committee meeting on the question of bar times. One member of the committee proposed that the bar should close at midnight and that the steward should notify all members on the premises that lights were to be out at 12.15a.m. However, the proposer eventually withdrew his proposition and it was decided to keep the existing bye-laws in this regard, though it was amended to include members who were also playing cards or billiards. In July 1922, the club committee had rules regarding the opening of the bar on Sunday printed and posted in the bar itself.

In August 1916, the committee ordered that any member taking a bottle of whiskey or any other drink from the club for his convenience be charged. A number of rules were passed in 1917 relating to the bar. In March, due to the 'shortage and difficulty of obtaining liquors', the committee withdrew the privilege enjoyed by members whereby they could take liquors for consumption off the premises.[14] A rule introduced in June meant that any club member who introduced a visitor was to remain on the club premises as long as the guest remained. In December 1917, the following notice was posted up in the club, 'Owing to shortage of liquor supplies the Committee think it advisable for the present that all members should abstain from treating other members in order to conserve our allowance.'[15]

In early January 1918, a temporary measure was introduced for the period of the war, whereby it was to be a rule of the club that no club member was to treat any other member to any excisable drink. The committee was to have the power to rescind or suspend the rule as or when they deemed it expedient. In addition, the club also introduced rules on admittance of dogs[16], cards[17], boats[18] use of rooms[19] and visitors[20].

MATTERS OF DISCIPLINE

The club minutes of the Sunday's Well Club go into some detail as regards incidents where rules of the club were broken or ignored. There were also instances of confrontations involving club members which necessitated the intervention of the committee.

In September 1909, the committee discussed a situation which involved the use of club money for charitable purposes. At the meeting in question it was proposed and seconded that voting one guinea, or any such sum of club money for charity purposes, was without precedence in the club. Since the committee did not have the power to vote money for that purpose, then the committee members should refund this money to the club funds. A Mr Crosbie suggested that if a general meeting of the committee would not sanction what the committee had voted for charitable purposes, then the committee would have to pay this money, since it had exceeded its powers. It was then proposed and seconded that the club committee take upon themselves the payment of a one-guinea subscription to the Poor Children's Excursion Fund voted at the previous meeting. Furthermore, it was decided that a resolution authorising the secretary to subscribe to the Barry Testimonial be rescinded.

In 1922, a serious matter arose which the club had to deal with, namely the conduct of some club secretaries and the inadequate auditing of the club accounts, which raised serious doubts about one secretary's integrity. On 21 February 1922, the club committee held a special meeting to deal with the matter and to discuss their unease with the secretary's conduct. The minutes of the meeting note how it had been resolved to pass a motion in view of the 'very unsatisfactory work of the club by the secretary', whereby if:

> ...the regulations as set down by the auditor and passed by the committee are not strictly carried out they will have no option but to dispense with his services. They have not overlooked his long service to the club and they all the more regret having to come to this decision.[21]

However, rather confusingly, the chairman then suggested that the committee appoint four individuals to meet the secretary on the following day, Wednesday, to inform him of the committee's decision, described in the minutes as a 'foregone conclusion'. The auditor's suggestion, which had the full support of the committee, was also to be conveyed to the secretary. There seems to have been no further mention of the affair in the minutes following those of this meeting.

While in the aforementioned episode it was not made clear from the club minutes exactly how the secretary had failed in his duties, the events of October 1923 point to the club secretary being remiss in accounting for sums of money. At a special meeting called on 26 October 1923, the chairman read a letter from the club auditors detailing the statement of accounts. In reply to the chairman, the auditor stated that since drafting the letter, he had looked up the cash in the secretary's hands and found a sum of £70 15s 6d unaccounted for. When asked for an explanation, the secretary admitted the shortage in cash, but said he would be able to make good the account from certain monies coming to him and with assistance from a friend. His only explanation for using club money was that his necessary expenses were in excess of his income. After some further questions he was asked to retire while the matter would be discussed in his absence. After a 'full discussion', the committee came to the unanimous decision that the explanations offered by the secretary were 'not satisfactory' and he was again asked to come before the meeting. When the secretary returned, the committee informed him of its decision that his explanations were not satisfactory and he was pressed to be more explicit. However, he could add nothing to what he had already said except that there was a further sum of £7 12s to be added to the 'deficiency' for cash received by him in connection with the club tournament. The secretary then handed over the up-to-date club receipts, as he had been directed to do, and was asked to retire while the committee further considered the matter.

The committee again discussed the matter 'from all points' and it was eventually proposed and seconded that in light of 'serious defections' of the secretary, the committee had no alternative but to dismiss him forthwith. In informing the secretary of his decision the chairman was also to notify him that if he desired to have the matter brought before the members of the club, a general meeting would be called for the purpose. Two individuals were to be approached to become joint secretaries of the club to carry out the duties of the secretary pending the appointment of a new one. The decision was made to notify the bank that Hurst had ceased to be secretary and that, until further notice, cheques would be signed by W. Olden or W. Williams instead of W. Hurst. Hurst was then called before the committee and informed of the decision of the committee to terminate his services forthwith under the terms of the decision reached. He was also asked to hand over club keys and papers to the new temporary secretaries and the meeting was then terminated.

As a postscript to the incident, the committee, when meeting on 3 November, debated the question of payment of the secretary's salary for the month of October. It was decided not to pay Mr Hurst the accrued salary to the date of his dismissal. However, an application had been received for the vacant post of secretary. The application from Captain M. Reilly was read and considered. The chairman asked the committee if they had any other names to suggest or had any other suggestions as to the making of an appointment. After some discussion it was proposed and seconded that the application of Captain Maurice Reilly be accepted and he was duly appointed. It was recorded that the appointment would be terminated on a month's notice on either side and duties of the post were also read out.

In March 1902, the club committee turned its attention to an incident involving a member of the committee who was charged by another member with assault. At a committee meeting on 17 March, it was decided that Mr Dorgan was to be written to and asked to explain a charge brought against him by Mr Cooke. In the meantime, the secretary was also to write to the complainant to inform him that the matter was being investigated. The following week, when the committee met again, it heard the contents of the letter from Mr Cooke to the club regarding the 'assault' on him by Mr W. Dorgan. In his letter, he referred to the 'grievous assault on by him by Mr William Dorgan', who was described as a 'member of your committee'.

Mr Cooke, when brought before the meeting, gave details of the incident, which centred on a dispute over the closing of a door because of a draught. He described how Dorgan had hit him on the eye, had cut his nose and broken one of his teeth and had then gone away without passing any remark. Cooke had received a letter of apology from Dorgan the following day, and this was read out at the meeting. Cooke also added that he had brought the matter up after being induced to do so by certain members of the club. Evidence was then heard from other members of the club, which described how Dorgan had wanted to keep the door of the card room open so as to let light into the bar, whereas Cooke had wanted the door closed.

In his description of the incident, Dorgan admitted that he had felt ashamed and sorry about his actions, but in his defence said that Cooke had called him a 'Coal Quay blackguard'. Another member of the club who gave evidence said that after the blow was struck by Dorgan, the remarks of Cooke were 'particularly low'. After hearing all the evidence, it was noted that the committee had adopted certain findings, but these were not found in the minute books.

In 1912, the club committee dealt with a dispute between two members over a game of cards. Mr Gibson had complained that Mr Cook had objected to him joining in a game of cards, in the process of which he called Gibson 'an old man' and said 'that he ought to stay at home'. Gibson had also charged Cook with sitting on the card table with 'felonious intent'.[22] Cook denied this had happened, but did say that during the incident he himself had charged Gibson with making a statement against him which might injure him with his employers, a remark that Gibson would not admit having made. Cook did admit, however, that he may have said that Gibson was an old man and should not come down playing cards. The committee, having heard the evidence, drafted a letter to Cook in which it concluded that Cook's behaviour was 'extremely reprehensible and calculated to create an atmosphere of discord and discomfort that cannot be tolerated'.

The minute books of the club include briefer accounts of other disciplinary incidents. A committee meeting in May 1902 discussed a letter from Mr Fred Dale in reply to a letter from the secretary, and Mr Dale appeared before the committee and corroborated what he had written. It was proposed and seconded that Dale's explanation be accepted and he was to be written to asking him to be more cautious in his observance of the club rules. While the committee accepted Dale's explanation, 'we condemn his demeanour before us this evening as being most disrespectful to the Committee'.[23] An amendment was proposed saying that Dale's explanation was not sufficient and that he be suspended from using the club premises for a week. However, this amendment was not carried and instead the committee took the view that, since it had been Dale's first offence, they were not disposed to take further action.

The following June, the committee dealt with some minor incidents of indiscipline. A Mr McCarthy wrote, explaining the breaking of the lock of the boathouse door. It was proposed and seconded that this explanation be accepted. Two individuals named Mason and Hamilton were censured for not being on duty at the time. Another letter was read from a Mr Dorgan in relation to the breaking of a rule. The committee decided to write to Dorgan to say the committee accepted his explanation but trusted that Dorgan would not let such an incident happen again.

In January 1908, the committee discussed the unauthorised writing of W.J. Cook's name on the Christmas Box List by some member, and the following statement was to be placed in the minute book, 'That we have heard Mr Cook on the subject and express our strong disapproval of the action of the member who put down Mr Cook's name without permission.'[24]

In July 1912, the committee heard of a complaint whereby a member brought a friend, presumably into the club premises, 'who was at the time under the influence of drink'.[25] The secretary was instructed to write to the member in question and intimate to him that if such an incident was to occur again, then the committee would be 'forced to take strong measures'. In June 1914, the committee had a letter read from an individual who admitted to damaging the shop netting by riding a motorcycle but offered to make good the damage. The committee took no action, but informed the individual in question that he was not to ride a bicycle on the grounds in future.

MATTERS OF FINANCE

Like other clubs, the minutes of the Sunday's Well Boating and Tennis Club record the financial expenditure of the club and the payments made to such individuals as employees and club secretaries for their services. We have already noted the rules dealing with membership and subscriptions, and the sometimes difficult task of collecting money owed.

However, what is of most interest is how the club fared in acquiring loans to procure club premises and the mechanisms by which such loans were given by banks to the club. The first instance recorded in the minute books of the club applying for a loan was discussed at a special committee meeting in December 1902. It should be noted at this point that such discussions were occurring against a background of discussions with the Cork Exhibition Committee on the erection of a club premises. (This was to be the subject of a court case and will be given special attention later.)

The meeting did discuss the means by which finance could be raised for any future building. The secretary reported that he had interviewed the manager of the Munster and Leinster Bank, who said the bank would not advance money on the security of the lease alone, but that they would be glad to place a sum of £500 at the disposal of the club on getting approved personal security from members. The question of raising money from other sources was discussed. It was proposed and seconded that two individuals be deputed to ascertain on what terms the Cork Mutual Building Society would advance the money necessary for the building and report to the adjourned meeting.

At a club AGM in the beginning of 1903, the means of raising money to build a clubhouse was again discussed. Mr Haynes, in his contribution to the meeting, felt that £400 would be required to build and furnish a clubhouse. He was of the opinion that money could be raised easily by a few members signing an overdraft, which could be paid off in a few years time. However, the chairman ruled Mr Haynes out of order.

In April 1903, against the background of a dispute with the executive of the Cork Exhibition, the question of security for a new clubhouse was again discussed by the committee. It was proposed and seconded that the club secretary inform the executive of the Cork Exhibition that the club was prepared to lodge a lease or give a legal mortgage. The club committee was of the unanimous opinion that the resolution of the general committee of 30 January, to meet with the executive of the Exhibition on the best terms, entitled the club to authorise the trustees to execute a mortgage of the leasehold interest on the terms suggested. It was then proposed and seconded that three trustees were to be authorised to execute the mortgage and deposit the lease.

In December 1904 and January 1905, the committee of Sunday's Well Boating and Tennis Club were involved in discussions with the Hibernian Bank on acquiring a loan. At a committee meeting on 29 December 1904, the secretary reported that the Munster and Leinster Bank had refused to negotiate a loan of £500 as a security of the club lease. As a result, a deputation from the club had met with the manager of the Hibernian Bank, who was to communicate with his directors and inform the club secretary on the result of these discussions. A letter was read from the manager of the Hibernian Bank stating that the directors of his bank had granted the advance required on his being satisfied as to the recreations of the club. The meeting decided at this point that since a full committee was not present, they would defer 'consideration of this most important matter' until a meeting on 2 January. At the same meeting, the secretary suggested that in order to pay back the loan on the clubhouse, he should take half his present salary until such time as the committee felt it was appropriate to pay the usual amount. It was proposed and seconded that the 'generous offer' of the secretary be accepted.

At the following meeting on 2 January 1905, a letter was read from the manager of the Munster and Leinster Bank on the question of the £500 loan. The committee decided that three trustees, together with the secretary, should meet Hogan, presumably the bank manager, and ask him to explain an aspect of his letter of 22 December. On 13 January, when the committee discussed the loan and the signing of documents, a list of members of the committee was written in the minute books, these individuals consenting to sign the relevant documents.

On 23 January, the committee was in possession of a letter from the manager of the Hibernian Bank, telling of how his directors were willing to make the balance of £500 to be given on the overdraft. But at this stage a problem arose, since one of the club members objected to becoming a guarantor. It was suggested that he be allowed to resign from the committee if his declining to sign the guarantee would in any way embarrass the committee in their negotiations with the bank. It was decided that a Mr Donegan and the secretary would tell the bank that one member of the committee had refused to sign any form of guarantee. However, the bank's terms were accepted by the committee. It was also proposed and seconded that if the bank had any difficulty with the member of the committee refusing to sign, then this member's resignation would be accepted and another member of the committee would be co-opted.

At the following week's meeting, Donegan reported how he and the secretary had waited on a Mr Horgan to discuss the refusal of a committee member to sign the guarantee of the overdraft. He told the meeting that Mr Horgan, presumably from the bank, stated there would be no objection and since Donegan had met Horgan, the form of guarantee had 'come down' and had been signed by the committee.[26] Not surprisingly, the committee also decided to transfer the club account from the Munster and Leinster Bank to the Hibernian Bank.

In 1909, the club were again interested in acquiring a loan, but they must have experienced less trouble this time, as the issue receives less coverage in the minute book. At a meeting in April 1909, the committee decided that the secretary would lodge sufficient money in the bank to take up the guarantee on the lease and that he would also enquire as to what security would be required for a further loan of £300. At a meeting in early May, the committee accepted the terms of the Hibernian Bank and authorised the continuance of the club lease. The committee was to sign the guarantee.

In 1924, the club had occasion to ask for a loan based on the lease and giving a guarantee, and once again there were some problems. At a special committee meeting a letter was read from the trustees indicating their desire to resign their positions and asking the club to nominate persons to whom they could assign the lease of the club premises. In response, the committee instructed the secretary to write to the trustees and inform them that a special committee meeting on fifth instant had decided unanimously that the resignation of the trustees not be accepted. Furthermore, it was the 'earnest request' of the committee that the desire of the trustees to have the matter put on the agenda for the next general meeting be reconsidered.[27]

A special general meeting in March 1924 was informed that the Hibernian Bank would advance the money required for an extension of the club, on lodging the lease with the bank. In addition, the club was to lodge a book of all club rules along with a resolution from the committee. There is also included in this minute entry a reference to a resolution of trustees which may also have been required. A vote of confidence was then passed to the trustees, though a letter of resignation was read from one of the trustees, who was elected an honorary member of the club. At a meeting on 11 March, it was resolved that the trustees be authorised to lodge the lease at the bank as security for an overdraft of £1,400 in connection with alterations to the club as decided at the special general meeting called for the purpose on 7 March. The meeting also elected another trustee to replace the individual who had resigned.

However, there were problems with this arrangement with the Hibernian Bank. At a special committee meeting on 25 April 1924, the club secretary read a letter from the directors of the bank asking for approved guarantees to cover the advance of £1,400 in addition to what had been offered by the club on the Cork Club premises. The meeting discussed the matter at length, after which two committee members and the secretary were to draft a reply. This draft reply stated that the committee did not see their way to sign any guarantees and they considered the security already offered to be sufficient. The reply also pointed out that the circumstances referred to when the committee had previously given personal guarantees were very different to those now existing, and the club requested a further reply from the bank by 1 May. There is no further documentation on the outcome of this impasse.

In terms of the finances of the club, there are other issues worth noting. There were, for example, the amounts passed to the secretary for his services and expenses. We have already noted how, in one instance, the club secretary decided to forego his salary to help the club. The following are some instances from the club minutes of the amounts passed to the secretary. On

21 April 1902, a cheque for £5 0s 2d was passed to the secretary for the April accounts and salary of the secretary for the month. On 30 June of that year, a cheque for over £7 was passed for that month's expenses and the salary of the secretary. At the beginning of August, a cheque for £3 2s 4d was passed to the secretary for the July accounts along with the secretary's salary.[28] On 13 October 1902, a cheque amounting to £6 6s 6d was passed to the secretary for the September accounts and the secretary's salary.

However, after a number of years, the gratuity being paid to the secretary came under review. In January 1913, a meeting had been called, as the chairman explained, to consider raising the secretary's salary. The chairman considered that the £30 that the secretary was receiving was 'extremely low' considering the time the secretary devoted to club affairs.[29] A number of people spoke at the meeting advocating an increase, after which it was proposed that the secretary's salary be raised to £52 per annum. It was to be retrospective to the beginning of that financial year. The resolution was carried unanimously. At a committee meeting on 4 February 1918, the meeting conformed with the direction of the AGM on the question of a gratuity to the secretary for 'excellent services rendered during the past nineteen years'.[30] It was then proposed and seconded and passed unanimously that £20 be passed to the secretary.

There were also references in the early minute books of the club to the rent paid for use of the grounds. On 13 October 1902, a cheque for £7 11s 8d was passed to a Mr Desmond for a half year's rent (to 29 September) and one year's rates. Correspondence between Mr Donegan and Mr Higley was read at a committee meeting on 7 November 1904 on the question of the rent. It was proposed and seconded that the rent for £43 15s from 1 January 1903 to 29 September 1904 be paid to a Maurice Healy, which was carried.

Finally, on the question of finance, it is significant that in February 1918 the club decided to invest £200 in war stock or bonds, and the trustees of the club were appointed 'to carry the matter out'.[31]

SUNDAY'S WELL BOATING AND TENNIS CLUB AND CHARITIES

The last point dealing with the finances of the club, whereby they invested some money in war stocks during the First World War, leads us to neatly to the issue of how the club contributed to benevolent funds. Invariably, the monies given by the club to charities was to those linked to the First World

War. This may not be such a surprise when one considers the remarks of the club chairman at the AGM of December 1915. As well as remarking that the club 'might congratulate themselves on having done so well financially', he added that 'they might feel very proud that so many members had joined the army'.[32]

Throughout the conflict, the club donated to war charities. At a committee meeting on 7 September 1914, a letter was read from the Lawn Tennis Association appealing on behalf of the National Relief Fund to have a card hung up on the clubhouse for subscriptions. It was resolved that a subscription card be sent for. However, at the next committee meeting, on 9 September, a letter was read from the Royal Munster Fusiliers Old Comrades Association Royal Relief Fund asking for contributions. The secretary was asked to reply to the letter saying that the club already had a card for the National Relief Fund, and that 'we cannot see our way' to put up a second card.[33] On 24 September, the club decided to give subscriptions to the Cork City and County Branch of the National Relief Fund and a circular was to be sent to members appealing for subscriptions to the fund.

On 19 August, a letter was read at a club committee meeting from the secretary of the Belgian Red Cross Society asking for subscriptions to the society. The meeting decided that the card to record subscriptions be put up in the club and that subscriptions be limited to 2s 6d. In September of the same year, the club resolved that they would provide tea for wounded soldiers on Wednesday 13 September. In 1918, the war provided a backdrop for more charitable action from the club. In June, a committee meeting decided to provide entertainment for wounded soldiers at a future date, and that a subscription list would be opened in the club to defray the expenses of such a venture. Earlier that year, in April, the club granted use of its courts for one day in aid of funds of the Police-Aided Clothing Society.

However, it would seem that unlike the cricket club, the tennis club were unwilling to give their facilities on a regular basis to other clubs and associations. A number of years later, in 1922, Revd Mellifont wrote to the committee asking for the tennis courts for a tournament on 9 and 10 June in aid of a home for the Protestant Incurables. However, the committee decided that the writer of the application be seen and have it explained the difficulties the committee had with the application. The committee wanted to inform the writer of their unanimous wish to give the grounds, but that they could not see their way to do so, since they feared that such an action would create a precedent.

SOCIAL ACTIVITIES

The minute books of Sunday's Well Boating and Tennis Club indicate that there was a very active social side to the club, involving boating, reading facilities, music, card playing, draughts, croquet and billiards. The club had of course not neglected the playing facilities. At the club's AGM in December 1908 the chairman expressed the opinion that the club was in a very prosperous condition; that it was becoming 'solidified' and was one of the institutions of Cork.[34] In December of the following year, the club chairman expressed the view that he 'did not think there was any club in the four quarters of Ireland that would show such a record both in tennis and every other way'.[35] The same meeting was also told that a 'good many' of the members had been in favour of a hard court. It was proposed that the club committee be instructed to look into the feasibility of the construction of a hard court for tennis, and this proposal was seconded.

We have already noted that the club had bar facilities, and the ways in which they tried to regularise the running of the bar and the availability of alcohol. A committee meeting in April 1917 set the prices for various drinks available at the club, which were as follows: stout, 5d per bottle; Bass, 5½d; Cork whiskey, 8d per glass; Glenlivet, 9d per glass; White House, 10d; gin, 9d, and brandy, 2s 6d. The availability of such drinks gives an indication of the social tone of the club, as do a number of other entries from the club's minute books. In March 1909, the committee asked the secretary to buy carpet for the committee room, the cost not to exceed £4 10d. The secretary and other individuals were also to acquire some pictures for a room in the club.

As the name of the club shows, there was a boating aspect to their activities, though this seems to have been purely a leisure pursuit, without any indication of competition such as racing boats or rowing. References to boating in the club minute books refer to instances where boats were purchased or the boating facilities improved, and to boating and other water activities.

At the second AGM of the club, the secretary's report referred to how two fine Thames Wherries had been purchased from Messrs Salter Brothers of Oxford at a cost of £32, which had been greatly availed of by members till late in the season. In May 1902, a cheque for £32 was passed to Salter Brothers as payment for two Thames Skiffs. At the same meeting, the secretary was to see a Mr Atkins on the question of more members using boats. In May 1911, the committee decided to purchase a punt, though the cost was not to exceed £4. In April 1912, the club resolved to purchase backs for boats and four pairs of oars. We can see how, as the summer approached, the club invested in such equipment. The club also endeavoured to improve the facilities for boating. The secretary's report to the AGM in January 1902, recorded how in the previous year there had been the piling and building of another 100 feet of the retaining wall on the river frontage. He also remarked on the extension of the west-end slip by eight feet, to the level of water at low tide, to facilitate the coming and going of the gigs.

In 1908, the club expressed its concern about the state of the River Lee passing next to its facilities. In July, the committee sent a letter to the Lord Mayor, Rt Hon. Thomas Donovan. The letter reminded the Mayor of his promise to urge Cork Distilleries Company on the need to complete the contemplated work upon their weir. There was a reference to the removal of floodgates and the fact that the river had fallen two feet below its normal height, meaning that all the drains leading into the river had been exposed, and there was 'unquestionably a serious danger to public health'.[36] The club also brought to the attention of the Mayor the dilapidated condition of the lower weir, which was described as lately 'coming to pieces', gradually lowering the level of the river. The committee noted that the state of the weir had 'greatly injured the beauty of the river in this neighbourhood'. In addition, the letter referred to how some club members had been informed of a clause 'released' to the firm of Beamish & Crawford, binding that firm to keeping the lower weir in repair. Mentioning the interest of citizens, children and 'especially the large number using the Fitzgerald Park', the committee urged the Mayor 'to investigate the move in this matter'.

The club held various entertainments on the river. In June 1904, the committee ordered the secretary to advertise gig races, as well as a wherry and tub race. A donkey cart was to be used to advertise the events. Printing was to be carried out with the words 'Aquatic Sports' and 'Tonight', and notices were to put in the advertisements of Thursday and Friday. A whole day for ladies was switched from Wednesday to Monday, and the secretary was to purchase a large earthenware teapot and two dozen cups and saucers. At the next week's meeting, races to be advertised included an inter-club swimming race, a ladies' whirl race and a tub race. On 27 June, a subcommittee was formed to carry out weekly amusements on the water for the band promenade.

Like other clubs mentioned previously, this club was also involved in holding band promenades. The first reference to music in the club minutes occurs at the end of the AGM in January 1902, when, at a gathering after the meeting, someone played the piano. The club also had possession of a bandstand which was often requested by other clubs and organisations. In July 1902, the committee wrote a letter to a Mr Russell, saying that they could not give the loan of a bandstand because the application had not been put before them on time. In October 1904, the secretary reported an application from a Mr John Lyons for the loan of the bandstand tops for Blackrock, which the committee assented to. The club also held its own band promenades. In May 1904, the committee decided that a weekly band promenade was to be held on Fridays in June. In another instance, this time in May 1905, band presidents were to be communicated with and asked to give their vacant dates. The club also considered putting on other entertainments. In July 1904, the secretary was asked by the committee to find out the extra cost of a torchlight tattoo, as well as having pipers and sword dancing.

Other pastimes engaged in by club members included cards, billiards and draughts. In May 1905, the secretary was asked to get estimates for six card tables and four slides at such Cork shops as the Munster Arcade and Cash and Grant. Towards the end of 1910, the club was interested in replacing their billiard table. In November, the committee resolved that the billiard table be advertised for sale. In December, the secretary was authorised to sell the billiard table for the best price he could get, but it was not to be delivered until the new table had been set up. In April 1912, the secretary was to make an offer of 2s 10d for twelve pool balls from the Church of Ireland Association. In an interesting aside on the purchase of the billiard table, the club received a letter from the Cork District Council in June 1912 on the importation of the table. The secretary was to answer the letter and say that the firm responsible for the table had provided it at a factory in Belfast. In February 1914, the club resolved to get two more screens for the card room, as well as a draught board and a set of draughts.

What is particularly instructive in studying the entertainments of the tennis club is the list of titles of papers and magazines which the club held at its premises. The club also held books, and in October 1905 the committee expressed thanks to a Mr Dixon for a handsome presentation of books. In December of that year, the committee discussed the question of papers and resolved to get in such titles as *The Sphere, Sporting and Dramatic,* and the *Irish Field.* These same titles would be sold at the general meeting after being held to be rented for twelve months. In December 1908, additional titles were to be acquired for club members, namely, *Daily Mail, The Irish Times,* and *Trips* magazine. A sale of newspapers and magazines at the AGM in December 1909 consisted of the following titles: *Sphere, Sporting and Dramatic, Tatler, Sketch, Fries,* and *Strand.*

At the club's AGM in December 1911, it was proposed and seconded that *The Bystander* and *Punch* be taken instead of two magazines, and *The Motorboat* was to be added to the list of papers. The following publications were sold to members: *The Sphere, 6s; Sporting and Dramatic, 6s 6d; Tatler, 7s 6d; Sketch, 6s 6d; Bystander, 6s,* and *Punch, 5s 3d.* The minutes also listed the members who had purchased the publications. These publications were also auctioned at the club's AGM on 22 December 1914. Extra publications which were auctioned at the AGM in February 1919 were *Strand, Graphic* and *Windsor.*

In concluding our glimpse in to the social and entertainment side of the club, one or two remaining points from the minute books are worth noting. For example, on 30 January 1904, there was a suggestion that the club members should form a harrier club. There was a further suggestion at the same meeting that the members should have a dinner every year.

SUNDAY'S WELL BOATING AND TENNIS CLUB VERSUS CORK EXHIBITION

A major portion of the minutes of the Sunday's Well Tennis Club was taken up with communications relating to a protracted and byzantine dispute between the club and the Cork Exhibition, the issue extending from 1902 to 1905.

The kernel of the dispute, as revealed in the club minutes and in accounts in the local press, centred on the building of a clubhouse and a boathouse. Specifically, there was friction regarding who held responsibility for the construction of these facilities and for defraying the costs, and whether or not contractual obligations had been entered into and had been fulfilled. The issue was contentious, and despite the urgings of many local leaders and the press to have both parties settle the dispute amicably, it was in fact taken to the courts in Dublin 1904. There was extensive coverage both of the court case and of local discussion relating thereto carried in the *Cork Examiner* throughout these years.

While the legal issues as rehearsed in court, the minute books and local newspapers are complex and not warranting detailed discussion here, the dispute provides some interesting insights of wider significance regarding local elites and social sensitivity in Cork sporting circles. The fact that the parties insisted on bringing it to the courts is itself significant and cannot be accounted for simply by referring to the dissatisfaction of the tennis club with the quality of the facility (clubhouse and boathouse) that had been erected by the Cork Exhibition Executive. There can, of course, be no doubting the fact that they were dissatisfied, and the issue of whether or not sufficient money had been spent and sufficient care taken in the construction of the clubhouse/boathouse was a very real issue. But the protracted and bitter nature of the dispute and the harsh words spoken suggests there was more to the dispute than the question of the clubhouse.

Specifically, on the basis of the evidence in court and on the joy expressed by the tennis club when they won their case, there appears to be a good case for saying that this was a matter of wounded dignity and hurt on the part of the tennis club – that they had not been taken seriously by the 'great and good' of the wealthy elite who presided over the Cork Exhibition Executive.

Members of the tennis club seem particularly sharp in their references to Sir Edward Fitzgerald, principally, it seems, because of his superior position and his superior attitude; he felt he knew best what was needed by different groups in Cork and he invariably expected his views and opinions to be deferred to.

The newspaper account of the court action highlights these attitudes, both on behalf of Sir Edward Fitzgerald and the tennis club committee. The attitude of Fitzgerald can be gauged by the opening statement in the case by counsel for the plaintiffs (the Exhibition). Mr Healy, KC, referred to 'a dispute with a man who did all that might be kept for the locality and not to be troubling a Dublin jury with the great conflict between Mr Donegan, solr., and Sir Edward Fitzgerald about the windows of the Boat Club'.[37]

However, in contrast, the resentment of the tennis club towards Fitzgerald can be measured by the remarks of counsel for the club. When opening the case for the club, Mr O'Shaughnessy stated that the case had come about because, 'The great Poo Bah of Cork [laughter] thought he would carry out this thing as he liked as he did some other things and that any building the Exhibition Committee provided for the Boat Club was good enough.'[38]

O'Shaughnessy, when continuing his argument, stated that the 'respectable people – the members of the Boat Club – had come into court rather than that the foot of Sir Edward Fitzgerald should be put upon their necks'. He also felt that the result of the case would put an end 'to that fetish worship which for some time past had induced a great many people to prostrate themselves before Sir Edward Fitzgerald and it would also put an end to the involvement in favour of those "honorary industries" which improved no one but the honorary persons connected with them.'

When the club met after the court judgement in its favour, the report of the club solicitor was received with 'prolonged applause', while a 'hearty vote of thanks' was passed to Donegan, the club solicitor, for 'his great services'.[39]

It was also decided that Mr Lawrence, BL, who had acted as counsel for the club, be elected an honorary member. Here one notes the joy of the club that their stance on the clubhouse and the boathouse had been vindicated.

While it is impossible to characterise this incident in terms of class tension, it does reveal the subtle distinction between those who were respectable and loyalist (as the tennis club committee generally was) and those who were a few notches above them in wealth in the city, but whose authority and influence was resented and in this instance resisted.

It is evident that the Sunday's Well Boating and Tennis Club was a middle-class organisation in its rules and regulations, but its matters of discipline were firmly based on notions of proper behaviour (manners between members, disapproving attitude to misbehaviour particularly if under the influence of drink, a general emphasis on respectability and consideration of others).

It is also clear that its political sentiment was broadly loyalist, particularly during the war years, and this is also clear from magazines and reading material for its clubhouse. Here, one can also note how members of the navy, army, Indian and foreign colonial services residing in Cork at a particular period were to be admitted to the club without ballot. However, as we have also seen, tensions could arise within the club which could, in turn, reveal social divisions between members.

The respectable and relatively wealthy membership base of the club is reflected in its successful efforts in the early years to secure the substantial overdraft of £500 from the Hibernian Bank, based on club members becoming guarantors. In subsequent efforts to obtain further sums, however, there were some difficulties.

Finally, the committee were highly sensitive about their status, in social as well as organisational terms. Indeed, as we have seen, they were prepared to assert that dignity and self-esteem even to the point of forcing a court case in Dublin against the worthies of the Cork Exhibition, an episode that was divisive and deeply embarrassing to the general civic leaders of the city. The tennis club and its membership meant themselves to be taken seriously.

VI

ROWING

While the location of Cork ensured that boating (for leisure and commerce) was a tradition as old as the city itself, actual competitive rowing clubs, with premises, rules, regulations and competitive intentions, are a much more recent phenomenon. The oldest of the clubs for which records are available is the Lee Rowing Club. The following account relies to a large extent on the minutes of this club, supported by newspaper accounts of rowing in Cork and whatever secondary sources are available.

A brief study of the local Cork press at the end of the nineteenth and beginning of the twentieth centuries revealed a number of references to rowing, and various clubs and competitions in the city and its surrounds. We have already noted how the Sunday's Well Tennis Club was originally a boating club, which was associated with regattas, first of these having been held the mid-nineteenth century. The coverage of rowing was, particularly in the case of the *Cork Sportsman*, couched in a very conversational and opinionated style. For example, in a piece from July 1897 entitled 'Correspondence', the writer expresses disappointment at a recent showing by the Lees club, noting that there seemed to be 'a plentiful supply of men and boats', but criticising club officers for not getting the best out of both.[1]

Coverage of rowing in the local press in the early twentieth century suggests that the sport was quite popular. In July 1906, the *Cork Examiner* referred to the upcoming Fermoy Blackwater Regatta, which would have the 'cream of rowing'.[2] The clubs scheduled to take part included Glenbrook, Cork Harbour Rowing Club and City of Cork Rowing Club. The event would also include pleasure boat races and music by the Royal Irish Regiment during the day.

A further indication of the strength of the sport is to be found in a piece written by the columnist under the name of 'Back-Wash' in the *Cork Sportsman* on 13 June 1908.[3] The columnist noted that it had been many years since as much interest had been shown in rowing in Cork as was being shown during that season. For example, Shandon Boat Club had been training for the previous four weeks, while 'Lee Rowing Club have two junior eights on the water every night'. There was also a reference to the teams of Cork Boat Club, 'I have not seen a crew from the City of Cork Rowing Club but I hope they are training down the Lough, as I should be sorry to see this club go down.'

On the following week the same writer commented again on the level of rowing activity in Cork:

Since my last note, oarsmen on the Lee have been busy, and every night the Light Blue, Red and Black, Chocolate and White can be seen rowing courses, fast starts, or paddling, followed by their respective coaches and a fleet of enthusiasts on cycles. It is a great revival of the grand old sport in Cork; aye, the purest of all sport, as there are few sportsmen of any kind who 'play the game' as oarsmen do.[4]

As the summer of 1908 passed, the rowing correspondent on the *Cork Sportsman* kept readers up-to-date on the competitions and the preparations which clubs were making for same. In June, under the heading 'Acquatics', the correspondent expressed the desire to keep readers up-to-date on the Cork Boat Club and Cork City Challenge Cup, and he also gave the following advice, 'A word to coxswains. The rule of the river is: – crews going down must on all occasions give way to crews coming up, whether rowing a course or not.'[5]

In the previous week's issue, under the heading of 'Swimming Notes' and a subheading, 'The Clubs', the writer had made the following comment, 'Some of them are rowing like blacks every evening in our local clubs, while others content themselves with an occasional "dip" and then wheel down the Marina to criticise their clubmates who aspire to the Leader Cup, Arnott Cup, etc.'[6]

Two of the biggest rowing events referred to in the summer of 1908 were the Cork City Regatta and Queenstown Regatta. In July 1908, in the *Cork Sportsman* under the pseudynom 'Back-Wash' and in an article entitled 'A Friendly Hint', the writer noted how the Cork City Regatta of 'international fame' was approaching.[7] It was also referred to as the 'Premier Regatta of Ireland' and the piece told of how, on the day of the regatta, contestants often fasted all day, even though their race might not take place until nine o'clock in the evening. The following week the same paper noted that 'The Marina is thronged with people every evening'.[8] Pedestrians had complained about cyclists following the rowing, as each

The spectacle of a regatta by the Marina on the Lee. (Image courtesy of *Irish Examiner*)

club had a member who cycled in advance of their crew, blowing a whistle to signal the approach of a rival rowing crew, and it was noted that some professional oarsmen on the Lee had made a similar arrangement.

There then followed a very colourful passage setting the scene for the upcoming rowing competitions:

> Leander Cup: 'Who'll win the ship? Who'll win the ship?' It is the question of the day as far as Cork sportsmen are concerned; it is the question on the lips of every man who frequents the Marina after business hours; it is the cause of some heated arguments amongst the ladies who follow rowing; and was the cause of a hard fight between two school boys close to the Crinoline bridge on Saturday evening...

The article went on to say that those who would not be at the event 'will anxiously await the telegram announcing the result'.

In August 1908, the same paper ran an account of Queenstown Regatta. The event had taken place on the previous Saturday and was described thus:

From early morning crowds of pleasure-seekers poured into the town from all parts of Munster and well were they repaid for their journey, as the sport provided by the cream of energetic committees was of a first-class character, and dealt with every branch of aquatic amusement, from tug-boat racing to gig-racing...[9]

The correspondent 'Back-Wash', who penned the above, also made some observations relating to rowing in particular. He blamed the Cork Boat Club's poor season on their style of rowing, 'which gave the legs no share of doing their proper share of the work'. This piece seems to have been the final piece written on the local rowing season, as the following lines, under 'Au Revoir', indicate:

I hope all our oarsmen will live well during the winter and take as much exercise as they can get – football for preference – so that they will be in good form for the merry month of May next year, when it will be my pleasing duty to once again sound the 'call to arms' in these columns.

Throughout the early decades of the twentieth century, there were references in the local press to international rowing events, such as the Oxford–Cambridge boat race. In March 1900, the *Cork Examiner* carried a piece noting how Cambridge had rowed the full course in twenty-one minutes and eleven seconds (presumably against Oxford), and commenting on the weather conditions for the day.[10]

Other references to rowing clubs in the local press dealt with music events and concerts organised by the clubs. On 10 December 1894, the *Cork Constitution* advertised the Shandon Boat Club Concert, the programme of which appeared on that same morning, with the concert scheduled for the following evening. The band of the 10th Royal Hussars was to play and a scene from *Rip Van Winkle* would be introduced; there were also a 'number of dances embraced in the programme'.[11]

On 3 December 1898, the *Cork Examiner* informed readers of 'another band promenade' being held at the Marina on that same day.[12] The Working Men's Band were to play and the admission was described as being 'most moderate'.

The Lee Rowing Club, the minute book of which forms the primary source for this study of rowing, also held fundraising events. In 1934, the club was described as being 'sadly in need of funds' and was praised thus, 'This old established club may, not inaccurately, be described as a public institution, and being, as it is, a medium of periodic enjoyment for thousands who do not share in its membership, it has a very strong claim on public support.'[13]

The newspaper went on to predict that 'the fare to be provided is such that it will be surprising if the capacity of the theatre is not entirely taxed'. The price of admission was referred to as being 'unusually moderate', ranging from 9d to 3s, and the dearer seats could be reserved. In February 1936, Cork Boat Club hosted its annual dance at the Imperial Hotel, where the price of the ticket was described as being 'ridiculously cheap', at only 3s 6d.[14]

There is also reference in the press to an activity associated with the Lee Rowing Club that occurred in August 1908. Mr W. Kinmonth had boarded a ship for America to present a Mr J.J. Hayes with a gold watch and life membership of the Lee Rowing Club at the Irish American Athletic Club in New York. Hayes, a renowned athlete, had given an exhibition at the Lee Rowing Club sports in August 1908. Mr Kinmonth was now bringing a letter of thanks signed on behalf of the club. The signatories included Augustine Roche, MP, TC, and president of the club, as well as Mr McDonnell, Chairman of Cork County Council, and the aforementioned Kinmonth.

SUBSCRIPTIONS TO LEE ROWING CLUB

The issue of payment of subscriptions to this particular club is significant, as it provides information as to who took up membership of the club, while also giving an insight into the mechanisms employed to garner subscriptions, which seem to be unique when compared to other clubs and codes in this study.

Before studying club activity in collecting subscriptions for membership, it is worth noting the cost of membership of the club at the end of the nineteenth century. A look at the receipts book of Lee Rowing Club is instructive in this regard. Here one finds subscriptions from companies paying membership, presumably on behalf of their employees. For example, in Receipt Book No.1 and under the title 'Annual Subscribers', Messrs Cash & Co. paid a sum of £1, as did the Munster Arcade. Dwyer & Co. and Beamish & Crawford were other companies mentioned in this particular receipt book. There were companies with English addresses, such as Messrs J. Hale & Sons from Manchester, who subscribed a sum of £1 1s. Messrs J. Murphy, presumably the brewing company, paid a subscription of £5.

In Receipt Book No.2 there were subscriptions from other companies, such as Messrs John Daly & Co., who paid £1, while Cork Distilleries Company paid £3. Again, this documentation included subscriptions from English companies. There were subscriptions from Messrs E. Hughes & Co.

of Kidderminster and from Messrs Morton & Sons for the sum of £1, while Messrs Hall & Sons from Birmingham paid a sum of 10s. Subscriptions from individuals were usually for the sum of 10s, almost invariably with Cork City addresses. It is interesting to note that at the club's AGM in October 1887, a report on the club's finances mentioned that a sum of £20 5s 9d had been received from the 'English houses' in the previous year's receipts.[15] The AGM in April 1890 decided that a person joining the club for the first time should pay only 10s. The names of companies and addresses of individuals who contributed to the club will be looked at in greater detail later.

Lee Rowing Club had a much more pro-active policy with regards to collection of subscriptions than other sporting organisations in Cork. Other clubs in this book did sometimes have difficulty in gathering subscriptions, and letters were usually written to those in arrears in an attempt to collect subscriptions due. However, as we shall see, Lee Rowing Club decided on a more active approach, whereby members waited on other members and institutions to collect subscriptions. In one of the earliest available minutes of the club, dating from 1887, a member informed a committee meeting that he and the Lord Mayor had collected an amount over £6.[16]

The following July, it was decided that members of the committee would wait on members whose subscriptions had not been paid, and in the event of these individuals not paying their membership, their names would be posted up as defaulters. In May 1890, the minutes of a committee meeting noted that Messrs McCarthy and O'Callaghan had been selected to go on a deputation to the breweries. This was presumably to collect a subscription, since employees of the breweries rowed for the club. In July of that year, there is reference to Messrs Preacher and Dunworth forming a deputation to collect subscriptions. At the club's general meeting on 15 April 1890, two club members were deputed to call for subscriptions from two major businesses in Cork, namely the Arcade and Messrs Lyons & Co.

At a general meeting in October 1887 it was decided to form a committee to collect a 'few outstanding subscriptions'.[17] In June 1889, ten people were appointed to wait on subscribers. However, a club meeting held in May 1888 shows the extent to which the club relied on a personal approach to collect subscriptions. Firstly, the meeting heard how the captain of the club announced that both he and a Mr Murphy had been out collecting during the previous week and had collected over £20 in subscriptions. Interestingly, they informed the meeting that they had waited on Beamish & Crawford for a subscription and had been refused. Accordingly, a Mr E. Crean and a Mr

Goggin were appointed to wait on the company again. This E. Crean may well have been the same individual who was in charge of one of the rival GAA county boards in the 1880s.

In April 1889, the minutes of the club record the names of members who called on other members and instances when collectors had called on those whose subscriptions were due only to be told to call back in a few days. At another meeting in the same month, certain individuals were asked to call on other named individuals for subscriptions. In May, a J. O'Sullivan and a J. Whitaker were to call on the 'Arcade men' for the subscription of the previous year.[18]

One can see, then, that the club experienced difficulties in collecting subscriptions, and as a result, various measures were adopted to ensure payment. As well as the aforementioned personal visits undertaken by members, the club also wrote asking for subscriptions. In October 1887, the secretary read out to the committee a list of members he had written to requesting payment of subscriptions and some of the replies received that had included the 'desired amount'.[19] At a special committee meeting in 1889 the decision was taken to issue a circular to those who had not paid their subscription, requesting payment immediately, and that all members were to be written to at the first opportunity. This meeting had already decided to draw up a list of the annual subscribers who had not yet been called on and determined that a deputation was to go out during the following week to collect subscriptions. In one of the first entries in the minute book of the club, the committee decided to send notice of a second application to those members who had not paid their membership. The committee also resolved to read out the names of members who had not paid their subscriptions at the following meeting.

At the next meeting it was decided to wait for members who had not paid their subscriptions and in the event of subscriptions remaining unpaid, the names of defaulters would be posted up. However, there was not always full approval among the committee regarding this action of reading out the names of defaulting members. At the beginning of August 1887, there was a proposition before the committee not to read out the names of defaulting members at the following meeting, with an amendment that the original intention to read out the names be carried through. However the proposition not to read out the names was carried. On 23 May 1890, the committee approved a proposition to post up the names of defaulting members on that evening.

The issue of non-payment of subscriptions received particular attention at the club's AGM in April 1890. There was a long discussion on members who had not paid, after which it was decided to have these individuals expelled from the club, with their names posted on the noticeboard. The following resolutions were then proposed and seconded:

That:

1. all subscriptions were to be paid before 20 May and that any members who had not paid by that date were not to be permitted to make use of the club,

2. members of the club who had not paid the previous year's subscription be not allowed to enter the club 'in any pretext whatsoever',

3. the names of these defaulting members were to be posted up in the club and all other members were to take notice of such a rule by not bringing any such members into the club, as they were liable to be ordered out under these regulations.

ADDRESSES OF COMPANIES AND MEMBERS

The primary source of documentation from the Lee Rowing Club contains both minute books and subscription lists of members, with names and addresses. The addresses in particular are noteworthy, as they provide information on the membership base of the rowing club and also indicate the types of employment in which members were involved. There are business addresses, as well as addresses of different types of member, be they honorary or rowing members.

Before studying the addresses of members, it is worth remembering that there were various types of members. In October 1887, the general meeting heard that the club had enrolled three rowing members and thirty honorary members. In April 1888, when individuals were proposed and elected for membership, along with honorary and rowing members there were also those proposed as junior rowing members. In the subscription lists of the club, it was sometimes specified after a name whether the individual who contributed was a rowing or honorary member. Occasionally, in brackets, was written 'E. Member' after a name.[20] Various amounts were paid by those who subscribed. In the subscription list of 1894, some members paid 10s while others paid 5s. These amounts did not always distinguish rowing from honorary members. In 1894, a Mr Davis paid £1, though he was marked down as a rowing member. Honorary members also paid £1, though there were honorary members who paid 10s. There was also a difference in the amounts contributed by companies. In 1894, Beamish & Crawford contributed a sum of £3, while, for example, Smithson Brothers gave £1 1s 0d and J. Taylor & Sons were recorded as paying £2 2s 2d.

We have already seen how the club actively collected subscriptions from companies and businesses in Cork. Let us now look at further instances of companies paying subscription fees, possibly on behalf of their employees or alternatively to support a pastime which they felt was either necessary or beneficial. In addition, we can note instances were members cite a business address when joining the club.

Apart from separate books listing the names of members who joined the club, the club minute book contains references from various meetings where individuals were passed for membership and records the addresses of such individuals. For example, a committee meeting in April 1888 recorded the names and addresses of individuals who had been either elected as members or proposed and seconded for membership. Two of the elected members had addresses at Cash & Company, as did two of those proposed and seconded for membership. There is an even earlier reference to a place of employment found in the first available minutes, where two individuals proposed at a committee meeting in July 1887 gave their addresses as the Butter Exchange (although the fact that they intended to become honorary members may indicate that they were not active in the club and were possibly in high positions in the Butter Exchange). In May 1890, a Mr P. O'Leary who was proposed as a member gave his address as 'Buttermarket', but it is unclear from the minute book what type of membership he was taking up. In the following month, a Mr Desmond of the Butter Market was elected a member of the club. Another elected member gave his address as the Arcade. This was also known as the Munster Arcade and was a significant membership base for the club.

When one turns to the membership lists of the club in the 1890s, one can see the preponderance of business addresses given by those who had joined Lee Rowing Club. The membership list for June 1894 contains business addresses given by members as well as many Patrick Street addresses, which suggests that these were business locations also. There were membership subscriptions from businesses themselves in the June 1894 list and these included Beamish & Crawford, Grant & Co., Lane & Co., Daly & Co., L.L. Murphy & Co., Munster Arcade, Hogan & Sons, and Drapers' Club. Other addresses given by individuals who presumably worked in the relevant business houses included Perry & Sons, Queens Old Castle, Cash's, Dwyer & Co. and the Munster Arcade. Two individuals gave their address as 20 Patrick Street and two more as 30 Patrick Street. It is probable that these were business locations.

The receipt books of the club from 1898 and 1899 provide further evidence of the links between the club and business houses in the city. In what was entitled Receipt Book No.1, the club recorded subscriptions from various Cork businesses. These included Messrs Cash & Co., Munster Arcade, Messrs Egan & Sons, Messrs James J. Murphy (presumably brewers), Messrs J. Lyons & Co., Dwyer & Co. and Beamish & Crawford.[21] The No.2 Receipt Book recorded contributions from other companies. Among these were Messrs John Daly & Co., Cork Distillers Co. Ltd. It is also significant that the membership lists of the club for 1898 include business addresses given by those who subscribed. Such businesses listed were Queens Old Castle, Grants and Munster Arcade. Also included were addresses such as Herald Office, London House and GPO.

As noted earlier, businesses with English addresses subscribed to the club. In 1894, individuals and businesses from Leeds, Manchester and Huddersfield contributed various amounts to the club. The list of annual subscribers for 1898 recorded a contribution of £1 1s from Messrs J. Hale & Sons of Manchester. Among a number of English contributions recorded in another receipt book for the same year were those from Messrs E. Hughes & Co., Messrs Norton & Sons of Kidderminster, and Messrs Hall & Sons of Birmingham.

There were a significant number of inner-city addresses given by members. These would suggest that members lived over premises in which they worked or alternately that they lived in inner-city accommodation. The minute books of the club refer to such addresses when recording the names of those who applied or were passed for membership. For example, in June 1888, club minutes for meetings in that month record such addresses, the majority of which were situated within the centre of the city. Of the four individuals elected on 5 June 1888, two gave an address of 11 Popes Quay, while the other new members lived in Mallborough Street and Old Georges Street. The minutes of a committee meeting on 15 June 1888 record a longer list of new members. City-centre addresses included Princes Street, Cove Street, Popes Quay and Grand Parade. North Mall was the address of another new member, situated just to the north of the River Lee. One of the new members lived in Ballinlough Road, which was a suburban address. In April 1890, two new members lived in Shandon Street and South Main Street.

Receipt books from 1898 in particular, show how members at the time lived in city centre addresses, again, quite possibly over the business premises in which they worked. In the list of annual subscribers for 1898, those who became members had addresses in: Bridge Street, Georges Street, Adelaide Street, Cornmarket Street, Paul Street, Leitrim Street, Princes Street, Winthrop Street, St Patrick's Hill, Lower Road, Alfred Street, Lavitts Quay, Malborough Street, South Main Street, Cook Street, Lower Montenotte and Balmorral Terrace, Rockboro Road, Hardwick Street, Richmond Terrace, Woburn Terrace, and Dunbar Street. A number of members gave Patrick Street addresses.

What also needs to be noted are the addresses given by honorary members of the club. These individuals may well have been owners or those in charge of the businesses in which the rowing members worked. In one of the earliest meetings recorded in the minute books, a Mr George Holland of the Munster Arcade was elected an honorary member. When the club committee elected a number of honorary members in May 1888, the individuals in question were referred to in the minute books as 'gentlemen'. For example, there was Mr W. Kinmonth of Woods Lane, Mr Lavallan of Princes Street and Mr John Cotter of the Cork Union. On the following June, three newly elected members were also referred to as 'gentlemen', and had addresses at Munster Arcade, Roches Road and Summerhill South respectively.

In 1899, the club had a list of honorary subscribers. Among these were representatives from businesses such as Messrs Egan & Sons, Messrs Cash & Co., Messrs Arnott & Co. and Cork Distillers Company. This particular list also recorded contributions from other individuals who may have been business owners or managers of businesses. There was, for example, a contribution of 10s from Mr W. O'Connor of Grant & Co., and the same amount from Mr J. Ryan and Mr Jack Aherne of Maylor Street. There were other amounts paid by individuals from Patrick Street on this honorary subscribers list.

OTHER ASPECTS OF MEMBERSHIP

There are a number of interesting points to note on membership of the club. The club seems to have had strong links with aldermen and mayors of Cork. For example, a club committee meeting in September was held in 'Alderman Horgan's'.[22] At the club's general committee meeting in July 1888, the Lord Mayor was in the chair. He also addressed the meeting 'at length' on the necessity of training hard. He addressed his comments especially to the young members and complimented the committee on the financial position of the club. At the club's general meeting in 1889, it was proposed and seconded that the club secretary write to the Mayor for his consent to act as president of the club. In April the committee had not received an answer from the Mayor consenting to be president and instead it was proposed that Alderman O'Brien take up the role.

The club was also anxious to be associated with significant political figures. Dr Tanner MP was elected an honorary member of Lee Rowing Club in April 1888. He was a notable figure in the Land League movement and was, as mentioned previously, a patron of the GAA club in Inniscarra. The same Dr Tanner was approached by the club again in 1890. At a committee meeting in July 1890, the club secretary was directed to write to C.S. Parnell, William O'Brien and Dr Tanner, asking for donations to clear off the debt of the club. Mr E. Crean is referred to a number of times in the minutes of the club. At a meeting in April 1888, Mr Crean TC addressed the members and stressed the necessity of attending well to rowing in the early part of the season. His name is also included in the 1899 list of honorary subscribers, described as 'E. Crean, Esq., MP', and his contribution was £5.[23]

FINANCES OF LEE ROWING CLUB

We have already looked at the issue of subscriptions and their collection, but what exactly was the financial state of the club towards the end of the nineteenth century? At the club's general meeting in October 1887, detailed reference was made in the minutes to the then financial position of the club. In the presentation of the accounts, the meeting was told that the debts of the club had been considerably reduced. When that committee had started in office the club liabilities stood at £241 1s, but had since been reduced to stand at £151 5s. It was also emphasised that a pleasure boat had been added to the club's fleet and it was forecast that the club would be more than out of debt in two seasons and would be 'second to none' in the line of boat clubs.[24]

The meeting was told that the committee had paid off all the bills contracted in the current season and it was noted that it would have been a 'great matter' if this had been done seasons ago, especially with regard to small bills. When the committee had come into office there were no documents or notebooks to inform them as to how the club stood, and subsequently a lot of care and trouble had been taken to find out the state of their finances. The committee had been obliged to communicate with those whom it suspected had amounts owing to them from the club, and when it was thought that everything was 'squared', new bills turned up. When the committee had money it did the best it could with the club creditors and it had settled accounts first with those who had given most inducements to do so.

The books, as it was reported, were now in a simplified form so that any member, no matter how unacquainted with bookkeeping, could, after a few minutes inspection, tell exactly how the club stood. Those creditors referred to as 'pressers' at that time, only amounted to four, and were as follows: Munster and Leinster Bank ('Old Bill') – £39; Munster and Leinster Bank – £92 7d; Messrs Ayling & Sons, London – £8 13s, and the secretary of Rochestown Regatta – £1 5s. There are other references in the minute books to some of these above creditors, such as the debt owed by the club to Messrs Ailing & Sons. In one of the first available minutes of the club, in August 1887, the club secretary read a letter from Messrs Ailing & Sons in reply to the ordering of a set of oars, in which they stated that an amount of £8 13s was due and settlement was requested. It was agreed that the secretary write to Ailing & Sons to cancel the order for oars, since the club would not have them in time for the Monkstown Regatta.

The club continued to experience financial difficulty. A letter was read at a committee meeting in March 1889 from Ailing & Sons demanding settlement of their account, but the committee decided to take no action since there were no funds at that time. However, in June the committee decided to pay Mr Ayling for the 'balance of bar' and to settle the account in August 'if possible'.[25] In the following year there were letters from creditors demanding payment of accounts, again including Ayling. The secretary was directed to write to these creditors informing them that after the Queenstown Regatta the committee would take steps to settle the accounts. The previous month the committee received a letter from Bisson Boatbuilder asking to have an old account cleared up. After a long discussion the committee decided to consider the case after the commencement of the following season.

Another expense of the club was the employment of individuals to take care of the boats, as well as a trainer for the crews. In one of the earliest available minutes of the club, the committee passed a sum of £2 to be paid out of the funds to help the trainer's fund. In July 1889, an individual was directed to write to Waterford on the question of Matt Taylor coming for a 'fortnight or so' to train crews and repair boats.[26] In the club's book of 'Honorary Subscriptions and Members Subscriptions 1898-1903', there are a number of payments recorded to various employees, though the payments to the boatman are listed for 1892. For the year 1892 the boatman was paid various amounts, ranging from 5s to 13s. This book also records a payment of 6s to a 'Murphy boy' for two weeks' work. The following entry notes a payment of

1s 6d to the *Cork Examiner* for an advertisement looking for a barman. When the general meeting of the club took place in 1894, payments to the boat-man were recorded in the club expenses. It notes that in the first week the boatman was paid 17s 6d, and 15s in the second week. Further down the list it records another payment of 15s in the fifth week.

Further expenses were incurred on repair to boats and in taking part in com-petitions. For example, the committee decided in May 1899 to employ a man to repair boats. The book 'Honorary Subscriptions and Members Subscriptions' included the expense of repairing a blue pleasure boat at the cost of 16s 6d. In August 1887, the committee passed a resolution whereby the expenses of the crew going to the Munster Regatta would be paid out of the funds of the club. There was also the expense of transporting boats to regattas. The club paid 5s to a 'Glenbrook Man ... for taking down boat".[27] At the AGM in 1894, one of the expenses listed was a sum of £3 for the Dublin Regatta.

ROWING COMPETITIONS

The expenses of the club also reveal where rowing competitions and regattas were held in the Cork area, and they also indicate the strength of the club in being prepared to compete in non-local regattas. The list of expenses read out at the club's general meeting in 1894 refers to regattas in which they competed. There was, for example, a sum of £1 4s paid to a Mr J. Bullen for expenses incurred at the 'Queenstown Regatta/Crosshaven'.[28] Further down the list, a sum of £3 0s 8d was given for the paid packet of '6 free boats' to Oxford. We have already referred to the expenses incurred in taking part in a Dublin Regatta. In July 1894, the club paid an entrance fee of £2 1s for the Cork City Regatta. There were also regattas being held at locations around Cork Harbour. In July 1887, the club decided to write to the secretary of the Monkstown Regatta con-cerning a race announced on the event's programme. In August of the following year, the committee discussed the issue of entering a crew for the Monkstown Regatta. There were other local competitions in which the club competed. In August 1890, for example, committee meeting minutes refer to the Marina Cup.

The club minutes also provide some insight into the kind of prizes that rowing clubs such as the Lee Rowing Club competed for in the latter decades of the nineteenth century. In one of the club minutes in August 1888, with regard to a challenge race in which the club would row against the Shandon club, there is a reference to a resolution that money drawn to back the 'challenge race' be the first money paid for the following season.[29] There had been a reference at a previous committee meeting to a letter received from the secretary of Shandon Boat Club offering to row a race for the Aspirants Cup over again. D. McCarthy was to be replaced by any other of the members qualified to row under the conditions of the race. The meeting passed the resolution, accepting the challenge. Later meetings of the club discussed the outcome of the race, which, according to the minutes, the Lee club had won. It was proposed and seconded that the £25 won by the crew on Thursday 16 August be given in prizes to the crew and cox. It was also proposed and seconded that the prizes be purchased from W. Egan. On 4 September, there was a 'long discussion' on the issue of the prizes. Several members assented that the committee had decided to give out medals and were at liberty to get 'whatever they pleased' and it was finally proposed and seconded that the matter be passed over.[30]

MATTERS OF DISCIPLINE

A number of disciplinary issues do arise in the minutes of the Lee Rowing Club, though some were of a minor nature. There were examples of indiscipline whereby some club members were not attending to training as well as they ought to, or where individuals did not come to row. At a committee meeting in June 1890, the chairman urged members to practice and not to be 'coming down' a week or a fortnight before the regatta to row in races.[31] In July, a committee meeting heard of a member being reported by another member for refusing to obey his orders. In August of that year a Mr Dunworth complained that a member had taken down and broken notices hanging up in the club.

There were also more serious matters which the committee had to address. At a club general meeting in June 1888, the captain brought before the meeting the case of an individual who had been a member of the club in the previous year and who had refused to pay his subscription. The same person had obtained keys from the caretaker and had entered the club at 'a very early hour of the morning' and removed a skiff.[32] This was his personal property, but the committee had decided to keep it in lieu of his subscription. The meeting agreed unanimously to expel this person from the club.

Finally, there were references to racing crews of the club not turning up to row for competition. In June 1888, a special committee meeting was called by the captain to discuss why a crew entered for a regatta at Monkstown had not travelled. However, an explanation from the crew was forthcoming and the matter was allowed to drop. Also in June 1889, the committee approved the action of the captain in not allowing the senior crew to row in Queenstown.

There are a number of comments that can be made on the sport of rowing, particularly pertaining to the end of the nineteenth century and early decades of the twentieth. One issue is that relating to the collection of subscriptions for the Lee Rowing Club. While the club shared the problem of collection of subscriptions with other codes and sports, there were a number of unique factors regarding rowing.

It has already been noted how the club actively sought subscriptions from the city's businesses and their employees. However, what seems to have worked in the club's favour was an apparent willingness on behalf of businesses and industries to pay subscriptions to the club, no doubt on behalf of their employees. One can also note the payments for honorary membership by individuals who looked favourably on the sport of rowing. One can surmise that such a benevolent attitude towards the sport was based on the fact that the risk of injury was much less than in other contact sports and was therefore more amenable to employers. (Here one can note a reference in the chapter on the GAA where employees who worked behind counters risked injury in football matches.) Employers were also favourable to rowing because there was much less chance of disputes of a fractious nature or incidents of ill-discipline taking place, compared, for example, to football or hurling; the minutes of the Lee Rowing Club reveal very few major incidents of indiscipline.

The club was also anxious to build on such goodwill, as witnessed by its efforts to ensure patronage by such notable political figures as Charles Stuart Parnell, William O'Brien and Dr Charles Tanner, as well as various Lord Mayors.

The rowing clubs of Cork also had a social function, as one notes newspaper accounts of band promenades down by the river along with events like pleasure-boat races. Clubs also held social events such as nights of entertainment at the Opera House, for example, in order to raise funds. The employment of a barman by the Lee Rowing Club also reflects the clubs social capacity.

Finally, there is the interesting question of professionalism in Cork rowing. The question was a particularly vexed one in Britain, where rowing for money was frowned upon by those who wanted to uphold the amateur ethos. Here, it is interesting that a club team had won a money prize and there was subsequent debate on the distribution of same. One could also possibly note a hint of professionalism in the expense the Lee Rowing Club incurred in hiring a trainer and the setting up of a trainer's fund.

CONCLUSION

The time frame of this book coincides with the development of organised sport in Great Britain, the continent and North America. In a number of ways Cork mirrors this development. We have seen how, in the development of field sports, games became more and more organised, with proper enclosures, though as in the case of the GAA and soccer, some grounds were not always able to cope with the number of spectators. It was also the case, as we have seen, that having to pay to watch matches was something that many were unwilling to do.

The growth of newspapers, such as the *Cork Sportsman*, *Cork Examiner* and *Cork Evening Echo* fostered, cultivated and reflected an interest in sport among Cork's sporting public. Newspapers began to print pictures of players in the run-up to games and were not slow to give advice or reprimand players or spectators for unsporting behaviour. Also, in the case of Sunday's Well Tennis Club, newspapers were provided for the entertainment of the members. The whole idea of sport as spectacle took root in Cork and surrounding districts. Bands began to play before and during matches, and trains allowed the sporting public to attend matches outside the city and outside the county.

National politics did impinge on Cork sport during these years. In the early years of the GAA, the issue of republican versus clerical influence on the association saw teams taking opposite stances. The ban on foreign games was an issue at various Cork GAA conventions, with players banned for playing or attending other sporting code events. The period from 1918 to 1922 saw games suspended, while, for example, the secretary of the Cork County Board, Padraig O'Caoimh was imprisoned. Even a golf club such as Douglas was not immune, when it had to rebuild its clubhouse after it had been mistakenly burned down – the perpetrators had intended to attack Cork Golf Club because of its association with the British army.

This leads us to one of the most significant aspects of Cork's sporting history, namely the influence of the British military and navy. The majority of the earliest clubs to play soccer were garrison teams, while members of the British army were also to the fore in the early years of cricket activity, as well as in golf. In addition, they were among the individuals given preference for membership in the various clubs around Cork.

Preferential treatment was also given to those from particular walks of life. For example, bank employees asked to join clubs at preferential rates, such as in the Monkstown club in the 1930s. The Douglas club facilitated golf outings from various professions. In addition, certain sports were associated with a sense of respectability. For example, the rugby writer and historian Edmund Van Esbeck, in his history of Cork Constitution, explained that club members came from the better-off section of society. The golf, tennis and cricket clubs in this study had standards of discipline and behaviour which were to be adhered to, and they also provided extra-curricular activities such as billiards, cards, etc. for members.

Finally, there were the links between sport and work. This is particularly noteworthy in Cork's rowing history and in the way in which the Lee Rowing Club regularly asked for subscriptions from the various commercial houses in the city whose employees rowed for the club. There were inter-firm tournaments held for GAA players, such as on the Wednesday half day, and the reference to the Bankers Rugby Club gives an insight into the runnings of a work-based rugby club.

So Cork, synonymous with sporting prowess, reflected the greater social development of sporting participation and attendance, nationally and internationally, but also had its own unique character, something which this book has attempted to shed light on.

BIBLIOGRAPHY

Austin, Revd Bro., (ed.), *Presentation Brothers College, Cork, 1887-1954: The Story of Pres* (Cork, 1954).

Bailey, Peter, *Leisure and Class in Victorian England: Rational Recreation and the Contest for Control* (London, 1978).

Beecher, Seán, *The Blues: A History of St Finbarrs National Hurling and Football Club*, edited by John O'Mahony (Cork, 1984).

Beecher, Seán, *Day by Day: A Miscellany of Cork History* (Cork, 1982).

Bielenberg, Andy, *Cork's Industrial Revolution: Development or Decline* (Cork, 1991).

Butler, Bryan, *The Official History of the Football Association* (London, 1991).

Carter, Plunkett, *Century of Cork Soccer Memories* (Cork, 1985).

CBC Cork: Diamond Jubilee Souvenir, 1888-1848 (Cork, n.d.).

Chubb, Holly R. & Chubb, Michael, *One Third of Our Time* (New York, 1981).

Cooke, Richard T., *The Mardyke, Cork City's Country Walk In History* (Cork, 1990).

Cooke, Richard T., *Cork's Barrack Street Silver and Reed Band: Ireland's Oldest Amateur Institution* (Cork, 1890).

Corr, Donoughue, *A History of the GAA in Midleton* (Cork, 1986).

Creedon, Colm, *Cork, Bandon and South Coast Railway, Vol. 2, 1900-1950* (Cork, 1989).

Cronin, Jim, *Cork GAA: History, 1886-1986*, edited by John Joe Brosnan and Diarmuid Ó Murchadha (Cork, 1988).

Cronin, Maura, *Country, Class or Craft? The Politicisation of the Skilled Artisan in Nineteenth-Century Cork* (Cork, 1994).

Cronin, Maura, 'Work and Workers in Cork City and County', in Patrick O'Flanagan & Cornelius G. Buttimer (eds), *Cork, History and Society: Interdisciplinary Essays on the History of an Irish County* (Dublin, 1993), pp721-758.

Cronin, Maura, 'From the Flat O'The City to the Top of the Hill: Cork Since 1700', in Howard B. Clarke (ed.), *Irish Cities* (Cork, 1995), pp55-68.

Crump, Jeremy, 'Athletics', in Tony Mason (ed.), *Sport in Britain, A Social History* (Cambridge, 1989), pp44-47.

Cunningham, Hugh, *Leisure in the Industrial Revolution, c.1780-c.1880* (London, c.1980).

d'Alton, Ian, 'Keeping Faith: An Evocation of the Cork Protestant Character, 1870-1920', in Patrick O'Flanagan & Cornelius G. Buttimer (eds), *Cork, History and Society: Interdisciplinary Essays on the History of an Irish County* (Dublin, 1993), pp759-792.

De Búrca, Marcus, *The GAA: A History* (Dublin, 1999).

Deasy, Paddy, 'The Early Years', in Liam Ó Tuama, *Spirit of the Glen, Cumann Lúthchleas Gael: Fánaithe an Ghleanna, Glen Rovers Hurling Club, Blackpool, Cork, 1916-1923* (Cork, 1974), pp4-9.

Diffley, Sean, *The Men In Green: The Story of Irish Rugby* (London, 1993).

Dodd, Christopher, 'Rowing', in Tony Mason (ed.), *Sport in Britain, A Social History* (Cambridge, 1989), pp276-307.

Fahy, A.M., 'Place and Class in Cork', in Patrick O'Flanagan & Cornelius G. Buttimer (eds), *Cork, History and Society: Interdisciplinary Essays on the History of an Irish County* (Dublin, 1993), pp759-792.

Francis Guy's County and City of Cork Directory for the years 1875-1876

Francis Guy's Directory of Munster; Comprising the Counties of Clare, Cork, Kerry, Limerick, Tipperary and Waterford, 1886.

Gallagher, Frank, 'Memories', in *Presentation Brothers College, Cork, 1887-1954: The Story of Pres* (Cork, 1954), pp49-51.

Gibson, William H., *Early Irish Golf: The First Courses, Clubs and Pioneers* (Naas, Co. Kildare, 1988).

Grenagh GAA 50th Anniversary Committee, *Cumann Iománaíochta agus Peil an Grianach: Golden Jubilee History 1934-1984, Grenagh Hurling and Football Club* (Grenagh, Co. Cork, 1984).

Guy's City and County Cork Almanac and (County and City) Directory, 1890-1935.

Harley, Walter, 'Memories', in *CBC Cork: Diamond Jubilee Souvenir, 1888-1948* (Cork, n.d.), pp21-23.

Henchion, Richard, *Cork Centenary Remembrancer, No. 1, 1887-1987* (Wilton, 1986).

Holt, Richard, *Sport and Society in Modern France* (London, 1981).

Holt, Richard, *Sport and the British: A Modern History* (Oxford, 1989).

Horgan, Tim, *Cumann Iománaíochta agus Peile na Brian Diolunaig: A Club History* (Cork, n.d.).

Hourihan, Kevin, 'Evolution and Influence of Town Planning in Cork', in Patrick O'Flanagan and Cornelius G. Buttimer, (eds), *Cork, History and Society: Interdisciplinary Essays on the History of an Irish County* (Dublin, 1993), pp941-962.

Howkins, Alun & Lowerson, John, *Trends in Leisure* (Sports Council Social Science Research Council, 1979).

Kennedy, Máire, 'Cork Library Society of 1801', *Journal of Cork Historical and Archaeological Society, Vol. 94* (1989), pp57-73.

Kelleher, D.C., 'An Old Pres Boy Looks Back', *Presentation Brothers College, Cork, 1887-1954: The Story of Pres.* (Cork, 1954), pp45-46.

Kidney, John M., *Skull and Cross-bones: The Cobh Rugby Story* (Cobh, 1990).

Lowerson, John, 'Angling', in Tony Mason (ed.), *Sport in Britain, A Social History* (Cambridge, 1989), pp12-43.

Lowerson, John, 'Golf', in Tony Mason (ed.), *Sport in Britain, A Social History* (Cambridge, 1989), pp187-214.

MacSweeney, Margaret & Reilly, Joseph, 'The Cork Cuverian Society', *Journal of Cork Historical and Archaeological Society, Vol. 63* (1958), pp9-14.

Madden, Paddy, *The Rockies: A History of Blackrock Hurling Club,* edited by Declan Hassett, (Cork, 1984).

Mandle, W.F., *The Gaelic Athletic Association and Irish Nationalist Politics, 1884-1924,* (London, Dublin, 1987).

Mandle, W.F. 'IRB and the Beginnings of the Gaelic Athletic Association', *Irish Historical Studies, Vol. 20* (1977), pp 418-438.

Mason, Tony, 'Football', in Tony Mason (ed.), *Sport in Britain, A Social History* (Cambridge, 1989), pp146-186.

Mason, Tony, *Association Football and English Society, 1863-1915* (Brighton, 1980).

Mason, Tony, *Sport in Britain, A Social History* (Cambridge, 1989).

Menton, W.A., *Golfing Union of Ireland, 1891-1991* (Dublin, 1991).

Minute Books of Bankers Rugby Football Club.

Minute Books of Cork County Cricket Club.

Minute Books of Douglas Golf Club.

Minute Books of St Finbarr's Temperance Abstinence Hall.

Minute Books of Sunday's Well Boating and Tennis Club.

Mulqueen, Charles, *Murphy's Story of Munster Rugby* (Cork, 1993).

Murphy, Maura, 'The Working Classes of 19th Century Cork', *Journal of Cork Historical and Archaeological Society, Vol. 85* (1980), pp26-51.

Newham, A.T., *The Cork and Muskerry Light Railway* (Oxfordshire, 1968).

O'Brien, Tim, *Muskerry Golf Club: A Cork 800 Anniversary Publication* (Cork, 1985).

Ó Caithnia, Liam P., *Báirí Cois in Éirinn* (Dundalgan, 1984).

Ó Caithnia, Liam P., *Scéal na hIomána: Ó Thosach Ama Go 1884* (Baile Átha Cliath, 1980).

O'Connell, Liam, *Story of Erin's Own*, (Cork, n.d.).

O'Donovan, Teddy, 'Bringing Home the Cup', in Liam Ó Tuama, *Spirit of the Glen, Cumann Lúthchleas Gael: Fánaithe an Ghleanna, Glen Rovers Hurling Club, Blackpool, Cork, 1916-1923* (Cork, 1974), pp117-118.

O'Flanagan, Patrick & Buttimer, Cornelius, G., *Cork, History and Society: Interdisciplinary Essays on the History of an Irish County* (Dublin, 1993).

O'Kelly, David, *The Nemo Rangers Story* (Cork, 1986).

Ó Maolfabhail, Art, *Camán: Two Thousand Years of Hurling in Ireland: An Attempt To Trace The History of the Stick and Ball Game in Ireland During the Past Two Thousand Years* (Dundalk, 1973).

Ó Riain, Maurice, *Maurice Davin (1842-1927): First President of the GAA* (Dublin, 1994).

O'Toole, Pádraig, *The Glory and the Anguish* (Loughrea, 1984).

Ó Tuama, Liam (ed.), *Spirit of the Glen, Cumann Lúthchleas Gael: Fánaithe an Ghleanna, Glen Rovers Hurling Club, Blackpool, Cork, 1916-1923* (Cork, 1974).

Ó Tuama, Liam, 'March of Champions', in Liam Ó Tuama (ed.), *Spirit of the Glen, Cumann Lúthchleas Gael: Fánaithe an Ghleanna, Glen Rovers Hurling Club, Blackpool, Cork, 1916-1923* (Cork, 1974), pp29-41.

Ó Tuama, Liam, *The Nicks of Time: Cumann Peile San Nioclás: 1901-1993* (Cork, 1993).

Pettit, S.F., *The Streets of Cork* (Cork, 1982).

Power, John, *A Story of Champions* (Cork, 1941).

Puirséal, Pádraig, *The GAA In Its Time* (Dublin, 1982).

Sheehan, Tim, *Sweet Inniscarra: A History of Gaelic Games and Social Life in Inniscarra since 1840* (Cork, 1984).

Sheehan, Tim, 'Historian Tim Sheehan of Dripsey Recalls the Barter Legend and the Origins of Muskerry Golf Club', in Tim O' Brien (ed.), *Muskerry Golf Club: A Cork 800 Anniversary Publication* (Cork, 1985).

Shipley, Stan, 'Boxing', in Tony Mason (ed.), *Sport in Britain, A Social History* (Cambridge, 1989), pp78-115.

Shubert, Adrian, *A Social History of Modern Spain* (London, 1990).

St Ledger, Alice, *Monkstown Golf Club, 1908-1983* (Monkstown, Co. Cork, 1983).

Twomey, Jim, 'The GAA and Its Times In the Parish of Ballincollig', *Journal of the Ballincollig Community School Local History Society* (1987), pp2-7.

Vamplew, Wray, 'Horse-Racing', in Tony Mason (ed.), *Sport in Britain, A Social History* (Cambridge, 1989), pp215-244.

Vamplew, Wray, *Pay Up and Play the Game: Professional Sport in Britain, 1975-1914* (Cambridge, 1988).

Van Esbeck, Edmund, *One Hundred Years of Cork Constitution Club* (Cork, 1992).

Walker, Helen, 'Lawn Tennis' in Tony Mason (ed.), *Sport in Britain, A Social History* (Cambridge, 1989), pp245-275.

Walvin, James, *Leisure and Society, 1830-1950* (London, 1978).

Williams, Gareth, 'Rugby' in Tony Mason (ed.), *Sport in Britain, A Social History* (Cambridge, 1989), pp308-343.

Williams, Jack, 'Cricket' in Tony Mason (ed.), *Sport in Britain, A Social History* (Cambridge, 1989), pp116-145.

ENDNOTES

C.C.: *Cork Constitution*.
C.E.: *Cork Examiner*.
C.E.E.: *Cork Evening Echo*.
C.S.: *Cork Sportsman*.

I

[1] Madden, *Rockies*, p.12.
[2] Sheehan, *Inniscarra*, p.19.
[3] Ó Maolfabhail, *Camán*, pp31-32.
[4] *Cork Constitution*, 31 March 1831, cited in Seán Beecher, *The Blues, A History of St Finbarrs National Hurling and Football Club* (1984), p.17, hereafter cited as Beecher, *Blues*.
[5] Beecher, *Blues*, p.26.
[6] Ó Caithnia, *Scéal na hIomána*, pp554-555.
[7] De Búrca, *GAA*, p.23.
[8] Cronin, J., *Cork GAA, A History, 1886-1986*, p.11, hereafter cited as Cronin, *Cork GAA*.
[9] Mandle, *The GAA and Irish Nationalist Politics, 1884-1924*, p.3, hereafter cited as Mandle, *GAA*.
[10] Henchion, *Cork Centenary Remembrancer No.1 1887-1987*, p.63, hereafter cited as Henchion, *Remembrancer*.
[11] Beecher, *Blues*, p.28.
[12] *C.E.*, 16 April 1888.
[13] Beecher, *Blues*, pp28-29.
[14] Beecher, *Blues*, p.26.
[15] *C.E.*, 18 July 1887.
[16] *C.E.*, 1 April 1889.
[17] Mandle, 'The IRB and the Beginnings of the Gaelic Athletic Association', in *Irish Historical Studies*, Vol. 20 (1977), pp418-419, hereafter cited as Mandle, 'IRB'.
[18] Mandle, 'IRB', p.425.
[19] Henchion, *Remembrancer*, pp161-162.
[20] Puirséal, *GAA*, p.81.
[21] Beecher, *Blues*, p.36.
[22] Sheehan, *Inniscarra*, p.38.

[23] *C.E.*, 29 July 1889.

[24] Beecher, *Blues*, p.35.

[25] *C.E.*, 8 April 1889.

[26] Beecher, *Blues*, p.44.

[27] Puirséal, *GAA*, p.96.

[28] De Búrca, *GAA*, p.61.

[29] *C.E.*, 1 June 1891.

[30] Power, *Champions*, p.62.

[31] Mandle, *GAA*, p.158.

[32] Beecher, *Blues*, pp74-75.

[33] *C.E.*, 17 January 1916.

[34] Cronin, *Cork GAA*, p.44.

[35] *C.S.*, 6 October 1911.

[36] *C.E.*, 4 January 1915.

[37] *C.S.*, 5 September 1908.

[38] *C.E.*, 1 August, 1898.

[39] *C.E.*, 19 March 1900.

[40] *C.E.*, 12 September 1904.

[41] Cronin, *Cork GAA*, p.62.

[42] *C.E.E.*, 29 January 1934.

[43] Horgan, *Brian Diolunaigh*, p.19.

[44] Sheehan, *Inniscarra*, p.55.

[45] *C.E.*,19 September 1904.

[46] *C.S.*, 29 January 1910.

[47] *C.S.*, 11 July 1897.

[48] *C.S.*, 5 September 1908.

[49] *C.E.*, 27 January 1913.

[50] *C.S.*, 29 January 1910.

[51] *C.S.*, 11 October 1911.

[52] *C.E.*, 10 February 1908.

[53] Puirséal, *GAA*, p.53.

[54] Cronin, *Cork GAA*, p.30.

[55] *C.E.*, 10 February 1908.

[56] Beecher, *Blues*, p.112.

[57] *C.S.*, 11 October 1911.

[58] Madden, *Rockies*, pp36-37.

[59] Mandle, *GAA*, p.158.

[60] *C.E.*, 29 January 1913.

[61] Horgan, *Brian Diolunaig*, p.24.

[62] *C.S.*, 29 January 1910.

[63] Madden, *Rockies*, p.62.

[64] *C.E.E.*, 26 January 1934.

[65] *C.E.*, 15 April 1901.

[66] Twomey, *Ballincollig*, p.2.

[67] *C.S.*, 22 January 1910.

[68] *C.E.*, 4 January 1915.

[69] Mandle, *GAA*, p.189.

[70] O'Toole, *GAA*, p.118.

[71] Cronin, *Cork GAA*, p.77.

[72] De Búrca, *GAA*, p.164.

[73] *C.E.*, 10 April 1888.

[74] Madden, *Rockies*, p.21

[75] *C.E.*, 19 October 1908.

[76] *C.S.*, 6 October 1911.

[77] *C.E.*, 22 April 1895.

[78] *C.E.*, 2 March 1914.

[79] *C.E.*, 16 March 1897.

[80] *C.E.*, 3 September 1906.

[81] *C.E.*, 1 April 1889.

[82] *C.E.*, 8 April 1889.

[83] *C.E.*, 1 November 1897.

[84] *C.E.*, 12 August 1895.

[85] Madden, *Rockies*, p.19.

[86] *C.C.*, 26 September 1896.

[87] *C.E.*, 6 September 1896.

[88] Power, *Champions*, p.46.

[89] Deasy, 'Early Years', p.4.

[90] Horgan, *Brian Diolunaig*, p.26.

[91] Sheehan, *Inniscarra*, p.278.

[92] *C.S.*, 11 October 1911.

[93] *C.S.*, 19 October 1911.

[94] *C.E.*, 6 March 1905.

[95] *C.E.*, 22 April 1895.

[96] *C.S.*, 29 January 1910.

[97] *C.E.*, 19 August 1886.

[98] *C.E.*, 10 April 1888.

[99] *C.E.*, 16 April 1888.

[100] Horgan, *Brian Diolunaig*, p.10.

[101] *C.E.*, 28 July 1890.

[102] *C.E.*, 16 April 1888.

[103] *C.E.*, 3 September 1906.

[104] *C.S.*, 4 July 1897.

[105] *C.E.*, 16 March 1914.

[106] O'Connell, *Erin's Own*, p.47.

[107] Corr & O'Donoghue, *Midleton*, pp50-51.

[108] *C.E.*, 22 April 1895.

[109] Ó Tuama, *Nicks*, pp14-15.

[110] *C.E.*, 28 July 1890.

[111] O'Connell, *Erin's Own*, p.31.

[112] Madden, *Rockies*, p.21.

[113] *C.E.*, 12 September 1904.

[114] Teddy O'Donovan, 'Bringing Home the Cup', Liam Ó Tuama, *The Spirit of the Glen*, p.117.

[115] Ó Tuama, *Nicks*, p.24.

[116] *C.E.*, 28 July 1890.

117 *C.E.*, 4 February 1907.
118 *C.S.*, 29 January 1910.
119 Grenagh, p.26.
120 *C.S.*, 8 August 1897.
121 O'Connell, *Erin's Own*, p.28.
122 *C.S.*, 1 January 1910.
123 *C.E.*, 3 September 1906.
124 O'Connell, *Erin's Own*, p.38.
125 *C.S.*, 4 July 1897.
126 *C.S.*, 22 January 1910.
127 *C.E.E.*, 21 March 1936.
128 *C.S.*, 22 January 1910.
129 *C.E.E.*, 26 January 1934.
130 Horgan, *Brian Diolunaig*, p.10.
131 *C.S.*, 29 January 1910.
132 *C.E.*, 16 August 1886.
133 *C.E.*, 21 September 1896.
134 *C.S.*, 8 January 1910.
135 *C.S.*, 29 August 1908.
136 *C.S.*, August 1908.
137 *C.E.*, 12 September 1904.

II

1 *C.S.*, 19 October 1908.
2 Carter, *Memories*, p.34.
3 *C.E.*, 11 December 1911.
4 *C.S.*, 11 October 1911.
5 *C.E.E.*, 26 January 1934.
6 *C.E.*, 22 February 1926.
7 *C.E.*, 11 January 1926.
8 *C.E.E.*, 20 January 1933.
9 *C.E.E.*, 12 January 1934.
10 *C.E.E.*, 9 February 1934.
11 O'Sullivan, 'Century of Soccer', *C.E.E.*, 13 April 1981.
12 *C.E.*, 7 February 1897.
13 *C.S.*, 19 October 1911.
14 *C.S.*, 22 January 1910.
15 *C.S.*, 12 December 1908.
16 *C.E.*, 11 December 1911.
17 *C.E.*, 3 March 1924.
18 *C.E.*, 18 January 1926.
19 *C.E.E.*, 12 February 1934.
20 *C.E.E.*, 12 January 1931.
21 *C.E.E.*, 12 January 1934.

[22] *C.E.E.*, 15 January 1934.
[23] *C.E.E.*, 4 February 1924.
[24] *C.E.*, 28 January 1924.
[25] *C.E.E.*, 13 March 1936.
[26] *C.E.*, 22 February 1926.
[27] *C.E.E.*, 23 March 1936.
[28] *C.E.E.*, 13 January 1934.
[29] *C.E.E.*, 17 April 1936.
[30] *C.E.*, 11 January 1926.
[31] *C.E.E.*, 16 January 1931
[32] *C.E.E.*, 18 January 1935.
[33] *C.E.E.*, 23 March 1936.
[34] *C.E.E.*, 24 April 1936.
[35] *C.E.E.*, 2 February 1934.
[36] *C.E.E.*, 19 January 1935.
[37] *C.S.*, 22 January 1910.
[38] *C.S.*, 29 January 1910.
[39] *C.E.E.*, 19 January 1935.
[40] Mulqueen, C., *Murphy's Story of Munster Rugby*, p.57, hereafter cited as Mulqueen, *Munster*.
[41] Kidney, *Skull and Crossbones: The Cobh Rugby Story*, p.1, hereafter cited as Kidney, *Cobh*.
[42] Diffley, *The Men in Green: The Story of Irish Rugby*, p.45, hereafter cited as Diffley, *Irish Rugby*.
[43] *IRFU Annual 1880*, cited by Van Esbeck, *100 Years of Cork Constitution Club*, p.17, hereafter cited as Van Esbeck, *Cork Constitution*.
[44] Kidney, *Cobh*, p.5.
[45] Minute Book of Bankersfinbarr Rugby Football Club, December 1922.
[46] Van Esbeck, *Constitution*, p.16.
[47] Van Esbeck, *Cork Constitution*, pp82-83.
[48] Ryan, 'Early Days in Christian Brothers', in *CBC Cork, Diamond Jubilee Souvenir*, p.18.
[49] McSweeny, 'Reminiscences of CBC', in *CBC Cork, Diamond Jubilee Souvenir*, p.27.
[50] Harley, 'Memories', in *CBC Cork, Diamond Jubilee Souvenir*, p.22.
[51] Kelleher, 'An Old Pres Boy Looks Back', in Austin, *The Story of Pres*, p.46.
[52] Gallagher, 'Memories', in Austin, *The Story of Pres*, p.50.
[53] *C.E.*, 19 March 1900.
[54] Van Esbeck, *Cork Constitution*, p.44.
[55] *C.S.*, 11 October 1911.
[56] *C.E.*, 10 September 1904.
[57] *C.E.*, 12 September 1904.
[58] Kidney, *Cobh*, p.11.
[59] *C.E.*, 19 April 1894.
[60] *C.E.*, 30 April 1894.
[61] *C.E.*, 15 April 1901.
[62] *C.E.*, 6 March 1905.
[63] *C.E.*, 19 February 1917.
[64] Kidney, *Cobh*, p.17.
[65] Van Esbeck, *Constitution*, p.69.
[66] Mulqueen, *Munster*, p.70.
[67] Kidney, *Cobh*, p.13.

III

[1] Minute Book of Cork County Cricket Club. 7 July 1877.

[2] *ibid.*, 12 April 1891.

[3] *ibid.*, 8 April 1892.

[4] *ibid.*, April 1902.

[5] *ibid.*, 29 March 1904.

[6] *ibid.*, 13 December 1913.

[7] *ibid.*, 24 November 1916.

[8] *ibid.*, 1 July 1881.

[9] *ibid.*, 26 February 1875.

[10] *C.S.*, 13 June 1908.

[11] *C.S.*, 20 June 1908.

[12] *ibid.*, 29 April 1898.

[13] *ibid.*, 6 September 1898.

[14] *ibid.*, 2 May 1926.

[15] *ibid.*, 23 June 1915.

[16] *ibid.*, 16 July 1915.

[17] *ibid.*, 24 November 1916.

[18] *ibid.*, 12 April 1924.

[19] *ibid.*, 20 July 1925.

[20] *ibid.*, 29 April 1898.

[21] *ibid.*, 19 February 1903.

[22] *ibid.*, 16 April 1926.

[23] *ibid.*, 29 July 1927.

[24] *ibid.*, 29 July 1927.

[25] *C.E.*, 16 August 1886.

[26] *C.S.*, 29 August 1908.

[27] *ibid.*, 25 June 1894.

[28] *C.S.*, 1 August 1898.

[29] *ibid.*, 15 June 1891.

[30] *C.E.*, 15 June 1891.

[31] *C.S.*, 20 June 1908.

[32] *ibid.*, 5 September 1908

[33] *ibid.*, 22 August 1908.

[34] *ibid.*, 20 June 1908

[35] *ibid.*, 1 August 1908

[36] *ibid.*, 11 July 1908.

[37] *ibid.*, 22 August 1908.

[38] *ibid.*, 4 July 1908.

[39] *ibid.*, 15 August 1908.

[40] *ibid.*, 1 August 1908.

[41] *C.E.E.*, 15 January 1934.

[42] *C.C.*, 1 September 1886.

[43] *C.S.*, 13 June 1908.

[44] *ibid.*, 1 August 1908.

[45] *ibid.*, 29 August 1908.

[46] *ibid.*, 13 June 1908.
[47] *ibid.*, 10 December 1904.
[48] *ibid.*, 24 May 1907.
[49] *ibid.*, 14 December 1912.
[50] *ibid.*, 3 April 1908.
[51] *ibid.*, 9 April 1908.
[52] *ibid.*, 3 April 1875.
[53] *ibid.*, 10 April 1880.
[54] *ibid.*, 2 April 1925.
[55] *ibid.*, 5 April 1884.

IV

[1] *The Field*, 16 June 1883, in Gibson, *Early Irish Golf*, p.43.
[2] *Belfast Newsletter*, 1 November 1886, in Gibson, *Early Irish Golf*, p.44.
[3] *Belfast Newsletter*, 1 November 1886, in Gibson, *Early Irish Golf*, p.169.
[4] *The Irish Times*, 6 January 1906, in Gibson, *Early Irish Golf*.
[5] Minute Book of Douglas Golf Club, 1 May 1925.
[6] *ibid.*, 13 November 1928.
[7] St Ledger, *Monkstown*, p.17.
[8] Minute Book of Monkstown Golf Club, 12 May 1912, cited in St Ledger, *Monkstown*, p.9.
[9] Minute Book of Douglas Golf Club, 7 July 1931.
[10] *ibid.*, 13 December 1927.
[11] *ibid.*, 1 July 1928.
[12] *Irish Field*, 1 May 1926, cited in Douglas Golf Club Booklet.
[13] Minute Book of Douglas Golf Club, 31 May 1921.
[14] *ibid.*, 30 November 1923.
[15] *ibid.*, 25 March 1925.
[16] *C.E.*, 18 January 1902.
[17] *ibid.*, 1 March 1924.
[18] Minute Book of Monkstown Golf Club, 25 October 1923, cited in St Ledger, *Monkstown*, p.22.
[19] Minute Book of Douglas Golf Club, 8 May 1928.
[20] *C.E.*, 15 May 1902.
[21] *C.E.*, 24 February 1902.
[22] Minute Book of Douglas Golf Club, 3 June 1921.
[23] *ibid.*, 11 January 1924.
[24] *ibid.*, 30 April 1924.
[25] *C.C.*, 27 November 1894.
[26] St Ledger, *Monkstown*, p.13.
[27] Minute Book of Douglas Golf Club, 8 April 1931.
[28] St Ledger, *Monkstown*, p.7.
[29] *ibid.*, 17 July 1924.
[30] *ibid.*, 30 November 1923.
[31] Minute Book of Douglas Golf Club, 11 September 1928.
[32] Menton, *Golfing*, p.156.

[33] Menton, *Golfing*, p.8.

[34] Minute Book of Douglas Golf Club, 11 May 1925

[35] *The Field*, 16 June 1883, in Gibson, *Early Irish Golf*, p.43.

[36] Menton, *Golfing*, p.13.

[37] St Ledger, *Monkstown*, p.13.

[38] Minute Book of Douglas Golf Club, 8 May 1930.

[39] *ibid.*, 19 March 1928.

[40] *ibid.*, 27 August 1925.

[41] *ibid.*, 6 October 1925.

[42] *ibid.*, 3 September 1929.

[43] *ibid.*, 25 May 1931.

[44] St Ledger, *Monkstown*, 10 July 1928.

[45] *ibid.*, 26 May 1924.

[46] *ibid.*, 14 July 1924.

[47] *ibid.*, 10 May 1927.

V

[1] Cooke, *The Mardyke: Cork City's Walk in History*, p.63.

[2] *ibid.*, pp66-67.

[3] *C.E.*, 30 August 1886.

[4] *C.E.*, 12 August 1895.

[5] *C.E.*, 25 July 1897.

[6] *C.E.*, 26 July 1890.

[7] Minute Book of Sunday's Well Boating and Tennis Club, 17 January 1902.

[8] *ibid.*, 27 June 1904.

[9] *ibid.*, 18 December 1914.

[10] *ibid.*, 1 August 1905.

[11] *ibid.*, 9 December 1921.

[12] *ibid.*, 4 December 1905.

[13] *ibid.*, 19 December 1913.

[14] *ibid.*, 5 March 1917.

[15] *ibid.*, 10 December 1917.

[16] *ibid.*, 22 May 1905, 16 October 1905.

[17] *ibid.*, 19 June 1905, 5 December 1908.

[18] *ibid.*, 12 July 1920, 14 March 1922.

[19] *ibid.*, 2 December 1904.

[20] *ibid.*, 21 April 1902, 11 June 1917.

[21] *ibid.*, 21 February 1922.

[22] *ibid.*, 3 January 1912.

[23] *ibid.*, 28 May 1902.

[24] *ibid.*, 13 January 1908.

[25] *ibid.*, 18 July 1912.

[26] *ibid.*, 30 January 1905.

[27] *ibid.*, 5 February 1924.

[28] *ibid.*, 6 August 1902.

[29] *ibid.*, 13 January 1913.
[30] *ibid.*, 4 February 1918.
[31] *ibid.*, 4 February 1918.
[32] *ibid.*, 16 December 1915.
[33] *ibid.*, 19 September 1914.
[34] *ibid.*, 7 December 1908.
[35] *ibid.*, 16 December 1909.
[36] *ibid.*, 6 July 1908.
[37] *C.E.*, 3 June 1904.
[38] *C.E.*, 4 June 1904.
[39] *ibid.*, 6 June 1904.

VI

[1] *C.S.*, 1 July 1897.
[2] *C.E.*, 9 July 1906.
[3] *C.S.*, 13 June 1908.
[4] *C.S.*, 20 July 1908.
[5] *C.S.*, 27 June 1908.
[6] *C.S.*, 20 June 1908.
[7] *C.S.*, 4 July 1908.
[8] *C.S.*, 11 July 1908.
[9] *C.S.*, 22 August 1908.
[10] *C.E.*, 19 March 1900.
[11] *C.C.*, 10 December 1894.
[12] *C.E.*, 3 August 1898.
[13] *C.E.E.*, 12 January 1934.
[14] *C.E.E.*, 15 January 1936.
[15] Minute Book of Lee Rowing Club, 18 October 1887.
[16] *ibid.*, 15 June 1887.
[17] *ibid.*, October 1887.
[18] *ibid.*, 1 May 1889.
[19] *ibid.*, 10 August 1887.
[20] Subscription Book List of Lee Rowing Club, 1894.
[21] Receipt Book No.1 of Lee Rowing Club, 1898.
[22] Minute Book of Lee Rowing Club, 11 September 1887.
[23] List of Hon. Subscribers to Lee Rowing Club, 1899.
[24] Minute Book of Lee Rowing Club, 18 October 1887.
[25] *ibid.*, 19 July 1889.
[26] *ibid.*, 19 July 1889.
[27] Hon. Subscriptions and Members Subscriptions for Lee Rowing Club, 1898–1903.
[28] Minute Book of Lee Rowing Club, 1894.
[29] *ibid.*, 13 August 1888.
[30] *ibid.*, 4 September 1888.
[31] *ibid.*, 20 June 1890.
[32] *ibid.*, 21 June 1890.